Reconceptualising Material Culture in the Tricontinent:

When Objects Write Back

Reconceptualising Material Culture in the Tricontinent:

When Objects Write Back

Edited by

Minu Susan Koshy and Roshin George

**Cambridge
Scholars**
Publishing

Reconceptualising Material Culture in the Tricontinent:
When Objects Write Back

Edited by Minu Susan Koshy and Roshin George

This book first published 2023

Cambridge Scholars Publishing

Lady Stephenson Library, Newcastle upon Tyne, NE6 2PA, UK

British Library Cataloguing in Publication Data
A catalogue record for this book is available from the British Library

ISBN (10): 1-5275-9283-9
ISBN (13): 978-1-5275-9283-4

To,
My Appachi, for being my grandfather, for all the colours
and balloons and *appooppan thaadis*!

and
My Ichayan, for the unexpected magic of love and for all
that you are! . . .

and
To those who showed me the enchantment of "things" . . .

I

"All these objects . . . how can I explain?"
—Jean-Paul Sartre

CONTENTS

ACKNOWLEDGEMENTS

The book, the work for which began several years back, is a very special one, not just in terms of its content, but also in terms of the background against which it took shape. The publication is nothing short of a miracle, considering that it was initiated at a time when I was facing severe setbacks. When the editing was almost complete, Kerala was hit by severe floods and the manuscript was washed away, forcing me and Dr. George to redo the entire work. Covid-19 was the next calamity, which led to extreme delays in the progress of this work. In the period that elapsed, we repeatedly thought of quitting this entire venture owing to personal tragedies. It was only God's grace that enabled us to complete this work. The fact that the book has reached this stage makes me believe in miracles! I thank all the powers in the universe that worked together to bring our efforts to fruition.

Words are not enough to convey my gratitude to the contributors. They have been very patient and considerate, especially during the floods and later, when progress was quite slow. Their trust prompted us to persevere. Many thanks for being so understanding!

All that I do and am is because of Appachi, my grandfather. It was he who taught me the power of words, who showed me the meaning of seemingly insignificant things. My interest in material culture itself stems from the mini-universe he made for me with dolls, coloured pieces of chalk and balloons, and *appooppan thaadis*, shaping an alternate world filled with his love. Thank you Appachi! And Ammachi, my great-grandmother, for introducing me to the magic of objects through her stories spanning decades!

Once in a lifetime there comes along a person who means the world to you, who can push you to do better, to reach for the stars. For me, it is my husband, Alok, who made me complete this work, which would otherwise have been left incomplete for another six months. The "limited period offer" and the chocolate cake were too tempting to refuse after all! A bunch of thanks to him for listening to my endless chatter, for believing that I would be able to complete the work and for never letting me quit.

Dr. Roshin George, the co-editor and my mother, deserves a very special note of thanks. This book was to be co-authored with another specialist in the field; however, he had to quit the project owing to unfortunate circumstances. At that time, it was my mother, who was then working on a similar area of study, who came to my rescue. I thank her for opening the world of literature for me, for being my best friend and confidante and for all the times she protected me. No words can explain how I would not be me without her! A special note of thanks to Appa for encouraging me to pursue my passion without restrictions, enabling me to reach greater heights, and also for frequently asking me about the progress of the publication. Vava, with her humour and sarcasm, has always been there for me, ensuring in her own ways that I did not leave the editing half-finished. I am grateful to her for making life fun!

No words are enough to thank Daddy, a one-in-a-million kind of person, a solid source of support, my best friend and cheerleader. And yes, I do intend to fill his custom-made shelves with books! Special thanks to Amma, a person I admire for her cool-headedness and love. It is very rare indeed when your mother-in-law is also your ally in mischief! Thanks to Achu for showing me that a person can remain at peace with himself even when obstacles seem insurmountable.

A bunch of thanks to Ganesh, for not allowing me to lose hope and for his practical wisdom which has sustained me over the years! Thanks for not letting me quit, for helping me deal with trouble, and for putting up with the unending stories. And to Raj, for being there throughout, for endlessly believing that his friend can never fail!

Cambridge Scholars Publishing has been gracious enough to accommodate our requests for extension. I was deeply touched by their response when informed of the floods in Kerala. Thanks a lot for your concern and generosity. I also thank Mar Thoma College for Women and St. Thomas College, Kerala, for being supportive workplaces for Dr. George and me.

I must acknowledge the help and support we received from the English and Foreign Languages University, Hyderabad, my alma mater. Although I completed my course five years earlier, EFL-U still remains home to me. The emotional support I received from my teachers is as important as the academic advice they provided me and it is rare that such emotional bonds exist in institutions of higher education. Thank you EFL-U for being my home even today!

—Minu Susan Koshy

INTRODUCTION

Material culture assumes great significance in cultures across the globe by virtue of its ability to trace everyday life and its nuances through the signifying metaphor of objects. The historical trajectories of nations, cultures, and communities function in tandem with that of the prevailing material culture(s) in as much as transformations in the latter sphere inevitably represent ruptures or shifts in the former. The stories that objects recount surpass the boundaries of time and space as they transcend both. They function as signifying metaphors, carrying multiple significations of lives lived through and with them. Material culture and object-oriented ontologies have occupied significant space in academia, contributing immensely to tracing alternate histories of communities and cultures.

Theoretical paradigms on material culture have explored the object and its relationship with the human subject as well as the social order in which it manifests itself at intersections of the spatial and temporal axes. The history of the object is also the history of the social order that produces it. As such, "thinging" the object also "things" the social order that produced it in the first place—that is, it foregrounds what had hitherto been relegated to the background. Theorists such as Mary Douglas and Baron Isherwood elaborated upon and highlighted the potential of objects to foreground "culture." Igor Kopytoff and Arjun Appadurai's contribution to the field of material culture studies and object-oriented ontologies also becomes significant from the vantage point of the object in as much as it possesses agency and a "life" of its own. Theoretical paradigms on material culture ranging from the Marxist approach to structural and semiotic approaches and the cultural approach among others have delineated material culture studies as an academic discourse carrying the potential to enable a tracing of alternate histories.

One of the major lacunae in material culture studies is the Eurocentrism that characterises the theoretical models. "Thinging" and "commoditising" were analysed in the context of Western countries and the models failed to consider the scenario in other parts of the globe, especially in the erstwhile colonies in the tricontinent comprising Asia, Africa, and Latin America— the three geopolitical entities characterised by a shared history of colonialism and a similar present as Third World countries. After the Tricontinental Conference of 1966, held in Havana, there was a heightened sense of fraternity between the three locales and the commonalities came to be highlighted. As nations with a shared history of having borne the burden of imperialism, Asia, Africa, and Latin America have followed similar trajectories in their movement towards integration into a global, and now "glocal," economy. As such, the material culture in these erstwhile colonies reveals marked traits of a colonial past and neo-colonial present, with the socio-political realities modifying and being modified by the rapidly transforming "objects" and "things" utilised by postcolonial subjects. The edited volume is an attempt at shaping a predominantly tricontinental model of engaging with material culture, marking a shift from existing Eurocentirc theoretical frameworks.

The first chapter, "Meaning of Objects in a Naturalistic *Lebenswelt*," locates objects as part of the naturalistic life-world, with the religio-metaphysical world becoming an entity satisfying the human desire for embeddedness that imparts meaning. The following chapter, "The Biography of a Stolen Benin Bronze Casket," attempts an object biography, tracing the Benin Bronzes and their journey, locating them at specific points in history, thereby throwing light on the peculiarities of African art. "Locating Latin American Matters through Francisco De Goya's *Linda Maestra*" is an attempt to highlight how books and bodies in Latin America have reclaimed agency and dignity. It further addresses how the Indian Hispanists may also do so through an embodied and a conscientious reading, arguing that Francisco de Goya's *Linda Maestra* becomes a metaphor of translation, transgression, and transduction. "No Signs and Graffiti in Contemporary Medellín: Significant Paradoxes in the Time of Peace" outlines a brief history of graffiti in Colombia and Medellín, reflecting on the relationship between graffiti and the discourse performed by urban norms and the peace settlement in Colombia. The essay "When a House is More Than a Home: The Liberatory Life of Objects in a Post-Apartheid Future" locates the house as a site where the disconnect between national politics and daily life manifests itself, pointing to the move away from a combative national politics to the politics of dispossession in a racist social order. "'Matter Out of Place': The Ontologies of Waste in Teju Cole's *Every Day is for the Thief*" attempts a scatological reading of Teju Cole's *Every Day is for the Thief*, examining how objects (and subjects) gradually exceed their utility value, transforming into objects of abjection.

Chapter 7, "Decentring the Centre: Examining the Materiality of Connaught Place," examines the indexical and symbolic materiality of Connaught Place, engaging with the question of whether it functions simply as a sign of colonial rule or whether its materiality and symbolic meaning have undergone transformations over the years. "Goalporia Folksongs as an

Epistemic Cultural Resource for Understanding the Postcolonial Uncanny" investigates the Goalporia Lokageet of Western Assam, specifically with regard to songs by Pratima Baruah Pandey, locating them within the greater discourse of the culture, ethnicity, folk consciousness, and history of the colonial past of Western Assam, examining how these folksongs are glaring manifestations of the exclusion of Koch Rajbongshis. "Biographies of Yaksha: Object, Style, and Agencies" interrogates the biographies of objects, tracing the transformations an object undergoes from being a product of cult practices to an object of art, with specific reference to the stone sculpture of Yaksha Manibhadra from Parkham. Cult practices are located as distinctive iconographical exercises, dictating the modes in which the life history of the object is reconstructed in diverse cultural and spatial contexts. "Food and Food Habits of the Tribals of Chotanagpur in Colonial India: Writings, Perceptions, and Discourse" explores the modes in which the food cultures of the tribals in Chotanagpur were recorded by colonial authorities, leading to the formation and consolidation of stereotyped notions about the community, further shaping the policies of the Empire in India. In "Conflict between Rights and Obligations in Food Commodification," the authors adopt a Gandhian approach to the issue of food commodification and patenting, interrogating the role of the state and policymakers in ensuring food security.

"'They Too Have a Story': Tracing the Biographies of the Looms at Suraiya Hassan Bose's Workshop" locates the looms at the House of Kalamkari Durries as sculptural objects and cultural artefacts, and explores its engagement with the weavers in the industry through their narratives, memoirs, and visuals. In "The Spiritual and the Material: Insights from Sarala's Mahabharata," the author traces the intersections between the material and the spiritual, examining how the two realms mould human existence and in turn are moulded by it, through a reading of Indian folktales. "Making of a 'Transgressive' Substance: The Case of Cannabis in Himachal Pradesh" investigates how cannabis assumes the status of a 'transgressive' object in the Kullu region of Himachal Pradesh and how the local subjects engage with it, through the theoretical framework of material sociology. The final chapter, "Perambulating Reeds: An Analysis of Tapan Sinha's *Harmonium*," traces the biographical life of a harmonium as it appears in the 1963 Bengali movie *Harmonium* by Tapan Sinha, locating it within the paradigms of postcolonial modernity. Through its multiple transformations, the harmonium becomes "different things in different scenes" (Brown 9), functioning simultaneously as a quasi-subject and quasi object (Latour 51).

On the whole, the book seeks to formulate an alternative view of material culture emanating from the tricontinent, altering and modifying existing theoretical paradigms to arrive at a better understanding of what "objects" signify in a postcolonial and polycolonial context through readings of literary and visual texts. The potential of objects in the tricontinent to write back to the centre constituted by Eurocentric notions of material culture, thereby highlighting the possibility of a tricontinental theory of material culture, is explored. The book engages with the potential of the "object" to define and redefine postcolonial subjectivities, along with its significance in the "glocalised" context to which the tricontinent has shifted.

MEANING OF OBJECTS IN A NATURALISTIC *LEBENSWELT*

JIBU MATHEW GEORGE

Historico-Philosophical Backgrounds

Beginning with definitions is a double-edged move. On the one hand, it serves the purpose of clarity, and helps set the terms of discourse. On the other, it sometimes renders the discourse itself vulnerable to getting bogged down in definitional issues, and, consequently, the discussion seldom makes substantial headway. As we know, many philosophical/theoretical discussions fall prey to such tendencies. Philosophical naturalism is no exception. Though all may not agree, doing philosophy, or any intellectual endeavour for that matter, involves much more than linguistic nitpicking and checking the semantic/syntactic validity of propositions. We need semantic clarity, nevertheless. Seeing such a double bind of mandatory conceptual clarity and nitpicking unfruitfulness, David Papineau, in the *Stanford Encyclopedia of Philosophy*, begins his own definitional endeavour contextualising naturalism with reference to "self-proclaimed" American naturalists of the first half of the early twentieth century—John Dewey, Ernest Nagel, Sidney Hook, and Roy Wood Sellars. With a view to aligning "philosophy more closely with science," "they urged that reality is exhausted by nature, containing nothing 'supernatural,' and that the scientific method should be used to investigate all areas of reality, including the 'human spirit'" (Krikorian; Kim). According to Papineau, "naturalism can be separated into an ontological and a methodological component. The ontological component is concerned with the contents of reality, asserting that reality has no place for [the] 'supernatural.' . . . By contrast, the methodological component is concerned with ways of investigating reality, and claims some kind of general authority for the scientific method."

What matters to us here, especially with regard to the question of meaning, is the ontological component. For the present purpose, an understanding of naturalism as a non-supernaturalistic world view suffices. Naturalism denies any meaning beyond this world. This implies that the world view (*Weltanschauung*) could be, and historically once was, a supernaturalistic one, and there indeed occurred a transition to one that was not. We are familiar with this long-established narrative of the Occidental intellectual and cultural trajectory as a linear succession of world views. With a phrase borrowed from Friedrich Schiller,[1] the "disenchantment of the world" (*Entzauberung der Welt*), Max Weber (1864–1920), a German sociologist, political economist, and philosopher, outlined a process that Western civilisation had been experiencing for several millennia, and which reached a highpoint with the scientific revolutions of modernity. In Weber's work, the phrase denotes, on the one hand, a development within the domain of religion from magic to paths to salvation completely devoid of magic, and on the other, an understanding of the world's occurrences increasingly by reference to natural forces—which are humanly controllable by rational calculation, physical laws, and mechanical principles—rather than to magical and supernatural powers (Weber/Kalberg xxii–xxiii). Charles Taylor contests the notion of secularisation, a concept that is not the same as but includes disenchantment,[2] as a simplistic narrative wherein science got rid of the supernatural element—which he categorises under "subtraction theories" (the supernatural just peeled away and the world became "natural"!). Instead, Taylor traces the origins of secularisation to the gradual emergence of an "exclusive humanism" (19). The "great disembedding" (146), as he calls the development, refers to a world view wherein this world suffices in itself ("the immanent frame"), without recourse to anything transcendent for a sense of "fullness" (5).

---

[1] Friedrich Schiller (1759–1805), poet, playwright, philosopher, and historian, in his *On the Aesthetic Education of Man* (1794), used the phrase to designate a shift from the holistic world view of the ancient Greeks to the fragmentation characteristic of modernity.

[2] Indeed, religion, supernaturalism, and enchantment are not identical but show overlaps and divergences. Marcel Gauchet sees disenchantment as a shift from the ubiquitous enchantment of what Weber calls "mysterious, incalculable forces" (322) to personalised and externalised gods, who are amenable to human influence. Similarly, Hans Joas points out that "the meaning of 'disenchantment' . . . is certainly not—as has frequently been assumed—secularization (what ever that exactly means), but 'demagicization,' a process that occurs when processes in the world lose their 'magical meaning'; they happen but do not 'mean' anything" (20). Nevertheless, the presence of a strong magical element in medieval Christianity and its co-existence with belief in a personal God problematise such a schematisation. This essay is premised more on the distinction between naturalism and supernaturalism than between two kinds of supernaturalism, namely that of magical forces and of personal gods.

A minor but significant qualification, however, ought to be made between a naturalistic world view and religious naturalism. According to Jerome A. Stone, religious naturalism "asserts that there seems to be no ontologically distinct and superior realm (such as God, soul, or heaven) to ground, explain, or give meaning to this world, but that *yet religious significance can be found within this world*" (1, emphasis added). Religious naturalisms abound in variety: pantheism, panentheism, panpsychism, materialism, monism, holism, process theology and emergentism, religious humanism, idealism, integrationism, contextualism, biotheology, naturalistic mysticism, operational theism, and Owen Flanagan's *eudaimonistic scientia* (a science of human flourishing; a neuro-scientific version of what Charles Taylor calls "exclusive humanism"). Feelings and concerns such as wonder and compassion, and meanings attached to entities in this world, which may as well be characterised as religious or spiritual, can be immanentised from a religious-naturalistic perspective. In other words, some of the meanings even here may have religious overtones but are innate to the world. Paradoxically, from such a historical perspective, naturalism is a back-formation, though it is certainly not so morphologically or etymologically. In part, this is a movement from the metaphysical to the cultural delineations of the larger entities and frameworks (we shall return to this theme shortly) that give meaning to the particulars of our *Lebenswelt*—literally, "life-world" in German—that is, reality as actually (often unconsciously) organised and experienced by an individual subject.[3] I say "in part" lest the alternative narrative be a gross simplification. The religio-metaphysical world view was meaningful to many, in the sense that it satisfied the human *penchant for embeddedness*, the desire or need to see one's experience as part of a larger framework, phenomenon, ensemble, or narrative—the horror of the "left to itself." The absence of the larger meaning-giving framework is the condition of the absurd. The immanent human world also has a penchant for embeddedness, for meaning, perhaps in a greater degree. This essay explores the dynamics of an alternative, secular embeddedness that imparts meaning in a naturalistic world. But in order to understand this alternative dynamics, we need to clarify its non-secular antecedents, though to some of us these may seem past their age of interest.

---

[3] *Encyclopaedia Britannica* defines *Lebenswelt* as "the world as immediately or directly experienced in the subjectivity of everyday life, as sharply distinguished from the objective 'worlds' of the sciences, which employ the methods of the mathematical sciences of nature; although these sciences originate in the life-world, they are not those of everyday life. The life-world includes individual, social, perceptual, and practical experiences."

I show in Chapter 1 of my book *The Ontology of Gods: An Account of Enchantment, Disenchantment, and Re-Enchantment* (2017) that if the term "supernatural" is to denote what it literally means—that is, beyond the established course of nature—it has to encompass a broader semantic field than assumed in ordinary usage. Then, the terminological reach of the supernatural covers not only entities such as deities, angels, demons, fairies, ghosts, and spirits but also heaven and hell, or any form of after life for that matter, and concepts such as *mana*, an impersonal power that can be transmitted or inherited; the law of *karma* (self-contained causality or fate); rebirth; and the transmigration of souls (metempsychosis)—even any underlying purpose, design, or intelligence guiding the world process, including human destiny. Strictly speaking, these are all *supra-empirical posits* (1, italics original).

Is any framework of meaning devoid of anything in the above catalogue a naturalistic one? When Śaṅkara posits the Brahman, the ultimate reality according to the *Advaita* (non-dualism) school of Hindu philosophy, or a Transcendentalist such as Ralph Waldo Emerson proposes an "over-soul" we are still within the discourse of non-theistic supra-empirical entities. While in the former case of metaphysical monism, the appearance of objects qua objects itself is an illusion (*maya*), in the latter case, the meaning of objects derives from their being permeated by the reality of "the over-soul" (or similar entities in other non-theistic formulations of ultimate reality).[4] R. Puligandla has argued that the concept of *adhyāsa*—the "superimposing on the formless, nameless non-dual Brahman [of] various forms and names" (616)—in Śaṅkara's *Advaita* is comparable to the kind Immanuel Kant envisions as the function of "categories" in creating "phenomena." In all these cases, that is, across the spectrum of supernaturalistic (in the above broader sense) world views, the meaning of particulars draws upon an enveloping general narrative—a meta-narrative, if you like. In the above case of non-dualism, even the meaninglessness of particulars—a meaningful meaninglessness—owes itself to the general narrative of meaning and meaninglessness. As a corollary, the source of meaning of objects is the fact (or assumption) of their being part of a larger narrative. My contention is that the meaning of objects in the naturalistic world view also owes itself to being part of larger narratives, life-worlds, and frameworks of meaning.

---

[4] In their edited volume entitled *Models of God and Alternative Ultimate Realities*, Jeanine Diller and Asa Kasher present a "philosophical exploration, critique and comparison of (a) the major philosophical models of God, gods and alternative ultimate realities implicit in the world's religions and philosophical schools, and of (b) the ideas of such models and doing such modeling *per se*" (1).

These meanings emerge from the objects, which are at the confluence of several trajectories—historical, material, existential, cultural, and so on.

It is certainly not the case that the meanings under a religious world view were exclusively supernatural. Take, for example, the European Middle Ages, generally considered a paradigmatic age of faith. Not everyone was a believer, but the general character of the age was religious. Charles Taylor's description of the medieval world view and its rationale are succinctly striking:

> One important part of the picture is that so many features of their world told in favour of belief, made the presence of God seemingly undeniable. . . .
>
> (1) The natural world they lived in, which had its place in the cosmos they imagined, testified to divine purpose and action; and not just in the obvious way which we can still understand and (at least many of us) appreciate today, that its order and design bespeaks creation; but also because the great events in this natural order, storms, droughts, floods, plagues, as well as years of exceptional fertility and flourishing, were seen as acts of God, as the now dead metaphor of our legal language still bears witness.
>
> (2) God was also implicated in the very existence of society (but not described as such—this is a modern term—rather as polis, kingdom, church, or whatever). A kingdom could only be conceived as grounded in something higher than mere human action in secular time. And beyond that, the life of the various associations which made up society, parishes, boroughs, guilds, and so on, were interwoven with ritual and worship . . . One could not but encounter God everywhere.
>
> (3) People lived in an "enchanted" world. . . . The enchanted world in this sense is the world of spirits, demons, and moral forces which our ancestors lived in. (25–26)

In short, the ordered cosmos, the occurrences therein, and a hierarchically ordered society confirmed the supernatural narrative, which, apart from the God of Christianity, also included angels, fairies, spirits, demons, and other similar entities. But even in the God-framed Middle Ages, people resorted, as their ancestors had done, to agricultural practices that were rational from an earthly point of view, fought battles using weapons and methods that were quite this-worldly, and, on occasions of ill-health, took recourse to medical solutions alongside spiritual "cures." It would be more accurate to say that the natural and the supernatural outlooks co-existed, inevitably and pragmatically, even in pre-secular life-worlds. Perhaps the former was enveloped within the latter, but had an autonomy of its own, however limited that might have been. Conversely, just as the meanings under a religious world view were not exclusively supernatural, we cannot rule out religious affinities and affiliations for the meanings we derive, create, or assign under a naturalistic order of things. Further, contemporary delineations of what is natural, supernatural, or "subnatural" could be a product of our own historically conditioned thinking. Contemporary criteria in this regard may be the result of naturalised (that is, taken-for-granted) Enlightenment perspectives.

In any case, the immanence of meanings in the world, that is, without reference to any theological or metaphysical framework, is the premise of the present discussion. Those who are familiar with the history of Occidental thought may recognise at least two milestones in this movement: one from ancient Greece, and the other from the transitional phase of European thought from the medieval to the modern. The first is the Aristotelian revision (a rejection, for hard-core Aristotelians) of Platonic notions of reality. According to Plato, the particular things in the world derive their reality from participation in the transcendental, universal world of Forms or Ideas. For Aristotle, the forms are immanent in the particulars:

> Aristotle turned Plato's ontology upside down. For Plato, the particular was less real, a derivative of the universal; for Aristotle, the universal was less real, a derivative of the particular. Universals were necessary for knowledge, but they did not exist as self-subsistent entities in a transcendent realm. Plato's Ideas were for Aristotle an unnecessary idealist duplication of the real world of everyday experience, and a logical error. (Tarnas 59)

The second milestone is deism, one of the powerful instruments of modernity and a harbinger of naturalism. Deism restricted the role of the deity to creation, envisioning a universe that works on its own uniform and impersonal laws, and is knowable through human reason. Deism paved the way for empirical exploration of the world for its own sake, and scientific discoveries that characterise modernity, which in turn, have led to naturalistic concerns in the wake of scientific explanations, including the question of whether there can be a post-supernatural (or non-supernatural) religion. The following sections of this essay will examine the trajectories of meaning on which secular attention came to be focused, and the philosophical implications and assumptions thereof. I argue that the meaning of objects derives from the ways in which reality is organised and experienced by historical subjects, the existential dynamism of the life-worlds of which they are part, and also the historical processes of which these objects are palimpsestic indicators.

The Subject and the Object

What is meaning? What does it mean to mean? In common parlance, we understand meaning as something that a word, a text, an action, an event, or the like expresses, indicates, or signifies. In our own post-structuralist critical climate, it is a commonplace that though meanings are mostly a matter of convention, they can vary from person to person and from culture to culture. More importantly, meaning is a matter of interpretation. If we may confine our discussion to objects for the time being, what could objects mean? Here, I use the word "objects" as synonymous with things. To reuse an orthodox example, a rose has a different meaning for a botanist than it does for a couple who have lost a child and have found a rose on the coffin.[5] Contrary to popular ideas, the former is not a detached, "meaningless" perspective. Martin Heidegger, one of the foremost philosophers of the twentieth century, distinguishes between two attitudes to the world and its objects: *present-at-hand* and *ready-to-hand*. The former is a detached, "scientific," observing attitude towards something without regard for the use it has for *Dasein*'s purpose. The latter is *Dasein*'s involved, ordinary, and often unconscious use of something to achieve his purpose. For Heidegger, however, there is no negativity attached to the *ready-to-hand* attitude. But the *present-at-hand* attitude is also not completely disinterested or neutral; it has a "mood."

The encounter between the subject and the object has been the chief concern, and one of the perennial fascinations, of epistemology. René Descartes, with whom modern philosophy is widely believed to have emerged, viewed it as a detached and disinterested relation between an autonomous subject and the object that is out there in the world. Heidegger, in his philosophical magnum opus *Being and Time* (1927), contested the Cartesian ideas of the subject and its epistemic endeavours. To Heidegger, knowledge and interpretation (*Auslegung*) are ontologically grounded in prior structures of understanding, which he called *Vorstruktur* (translated into English as "fore-structure"). These structures are a function of "being-in-the-world," of the *Dasein*'s having projected himself *there* (*Dasein* literally means "being there"). In other words, the "totality of involvements" (Ormiston and Schrift 121) in the world underlies knowledge and interpretation. The mode of knowing is part of the way of being. A German peasant's view of, and meaning for, a piece of hewn wood is embedded in the project of making a wine barrel. The modern idea of the unavoidable

---

[5] Alternatively, one can also make a distinction, as E. D. Hirsch does, between meaning and significance.

"interest-edness" (bias, if you like) of knowledge and understanding flows from Heidegger's fundamental ontology. We may use this ontological foundation of knowledge as the point of departure for further discussion.

Except in a pristine childhood, there is no ground zero for approaching anything under the sun. The subject is conditioned prior to the encounter with the object. This is no inherent epistemic disability but one of the conditions to be factored in, in understanding the dynamics of the subject–object encounter. In fact, the (meta-) knowledge of prior structures has been a liberating development in the history of ideas. The "perspectival" conditioning of the subject is not, however, the only factor that problematises the encounter. Characteristics innate to the object render it complex. The object is multidimensional. One cannot perceive or understand all the aspects of the object, at least all at once.[6] Change of metaphor—facet, dimension, part, side, or feature—does not help here; language is fundamentally metaphorical, and even while dealing with non-physical entities is compelled to rely on the physicality of the physical world for its metaphorical extensions. Quotidian experience teaches us that one cannot apprehend all the dimensions of a physical object. Probably, there *is* such a thing as what Immanuel Kant called the *Ding an sich* (the thing in itself), but access to it can only be selective, and, in Kant's objective idealism, mediated. Our perceptual apparatus has its limitations. But our cognitive apparatus, aspiring though it may be, with a broader field to grapple with, is even more limited. This is so not only because cognition is conditioned and "biased," as stated earlier, but also because thoughts, beyond our calculations, interact and create links, even remote ones, that bear on the understanding of the object under consideration. Our discussion here, particularly when it takes up cognition, operates in an area that is beyond Kantian "categories," which are more about the "basic" processes of perception and understanding.[7] Selectivity vis-à-vis the features of the object is one of the organising principles of cognition, analogous to the principles of perception.[8] If we survey the knowledge of the world generated

---

[6] Theoretically, it is possible sequentially, though not simultaneously.

[7] Kant's twelve categories are divided into four sets of three: (1) of quantity: unity, plurality, and totality; (2) of quality: reality, negation, and limitation; (3) of relation: substance-and-accident, cause-and-effect, and reciprocity; (4) of modality: possibility, existence, and necessity (qtd. in Russell 708).

[8] The Gestalt principles of perception include the figure–ground relationship (humans focus either on the figure or on the background against which the figure rests), the law of *prägnanz* (humans tend to interpret ambiguous or complex images as simple and complete), uniform connectedness (elements with uniform visual features are perceived to be more related than those with disparate characteristics),

in the history of humankind, we may discern that most of it stemmed from a pragmatic imperative.[9] The Greek word *pragmatikos* means "fit for business or action" (from *pragma*, meaning "deed" or "action"). The purpose for which knowledge is created, or to which it is appropriated, often determines the production of knowledge itself, and, as the Heideggerian example shows, inadvertently (to Heidegger, inevitably) solves the multidimensionality problem as well.

The Object as Work and Text

The above characterisation of the subject–object interface can persuade us to consider the meaning of an object as analogous to that of a (literary) text. We may even say that the object is a text. According to Roland Barthes's critical narrative, the transition from conventional criticism to post-structuralism is a movement from "work" to "text"—that is, a shift from looking at a novel or a poem or a play as an entity with fixed meanings, mainly decided by the author for eternity, to a view of the same entity as an endless play of linguistic signifiers, whose meanings are open. The work is about the past, to the extent that you want it to be. The text is about limitless future potential. The work is anchored in literary archeology. The text is futurological. As far as practical criticism is concerned, this distinction between the work and the text is one of the *données* or conceptual frames of reference. We say different sets of things—each set being internally diverse as well—on the same piece depending upon our decision to view it as either a work or a text.

The object in the work mode is about its history—production and labour. Since the history of the object does not terminate, as we shall see soon, with its reaching a finished state of production, we can even call the production history its "pre-history." Material objects indicate their points of origin (the production processes) as well as points of circulation and consumption, where they create or affect the life patterns of people. In Chapter 4 of my book *Ulysses Quotīdiānus: James Joyce's Inverse Histories of the Everyday* (2016), entitled "'Something Feeble in a Civilization': A Material History of the Everyday," I argue that

---

closure (humans tend to look for a single, recognisable pattern), proximity (elements placed close to one another are perceived to be more related than those placed apart), and similarity (similar things are perceived to be more related than dissimilar things).
[9] In the *Nichomachean Ethics* Aristotle made a distinction among *epistêmê* (theoretical knowledge), *technê* (craft), and *phronesis* (practical wisdom and ethics).

> The many everyday objects and material practices that are mentioned or ruminated on in [Joyce's] *Ulysses* trace a material history. They have a double character—synchronic and diachronic. At the synchronic level, these objects and practices give a "slice" of the material life of a city at a certain point of time in history at a specific location—Dublin at the beginning of the twentieth century here. . . . At the diachronic level, such pictures are diurnal specimens that bear the signatures of a longer material history. . . . The everyday accumulates and showcases previous work processes. Its commodities and practices register the slow evolution, achievements, and even deteriorations in lifestyle. (114–15)

For instance, "[Leopold] Bloom's thoughts on the silk industry in Ireland (8.621–3)[10] are a silent tribute to centuries of ordinary life at the two ends. On the one hand, they point to the history of silk production and the lives of silk workers. On the other, they indicate the changes in sartorial culture" (118). A typical Marxian argument concerned the concealment of the alienating production process, at the end of consumption: ". . . often finished products and their immediate exchanges conceal the relations of production from the terminal consumer. Bloom's ruminations on Ceylonese tea tell us nothing about the plantation workers on the island, though he thinks of 'Cinghalese spice-islands'" (13.1018).

The comparatively new paradigm of the text irretrievably dismisses an authorial cogito and replaces it with a reader cogito. Since language is "plurisignificative," as Jacques Derrida would have it, since the signifier and the signified have only a gliding relationship, readers have the freedom to derive new meanings, even those that the authors are incapable of dreaming. But the reader is not as autonomous as is assumed. Codes of interpretation are culturally acquired, and, therefore, envisage relativism only of a collective type. At the collective level, however small the collective may be, the olive branch signifies reconciliation; the white flag symbolises (symbolism being extended signification) surrender. Simple and otherwise inert objects can become potent symbols due to their being part of collective signifying systems. Consider, for instance, how cloth became an object of political discourse during the Indian independence movement. C. A. Bayley analyses Mohandas Gandhi's manipulation of the meaning of indigenously produced cloth as an instrument for sending political messages. This was possible because the influx of machine-made foreign cloth, made cheaper by 30–50 per cent through a discriminatory tariff regime, had ruined the indigenous weaving sector. Besides the production side, cloth is part of

---

[10] In keeping with the tradition of using the Gabler edition of *Ulysses*, episode and line numbers are cited instead of page numbers.

a "biomoral symbolism" (287) in India. It is also a ritual sign of class in the traditional social order.

At the individual level, the meaning of objects, like that of meaning of texts, is a matter of symmetry—between the subject and the object/the reader and the text. Not only meaning and interpretation but also our whole response to texts, even the very decision to pick a book from the racks (provided we have a modicum of "pre-understanding"), is a matter of experiential symmetry, real or imagined, between the text and ourselves. The idea of symmetry has witnessed a dramatic change since the enthronement of the reader in the place of the "dead" author. As Jenefer Robinson illustrates, "If I read in a novel a description of a handsome young fighter-pilot who dies in the Second World War, and fall into a tender reverie about my fiancé who flies a plane for Fed-Ex, my feelings of tenderness may have nothing to do with the way the fighter-pilot is depicted in the novel" (71). Robinson's theory leans towards the subjective side of the reader–text interface. Contemporary literary theory is right to a great extent in hailing the text as a network of reciprocal effects. Texts *for us* are partly about themselves and partly about ourselves. The reader–text symmetry may be explained in terms of meaning or succour to our lives, intellectual stimulation, antidote to ennui, and so on. In other words, the effects are a matter of encounter between the subject and the object. It is both constitutive of, and a result of, our *Lebenswelt*.

The encounter with the text is the cumulative climax of the reader's individual and collective experiences. The antecedents of this encounter include more factors than are often assumed. Many components synthesise and mutate to form our world view (and text-view)—heredity, history, tradition, codes, religion, class, education, linguistic and cultural repertoire, cultural and ethical norms, psychohistories, beliefs, interests, motives, tastes, moods, interpersonal relations, what others read (and watch), calculations, childhood experiences, and the spider and the moonlight. The last two are Nietzsche's items in his theory of eternal recurrence. Reading revives more ghosts than can be enumerated! Since many of these factors change in the course of a person's life, the symmetry is not a static one, but a dynamic, shifting, progressive symmetry.

Just as readers can appropriate texts and read meanings into them, so consumers can make meaningful use of what is offered to them, sometimes in contrapuntal ways. Consumers derive pleasures from commodities, which fulfil many functions in their individual lives. In the *Ulysses* example,

> [t]he material repertoire becomes a resource for everyday life. A cup of creature cocoa, Epp's mass-product, promotes comfort, fellowship, and hospitality. Similarly, Gilbey's invalid port and Plumtree's Potted Meat

stimulate desire between Boylan [Molly's concert manager with whom she has an adulterous affair] and Molly [Bloom's wife]. One may argue that these commodities are designed to penetrate private experience, and are meant to be domesticated and personalized. It is certainly so. But . . . the experiential history of ordinary people asserts itself within an impersonal material structure. Use can invest inert material objects with personal meanings and experiential value. Thus they have a prehistory and a personal, experiential history. . . . In course of time the commodities assume the status of experiential testimonies and tokens. They get associated with memorable experiences, pleasant and unpleasant. Food, clothing, utensils, furniture, and their like tell the tale not only of survival and material comfort but also of joys, passions, regrets, and the limitations upon each life. Living human relationships get embedded in them. Bloom fondly remembers the American soap that added the cosy smell to [his daughter] Milly's bathwater during a tubbing night (8.170–3). His drawer contains a Vere Foster's handwriting copybook with Milly's drawings (17.1775–8). Likewise, Molly's elephant grey dress is a vivid memory and a token of happy times past for her husband. But perhaps the most important object in this category is the warm chewed seedcake that Molly passed into Bloom's mouth on the day of the proposal (8.907). These objects are like "objective correlatives" of specific emotions and experiences for the human subjects in whose minds and lives they appear and play a part. They are metonymic indices of these complex emotions and experiences, and take on such a symbolic role by participating in the lives and thoughts of ordinary people. The lamb wool corselet that Molly knitted for Rudy, and with which she buried him (14.269); the new boater straw hat that Rudolf bought before his suicide (17.629–32); and the bowl of china into which Stephen's mother vomited the bile in her deathbed (1.108–10) are experiential tokens of a life that is unknown, in other words, of an unaccounted history. (146–47)

I would like to single out the new boater straw hat for further discussion. As I argue elsewhere,

> [t]hat Rudolf Bloom purchased "a new boater straw hat" (17.629–32) before his suicide speaks volumes about his inner life, which contrasts with the matter-of-fact manner in which Joyce makes Bloom recollect the scene of the bureaucratic inquest. The reality of inner life which precedes a death possesses an experiential intensity which is not accessible to another person. . . . even objects partake of the intensity of death.
>
>   Like Rudolf Bloom's hat, objects such as the lamb wool corselet and the bowl of china, strictly speaking, are "not memento mori, in the sense these are not reminders of mortality. They are reminders of a life. The operating factor is that they are framed by loss, by absence. Little things of ordinary human life matter because they are *framed by mortality*." ("James Joyce and the 'Strolling Mort'" 67–68, emphasis added)

My larger point is that objects in a naturalistic life-world derive their meaning from being at the meeting point of several meaning trajectories. I have illustrated only some of them; the above example may be characterised as existential. If we may alter the metaphor, the meanings arise from being part of several lived spaces. Owen Flanagan, whom I mentioned as the naturalistic proponent of *eudaimonistic scientia*, in his book interestingly entitled *The Really Hard Problem: Meaning in a Material World* (2007), discusses six zones or *spaces of meaning*—art, science, technology, ethics, politics, and spirituality (7). As said earlier, human beings, in their search for meaning, have a penchant for embeddedness, the desire or need to see one's experience as part of a larger framework, phenomenon, ensemble, or narrative. And human ingenuity is such that the frameworks, ensembles, narratives, and spaces keep multiplying and expanding. While there is a view abroad that secularisation took away a profound and time-tested framework, and created an absurd, that is, meaningless, world (the horror of the "left to itself") devoid of the old metaphysical moorings, the complexity of existence and human creativity have ensured a proliferation of frameworks—multiple avenues of embeddedness. The story of secularisation is, in fact, one of heterogeneisation of meaning-giving frameworks, ensembles, narratives, and spaces, a development that is arguably not limited to Flanagan's sextet.

References

Barthes, Roland. "From Work to Text." *Image—Music—Text.* Trans. Stephen Heath. New York: Hill & Wang, 1977. 155–64. Print.

Bayley, C. A. "The Origins of Swadeshi (Home Industry): Cloth and Indian Society, 1700–1930." *The Social Life of Things: Commodities in Cultural Perspective.* Ed. Arjun Appadurai. Cambridge: Cambridge UP, 1988. 285–323. Print.

Diller, Jeanine and Asa Kasher, ed. *Models of God and Alternative Ultimate Realities.* New York: Springer, 2013. Print.

Flanagan, Owen. *The Really Hard Problem: Meaning in a Material World.* Cambridge, MA: MIT Press, 2007. Print.

Gauchet, Marcel. *The Disenchantment of the World: A Political History of Religion.* Trans. Oscar Burge. Princeton, NJ: Princeton University Press, 1997. Print.

George, Jibu Mathew. *Ulysses Quotīdiānus: James Joyce's Inverse Histories of the Everyday.* Newcastle upon Tyne: Cambridge Scholars, 2016. Print.

—. *The Ontology of Gods: An Account of Enchantment, Disenchantment, and Re-Enchantment*. New York: Palgrave Macmillan, 2017. Print.

—. "James Joyce and the 'Strolling Mort': Significations of Death in *Ulysses.*" *Mortality: Promoting the Interdisciplinary Study of Death and Dying* 22.1 (2017): 60–74. Print.

Heidegger, Martin. *Being and Time*. Trans. John Macquarrie and Edward Robinson. Oxford: Basil-Blackwell, 1962. Print.

Joas, Hans. "The Axial Age Debate as Religious Discourse." *The Axial Age and Its Consequences*. Ed. Robert N. Bellah and Hans Joas. Cambridge, MA: Belknap Press of Harvard University Press, 2012. 9–29. Print.

Joyce, James. *Ulysses: A Critical and Synoptic Edition*. 3 vols. Ed. Hans Walter Gabler, Wolfhard Steppe, and Claus Melchior. New York: Garland, 1984. Print.

Kim, Jaegwon. *Mind in a Physical World*. Cambridge, MA: MIT Press, 1998. Print.

Krikorian, Yervant H., ed. *Naturalism and the Human Spirit*. New York: Columbia University Press, 1944. Print.

"Lebenswelt." *Encyclopaedia Britannica*. 12 August 2017. Web <https://www.britannica.com/topic/life-world>

Ormiston, Gayle L. and Alan D. Schrift, ed. *The Hermeneutic Tradition: From Ast to Ricoeur*. Albany, NY: State University of New York Press, 1990. Print.

Papineau, David. "Naturalism." *Stanford Encyclopedia of Philosophy*. Published 22 February 2007. Revised 15 September 2015. 7 August 2017. Web <https://plato.stanford.edu/entries/naturalism/>

Puligandla, R. "God and Ultimate Reality: An Analytical Interpretation of Śaṅkara's Philosophy." *Models of God and Alternative Ultimate Realities*. Ed. Jeanine Diller and Asa Kasher. New York: Springer, 2013. 615–24. Print.

Robinson, Jenefer. "Emotion and the Understanding of Narrative." *A Companion to the Philosophy of Literature*. Ed. Garry L. Hagberg and Walter Jost. Malden, MA: Wiley-Blackwell, 2010. 71–92. Print.

Russell, Bertrand. *A History of Western Philosophy*. New York: Simon and Schuster, 1967. Print.

Schiller, Friedrich. *On the Aesthetic Education of Man*. Trans. Reginald Snell. Mineola, NY: Dover, 2004. Print.

Stone, Jerome A. *Religious Naturalism Today: The Rebirth of a Forgotten Alternative*. Albany, NY: State University of New York Press, 2008. Print.

Tarnas, Richard. *The Passion of the Western Mind: Understanding the Ideas That Have Shaped Our World View*. London: Pimlico, 2010. Print.

Taylor, Charles. *A Secular Age*. Cambridge, MA: Belknap Press of Harvard University Press, 2007. Print.

Weber, Max. *Readings and Commentary on Modernity*. Ed. Stephen Kalberg. Malden MA: Blackwell, 2005. Print.

THE BIOGRAPHY OF A STOLEN BENIN BRONZE CASKET*

RUSSELL MCDOUGALL

In *The Roth Family, Anthropology, and Colonial Administration* (Left Coast Press, 2008), edited by Iain Davidson and me, we explored the relationship between anthropology and colonial administration through the lives of the remarkable Roth family: Walter, Henry, and Felix, three brothers, and their sons, George and Vincent. My own chapter in the book had a double focus: first on Felix's role in the sacking of Benin during the British invasion of 1897; and second, on his brother Henry's publication six years later of *Great Benin; Its Customs, Art and Horrors* (1903). The punitive expedition of 1897 is a foundational event in Nigerian history; and *Great Benin* is a foundational text in the development of European understandings of Africa. But there is one aspect of Felix and Henry Ling Roth's contribution that I had neither time nor space to consider, and that is the impetus for this chapter: their role in the collection and sale of the cultural and artistic treasures of the Oba's palace in Benin City—including the famous Benin Bronzes, created by the Edo people of present-day southern Nigeria in the time of the Benin Empire.

The British looted some four thousand objects from the Oba's palace, which were subsequently donated or sold and gradually dispersed around the world. (Admiral Rawson's report to the Admiralty recorded the seizure of almost a thousand bronze plaques from the palace, two hundred of which the British government reserved as a gift to the British Museum.) But this, as William Fagg notes, was only "the official booty," which the Foreign and Commonwealth Office put up for sale in London "to defray the cost of the pensions of the killed and the wounded" (21). There were of course also a substantial number of bronzes, ivories, woodcarvings and ironwork shared out among the officers, as was "the custom of war in the nineteenth century" (Fagg 21). This "unofficial loot" was not reported to the Admiralty; and

---

* An earlier and much abbreviated version of this essay was given at the 38th Annual AFSAAP Conference in Melbourne in October 2015.

much of it has remained in private hands, stimulating the global illicit trade in African antiquities.

This chapter makes no distinction between the official and the unofficial spoils of war. Neither does it attempt to track them individually to all the institutions (and private collections) that today contain them.[1] Also beyond the chapter's scope is the long history of Nigeria's efforts to retrieve its cultural heritage from those institutions.[2] Rather, what I provide here is an object biography, focused on just one item. I take my cue from Jeremy Coote and Elizabeth Edwards's argument concerning the visual documents preserved in the Pitt Rivers Museum at the University of Oxford, that the "dominant model" of scholarly focus on the objects in and of themselves has tended to obscure the ways in which they have made (and continue to make) history. A more useful model, they propose, might be one that focuses on the "trade routes" of objects, the ways by which they have travelled and survived, "the contexts and histories of their preservation and use," the networks that have affected them and their interpretation (35). In other words, object biography.

Biography traditionally has had a human focus, and the narrowness of that focus—usually on a single individual—has made its contribution to history contentious. It continues to be regarded primarily as a literary genre, a species of memoir, one of the lying arts. As I have argued elsewhere:

> Modern biographies tend to give readers mostly what they want for themselves—the revelation of a deeply meaningful and secret life. To ask after the secret lives of things, then, is one aspect of the genre's reinvention, moving it into the post-human realm, where human and the non-human categories of existence begin to blur. This is particularly of interest for frontier subjects, since the processes of othering across the divide have often

---

[1] The 2018 survey by Kate Brown for Artnet reveals "unsurprisingly" that the British Museum holds the vast majority of the objects that were plundered by its soldiers—700 in total. The remainder is concentrated in just six museums: the Ethnological Museum of Berlin holds 580; the Pitt Rivers Museum in Oxford, 327; the Weltmuseum in Vienna, 200; the Museum of Ethnology, Museum of Arts and Crafts in Hamburg, 196; the Dresden Museum of Ethnology, 182; and the Metropolitan Museum of Art in New York, 163. https://news.artnet.com/art-world/benin-bronzes-restitution-1322807, accessed 28 August 2019.

[2] The former Kingdom of Benin is now part of Nigeria, which for decades has been calling for the restitution of the Benin treasures looted in the 1897 sacking. A Benin Dialogue Group was established in 2007 with the aim of establishing a museum to reunite in Benin City the most significant of Benin's historical artefacts, currently dispersed in museums around the world.

included the animalizing of Indigenous peoples. (McDougall, *Ochre and Rust* 28)

Object biography is a genre that has emerged from material culture studies "as a way to reveal and understand object agency" (Schamberger 276). It raises questions about the interactions of people and things in ways that are "culturally and historically specific" (Schamberger 277).

My "subject" then is an object of Indigenous manufacture from Benin City (which now lies within the Edo State of southern Nigeria): a small Benin casket (of lidded bowl) on permanent display in the Pitt Rivers Museum in Oxford (Accession No. 1900.39.4). But objects do not make meaning of their own accord. As Chris Gosden and Yvonne Marshall argue, it is an object's "social interactions" with people that create its meanings (169–78). Indeed, while the object of this biography had a life of meaning both before and after them, my interest in it in the first instance arises from its associations with Felix Norman Roth and his brother Henry Ling Roth. Felix was the advance surgeon with the main column of the punitive expedition, and Henry was an ethnographer, author, and curator of the Bankfield Museum in Halifax, Yorkshire.[3] As I have written in "The Making of Great Benin":

> Felix and Henry Ling Roth provide a window onto a period that not only, as Basil Davidson says, prophesied the triumph of imperialism in Africa (30), but that also, not coincidentally, saw the emergence in Britain of African Studies. As J. D. Fage points out, there was "no concept of African Studies as a discrete activity" in Britain prior to the founding of the African Society in 1900 (369). Most of the Society's early members, like the Roths, were amateurs whose careers had in one way or another brought them into contact with Africa. Less than 10% of those listed as Society's members feature subsequently in the *Dictionary of National Biography* (371). Neither Henry nor Felix are among them. . . . (McDougall 73–74)

Yet, as Annie A. Coombes observes, Henry Ling Roth "figured prominently in the history of interpretation of Benin culture" (46). In fact, the review of *Great Benin* in the *Field* in 1903 praised it as probably the best and most complete work of its kind ever published," including 274 well-chosen illustrations, certainly the most complete of the kind that has ever been published" (46).

---

[3] The Pitt Rivers Museum contains five objects known to have been collected in the field by Felix Roth. Two were donated by him, two came through his brother, Henry, and one came via Charles Kingsley. Of these five, only three are from Benin. The other two are from Liberia.

Despite its occasional bad press, biography is less ego-centred than generally believed; it is relational. This is just as true for the biographies of objects as it is for human subjects. The forced migration of objects out of Africa culturally impoverished the source culture while enriching the destination cultures of Europe, giving birth to the modern museum in the process as a secularised "holy" site, where the display of the primitive was instrumental to the launching of European modernity.[4] These objects of course often have significant cultural value, to the people who made them and for whom they had a particular purpose, but they have acquired significant economic value as well. Nonetheless, I have chosen this particular object neither for its indigenous importance nor its economic value, but because of the nature of its relation to a specific historical moment, to the individual and institutional protagonists of that moment, and to other similar objects.

The consequences of the 1897 war on Benin were profound. It destroyed the power of the traditional chiefdoms, cleared the way for the trade monopoly of the Royal Niger Company of Sir George Goldie, and enabled the establishment of the new colony and protectorate of Southern Nigeria just two years later. It also had major implications for the European art movement. It is customary for art historians to date the "discovery" of African art by Western painters and sculptors to the first decade of the twentieth century. Properly speaking, however, as Dennis Duerden argues (29–47), we should distinguish between this discovery of African art in the early twentieth century, which refers quite specifically to the art of the Niger and Congo River basins, and the very different kind of revelation that preceded it at the end of the nineteenth century. The artefacts of this revelation were not the masks favoured by Fauvism and cubism. They were bronzes and ivories of Benin. In other words, the sacking of Benin led directly to the first entry of the African arts into the European category of the "beautiful." As Henry Ling Roth himself wrote: "The taking of Benin city opened up to us the knowledge of the existence of a hitherto unknown African craft, the productions of which will hold their own among some of the specimens of antiquity and modern times" (Ling Roth, *Great Benin* 217).

---

[4] Scholars generally agree that the modern museum took shape during the late eighteenth and early nineteenth centuries, although, as Tony Bennett observes, it was "only later—in the mid to late nineteenth century—that the relations between culture and government come to be thought of and organised in a distinctively modern way via the conception that the works, forms and institutions of high culture might be enlisted for this governmental task in being assigned the purpose of civilising the population as a whole" (19).

Nonetheless, his use of the word "craft" (as opposed to "art") in this context betrays some reluctance. That is to say, somewhat paradoxically, that the Benin metallurgists, while exhibiting supreme skill and admirable technique, were denied those nobler qualities of art—such as grace, invention, and imagination—which would have raised them up the evolutionary ladder to enter the category of civilisation, which of course was reserved for European societies. For the same reason, it was argued, the Benin knowledge of metallurgy could not be indigenous, and must instead have come from early contact with the Portuguese.[5] We now know that some of these objects date back to the thirteenth century.

Today the Pitt Rivers Museum contains over half a million artefacts, from all over the world. The museum was founded in 1884 when Lt.-General Pitt Rivers, an influential figure in the development of archaeology and evolutionary anthropology, gave his collection to Oxford University. The General's founding gift contained more than eighteen thousand objects, generally referred to as the Founding Collection. His subsequent donation—of pieces collected after 1880, and therefore containing all the Benin objects—is known as the Second Collection.

The museum acknowledges five objects collected in the field by Felix Roth, though he donated only two of these personally. The Accession Book Entry for the one I am focusing on states that it was acquired from Charles Kingsley, brother of Mary Kingsley, whose *Travels in West Africa* (1897) had made her a household name and an acknowledged expert. The Museum's record of provenance is confusing. It has the heading "MISS MARY KINGSLEY" and it opens with the statement that the specimens listed were "chiefly collected" by her in "W. Africa." It goes on to acknowledge, however, that the bronze artefacts were taken during the punitive expedition under Admiral Rawson and "brought by Dr. Felix Roth" (Pitt Rivers Museum Accession Book Entry 1900.39.4.). As a consequence, the Ross Archive of African Images (RAAI)—the definitive contemporary record of published images of African art 1590–1920—has to hedge its bets, stating that the casket may have been collected either "by Ms. Kingsley or by Felix Norman Roth" (Ross n.p.). In fact, Mary Kingsley knew little about Benin, and had never been there. The object *had* been in her possession before it came to the museum. She had bequeathed it—along with several other items—to her brother, with the codicil that they be transferred to the museum when he died. But when *she* died in June 1900 he surrendered his

---

[5] The first Portuguese visitor to Benin was probably Ruy de Sequeira in 1472. But the Oba at this time showed little interest in the Europeans. It was not until the arrival of John Affons d'Aveiro fourteen years later that "meaningful contact" was established, when the new Oba welcomed him to his court (Ediagbonya 207–8).

life interest in the objects she had left him and presented them directly to the Museum (Balfour, "Report of the Curator of the Pitt Rivers Museum"). The association of these objects with the untimely death of Mary Kingsley—she was only thirty when she contracted typhoid fever in Cape Town—led the curator of the Pitt Rivers Museum (1893–1939), to report that a "special if melancholy and pathetic, interest attached to them" (Balfour, "Report of the Curator of the Pitt Rivers Museum"). She had been dead only three months at the time the museum acquired the casket. Henry Ling Roth had published a studio photograph of it two years earlier in an article in the *Halifax Naturalist*, in which he had made clear that, while it was then in the possession of Mary Kingsley, it had been "brought home" by his brother (Ling Roth, *Examples of Metal Work* 33). By the time Ling Roth published *Great Benin*, however, she had died; and it was in the museum. So he altered the holding credit. He also added a further detail about its provenance, stating that Felix Roth had found it in Benin City "suspended from a wall in a house" (Ling Roth, *Great Benin* 223). We may safely assume that his brother confided this information to him directly.

But how did the casket come to be in the hands of Mary Kingsley? Ling Roth was quick off the mark, probably being privy to inside information through his brother, and he certainly had access to the artefacts that were warehoused at the Army and Navy Stores before they were dispersed. He also attended the exhibition of the loot at the United Service Institution; and he described (and illustrated) a number of items that he encountered there in a piece he published in Holland in 1900, titled "Stray Articles from Benin" (Ling Roth, "Stray Articles from Benin" 194–97). It is possible, in view of Ling Roth's museological connections, that he acted as his brother's agent in the sale of some of the objects he had taken in the field. In any case, we know also that Ling Roth was a great admirer of Mary Kingsley and that she included him in her West African network. She introduced him, for example, to the Liverpool merchant John Holt (of John Holt & Co.), who operated a fleet of ships importing palm oil, rubber, and cocoa from West Africa into England (Birkett 118). Ling Roth even named his son "George Kingsley Roth" in her honour. But Felix Roth also was a friend of the Kingsleys and the casket could have come into Mary Kingsley's possession either directly (from Felix) or indirectly (through Henry).

The history of its description and display tells us a good deal about the progress of European understandings of African art. The Pitt Rivers Inventory identification of 1900 lists the object as follows: "Brass casket with cover and suspending chain. Embossed with animal heads, lizards and a human head, which is positioned on the centre of the lid" (Pitt Rivers Museum, Oxford, Inventory No. 1900.39.4). In fact, however, the earliest known description of the casket is Ling Roth's in the *Halifax Naturalist* (June 1898), which also features (as I have indicated already) the first known photograph of it, as well as the author's own fine line drawings of its enchased lid and base. Ling Roth presented it as a curiosity (a "curious casket"). But although the design is "bold," he says, it is also "artistic"— which curiosities, by Victorian definition, were not. It may be worth digressing here to observe that the Benin artefacts arrived in Britain at the tail end of the Victorian period, when the period's ornate and cluttered style and its high moral purpose were under attack from all directions. The Aesthetic Movement was leading the charge, liberating art from moral and narrative content, from Ruskin's insistence on political and social relevance (Landow). The "primitive" arts of Benin, as Ling Roth perceived them, seemed to bridge this late Victorian divide. In this regard, he believed the casket was typical of the art of Bini (i.e., Edo) art: it was bold *and* it was beautiful. The influential Victorian art critic, John Ruskin, was of the view that "pure and precious ancient art"—by which he meant "primitive" art— did not exist in Africa (or in fact anywhere outside Europe) (76). By the early 1900s, however, many of the same objects that had previously been regarded as "artifacts of material culture" were being exhibited in Western art museums and galleries. They had become "works of art," entering the modernist discourse of "primitivism." Ruskin, of course, would not have agreed. As Jonathan Jones writes in the Guardian, he would have found the art of Benin, as he did many things, "disgusting and repellent." Ironically, however, "there never was a better embodiment of all he thought best in art."

Ruskin's brilliance was to argue for the rough, the rugged, the organic in art, which he saw as an expression of a flowing, holy communal life. The art of Benin was made, as Ruskin said art should be made, in a spirit of community and faith, by anonymous craftsmen (Jones).

A month after Ling Roth's piece in the *Halifax Naturalist*, Ling Roth published another article ("Notes on Benin Art") in the *Reliquary and Illustrated Archæologist: A Quarterly Journal and Review Devoted to the Study of Early Pagan and Christian Antiquities of Great Britain.* Of the eight objects described therein, five—taken by Felix Roth in Benin City— had found their way already into the Pitt Rivers Museum. One, a wall plate depicting two catfish, was in Ling Roth's own possession still; and one, described as a "morion" (i.e., a kind of helmet, mostly associated with the Spanish invasion of the Americas, but more generally known in England as a pikeman's pot, worn by the New Model Army during the English Civil War), was in Mary Kingsley's possession. But what is remarkable about the article in the *Reliquary* is that Ling Roth clearly regards these as objects of art. More to the point, he concludes that the art predates the arrival of Europeans in West Africa (Ling Roth "Notes on Benin Art" 161–72).

The workmanship, Ling Roth admits, is "somewhat crude," by which he means that the "relief" work is "roughly cast" (i.e., not well "finished") and the enchased work is "irregular." But the proportions are "all good"; and despite the great variety of the ornamentation there is no "overcrowding" (Ling Roth "Examples of Metal Work from Benin" 35; *Great Benin* 223).

In fact, the "general grouping" of the relief figures (serpents and tadpoles, the human face on the lid), "the toned background," and the "real beauty of the major portion of the design" Ling Roth judges as evidence that the maker must have been a true artist, "a man of considerable taste . . . not only as a negro, but as a man of culture" (Ling Roth "Examples of Metal Work from Benin" 35; *Great Benin* 223). Of course, Ling Roth had no idea what it might mean to be "an artist" in Benin, or even if such a concept existed there. Still, to speak of a Benin artist as "a man of culture" was radical. A man of culture at this time in England meant a man of gentility, gentlemanly sensitivity, and restraint—in short, a highly civilised man. A number of distinguished commentators, faced with the indisputable technological sophistication of the Benin artefacts and their clearly masterful naturalistic representation of human form, sought to master their "epistemological embarrassment" by generating theories of non-indigenous origin.[6] Mary Kingsley, for example, had conjectured that some of the items at least must have been made in Birmingham and taken to Africa as trade items. Ling Roth disagreed. The first Europeans to have contact with Benin were the Portuguese in the late fifteenth century. By the mid-sixteenth century, Benin metalworkers had developed their skills to a "high pitch of excellence." The intervening period, Ling Roth reasoned, was insufficient for the Edo to have progressed so far. Still, he could not believe that their skills in brass casting had evolved in isolation. So, while he was willing to credit the manufacture as indigenous, and to dismiss the idea of European influence, he believed that the Edo had probably learned their techniques from the ancient Egyptians, migrating along the trade routes into West Africa.

In his June 1898 article in the *Halifax Naturalist*, he had simply observed a coincidence of spirit symbolism in Benin and Egypt, concluding specifically that these coincidences "by no means" implied "any direct connection" (Ling Roth "Examples of Metal Work from Benin" 38). Indeed, the "whole design" of the casket," was "so harmonious," that in his view it

---

[6] Coombes observes: "The confusing conjuncture of praise and appreciation for the artifacts with the adamant refusal to accredit any cultural and social value to the Edo themselves, often resulted in convoluted and self-defeating arguments" (*Reinventing Africa*, 24).

might just as easily have originated with the Phoenicians or the Assyrians (Ling Roth "Examples of Metal Work from Benin" 35). A month later, however—in the *Reliquary* (171–72) (and subsequently in *Great Benin* 234)—he was ready to canvass the probability of direct contact between Egypt and West Africa. The corollary of this was that the art of the Edo "may not be indigenous" (Ling Roth "Notes on Benin Art" 172; *Great Benin* 234).

The first person to propose Egypt as an origin for West African culture—or more specifically, Yoruba culture—was the Anglican missionary Samuel Johnson. He had completed his celebrated *History of the Yorubas* as early as 1897. But the Church Missionary Society would not publish it, and passed the manuscript to another publisher, who lost it, so that it was left to Obadiah Johnson, Samuel's younger brother, to reconstruct it from his papers and it did not appear in print until 1921. Still, Ling Roth was well connected and may have received a report of Samuel Johnson's theory of Hamitic origins much earlier. Johnson had worked on the book for twenty years before he gave it up to the Church Missionary Society.

The qualities of the Benin casket that had initially convinced Ling Roth of its indigenous manufacture were precisely those that he could not explain. The human face on the lid, for example, he could only describe as "bizarre" (Ling Roth, "Examples of Metal Work" 34; *Great Benin*, 223). From the side of the casket a "strange unknown" animal looked out (Ling Roth, "Examples of Metal Work" 35; *Great Benin*, 223);[7] but there were also more familiar animals—cattle and pigs—suggestive of agriculture. British anthropology at this time was in the thrall of Social Darwinism; and the cultivation of nature was the agreed indicator of social progress. Agriculture was the origin of civilisation. The man of culture, generally speaking, was a man of the city; but he was also deeply "cultivated."

Here was an object, then, *both* cultured and bizarre. Ling Roth was particularly taken by the casket's hinge mechanism, and he provided precise and detailed line drawings of it (Ling Roth, "Examples of Metal Work" 36; *Great Benin*, 223). The history of hinges can be traced right back to prehistoric times. But with the invention of steam power and the manufacturing explosion of the Victorian Age (introducing a myriad of new machines that required hinges), the hinge became a technology of endless innovation and ethnographic fascination. In any case, it was the ornamentation of the casket that fascinated Ling Roth most of all, because this was the most "bizarre" element of it—which, as I have said, meant the most African. His drawings

---

[7] Ling Roth was of course not alone in his strangeifying of Benin culture. His quotations from early European chroniclers reveal a pattern of repetition of descriptors like "strange," beginning in the fifteenth century.

of the casket's lid and base are extremely intricate and must have been particularly painstaking to produce.

Ling Roth's third piece, "Primitive Art from Benin," appeared in the December 1898 issue of the *Studio: An Illustrated Magazine of Fine and Applied Art*. As one of the most respected and influential art journals published in Britain, this might seem the perfect place to make a case for the Benin ethnographic objects as "art"—although the *Morning Post*'s notice of the magazine describes Ling Roth's contribution as "curious" and his drawings as "quaint" (3). What makes it "curious" is that this is the first article ever published in an art magazine about the Benin objects. Manuela Husemann points out, however, that Ling Roth changed his approach for his publication in the *Studio*. Whereas previously he had used the word "art" without a modifier, in the *Studio* piece he referred to "primitive art" and "decorative art" throughout; and he downplayed the "fetish or symbolic value" (179), emphasising "the decorative qualities of the iconographic elements in the bronzes rather than their possible metaphoric or symbolic meanings" (Husemann 16). He did not revisit the casket specifically, but he extended the general characterisation of Benin ethnographic objects into the art realm—and, as Husemann suggests, this marked "a further step towards the domestication of the bronzes" (17). This required, despite its indigenous manufacture, that it be comparable with European models. Hence, Ling Roth argued, it must have been partly copied from European models and partly introduced from other areas of Africa. Its originality, indeed, stemmed from its hybridity. It was characterised by its "boldness, freedom, clearness in execution," but its originality was "due perhaps as much to a grotesque mixture of subjects as to the method in which they are handled" (Ling Roth "Primitive Art from Benin" 184; *Great Benin* 213). It could not be said to be highly evolved. Its focus was limited to "isolated aspects of religious or court ceremonial, historical events, and individual peculiarities of human, animal, or artificial form" (Ling Roth "Primitive Art from Benin" 184; *Great Benin* 213). Therefore, while it might often seem "bizarre" (or "foreign"), it nonetheless showed a complete "want of fantasy" (Ling Roth "Primitive Art from Benin" 184; *Great Benin* 213). In other words, it belongs to that early period of evolution in the fine arts described by Henry Balfour (curator of the Pitt Rivers Museum, 1891–1939) as the "age of realistic representation" (Balfour, "The Origin of Decorative Art" 107).

The Austrian ethnographer Felix Ritter von Luschan reproduced Ling Roth's drawings of the casket in his multi-volume magnum opus *Die Altertümer von Benin* (1919). He also reproduced Ling Roth's photograph of the casket. In fact, even Luschan's description of the casket relies heavily on Ling Roth's, although it is much more dramatic, observing that the middle of the lid is "occupied by a negro head, from whose ears and nostrils snakes issue forth, whose bodies continue on the side wall of the vessel. Each of them has swallowed a man, from which only the head and arms stick out" (Luschan 422). This sits oddly with Luschan's use of the superlative "zierlichster" to describe the hallmarking of the pattern, meaning the most delicate, or (as the Ross Archive of African Images puts it) "the daintiest" (422), much like Ling Roth's description of the inside chasing of the lid as "pretty" (Ling Roth, *Great Benin* 223). But Luschan was able to identify the animal that, twenty years earlier, Ling Roth could not: in the radially ordered divisions of the lid design, alternating with the snakes and lizards, he found "panthers"—which today we know are really leopards, going through a black colour phase.

It is surprising that Ling Roth had been unable to identify the leopard (or "panther") on the casket's lid. It is the traditional image of the Oba, an emblem of his power and authority, and a common motif in the royal arts of Benin. In his article in the *Reliquary* Ling Roth describes at length a leopard ornamenting the head of a brass staff his brother had brought back from Benin (Ling Roth, "Notes on Benin Art" 163). He also refers several times to "leopards" in Great Benin; and he cites a number of other authors, both contemporary and antiquarian, who had written about Benin leopards, whether as figures in bronze (in the case of Henry Ogg Forbes, director of Liverpool Museums, 1894–1911) or as real animals, kept chained in the Oba's palace (in the case of seventeenth-century Dutch armchair ethnographer Olfert Dapper) (Ling Roth, *Great Benin* 30, 74). Others also had published on the Benin "panthers."[8] Luschan himself had written about a Benin "panther" he had seen in a private collection in England, less than a year after the looting (Luschan 146–62).[9] The publication was in German. But Ling Roth was certainly able to read German, for earlier in his life he had studied in Germany (Griffin n.p.).[10] In any case, his brother, Felix, had brought a large bronze "panther" back from Benin. It was probably the most valuable of the four items he had sold to the Liverpool Museum soon after

---

[8] See, for example, Figure 140 in W. D. Webster, *Catalogue 21: Illustrated Catalogue of Ethnographical Specimens, in Bronze, Wrought Iron, Ivory and Wood, from Benin City, West Africa. Taken at the Fall of the City in February, 1897, by the British Punitive Expedition under the Command of Admiral Rawson* (Bicester, 1899).

[9] The image of the "panther" described in this publication is captioned as being in private hands in England. But Luschan notes that two similar panthers were already in Germany, in the collection of Sr. Majestät des Kaisers.

[10] As Helga M. Griffin writes, Henry Ling Roth was "educated at University College School, London, then studied natural science and philosophy in Germany."

his return (Kingdon 29).[11] Luschan featured this piece subsequently in *Die Altertümer von Benin*. Of its providence he observes that Felix Roth had found it on a household "altar." Every house in Benin City had a shrine, upon which various ritual objects of clay, ivory, and brass might be found—all (according to, the principal medical officer of the punitive party, Dr. Robert Allman) "smeared and crusted over with human blood" (Allman 44). The leopard that Felix Roth sold to the Liverpool Museum featured as a key object in the 1931 catalogue of the museum's African collection. But it was seriously damaged in the fire that consumed the museum after the bombing of Liverpool in 1941.[12]

As the director of the Africa and Oceania Department of the Ethnological Museum in Berlin, Luschan was able to build up a wonderful collection of Benin artefacts. Today the museum houses "the largest and arguably the most important collection of Benin art in the world" (Willett 46). Ling Roth found it "especially annoying" that the Germans had secured so many of the Benin artefacts, which by rights he says (without the slightest trace of irony) should not have been allowed to go abroad (Ling Roth, *Great Benin*, xix). (Of course, he meant that they should have stayed in England, not in Nigeria.) The modest prices at auction of the items sold in London after the sacking of Benin confirms that initially they were perceived more in the category of the curio than the work of art.[13] On the other hand, as H. Glenn Penny observes:

> Once ethnologists on the continent realised what was taking place, they threw immense energy into staking their claims. A virtual flood of letters whipped back and forth across their networks soliciting information from the traders and auction houses offering Benin artefacts for sale, and securing promises of monetary support from their governmental and private patrons. Luschan, among others, quickly left for the first auction in London. Dealings began small . . . [but] neither the size of acquisitions nor the costs remained small for long, and Luschan's willingness to make any sacrifice recognisably

---

[11] The date of sale was December 1897 (21.12.97. 3–6). Ling Roth surely knew of the Liverpool Museum's purchase of the leopard from his brother. A few months after it he successfully negotiated with the museum for the sale of several of his own Benin artefacts (19.4.98. 1–4, 26.4.98.2, 15.1.03.19).

[12] "Survivors: Fragments of Leopard Altar Figure," http://www.liverpoolmuseums.org.uk/wml/collections/blitz/survivors/item-482299.aspx, accessed 31 July 2019.

[13] Coombes, *Reinventing Africa*, shows how objects held in the African collections of ethnographic institutions like the Pitt Rivers Museum changed their meaning over time in accordance with the anthropological theories of their directors regarding human evolution (degenerationist, diffusionist, etc.).

changed as prices became daunting. Through the last months of 1897, and the first months of 1898, auctions of Benin artifacts became common in London. These "tournaments of value" sent prices soaring as the directors of ethnographic museums on the continent clamoured for acquisitions, their supporters committed vast funds, and the owners of Benin artifacts sensed their desire. (Penny 76–77)

The result of this "acquisition frenzy" was the redefinition of the Benin artefacts as scientifically "valuable" (Penny 78). But as the museum collections grew, their directors became more and more particular; and while the rarest items continued to be desirable, the more numerous lost their allure, and many designated now as "inferior" became unsaleable. In short, the novelty wore off (Penny 78). Or, as Penny puts it, "Benin had been consumed" (79). Still, Luschan could congratulate himself that, outside Africa, there were only two other objects comparable to the Pitt Rivers casket: one was in the British Museum;[14] the other he had in the Ethnological Museum in Berlin.[15]

The display history of the casket is worthy of note. It has been on permanent display at the Pitt Rivers Museum for most of its time there. Like most of the museum's permanent displays, it appears with objects that are grouped typologically. In other words, as Jeremy Coote and Chris Morton explain, they are "arranged by type or function rather than by culture" (40). As Coote and Morton point out, there is now a sizeable literature analysing "the ways in which museums have displayed African material culture" (40).[16] But none of this literature focuses specifically on the Benin casket, or on object biography per se. The casket was included, however, in the first

---

[14]   The British Museum identifies its casket (Af1954-23-296) as a "lidded bowl (with embossed human heads, lid with bells) made of brass, metal." https://www.britishmuseum.org/research/collection_online/collection_object_detai ls.aspx?objectId=615204&partId=1&searchText=benin&page=10, accessed 11 September 2019. A photograph of it appears in *Benin Kings and Rituals: Court Arts from Nigeria*, ed. Barbara Plankensteiner (Ghent: Snoeck, 2007), 428. See also Nigel Barley, *The Art of Benin* (London: British Museum Press, 2010), 84.

[15] Ethnological Museum (Berlin), ID No. III C 10885.

[16] For a detailed account of early African displays at the Pitt Rivers Museum, see Coombes, *Reinventing Africa*, pp. 142ff. Staffan Lundén provides a similar account of displays by the British Museum of its Benin objects, from the time it began to acquire them to the present, in his doctoral dissertation "Displaying Loot: The Benin Objects and the British Museum," Göteborgs Universitet, 2016.

special (i.e., temporary) exhibition ever mounted at the museum,[17] titled "Art from the Guinea Coast" (1965). This was put together by the newly appointed curator, Bernard Fagg, who, like his brother William at the British Museum, had spent a good deal of his professional life in Nigeria. (Before his appointment at Pitt Rivers, Bernard Fagg had been the government archaeologist for Nigeria, later its director of antiquities. He founded the first public museum there, the Jos Museum, which was for a time the National Museum.) The "Art from the Guinea Coast" exhibition consisted of a total of 120 "specimens of West African art" (3). One hundred of these were Nigerian, including twenty-four on loan from the British Museum's collection of Benin palace plaques. These were the first objects to be seen upon entering the Pitt Rivers Museum, for they flanked its entrance, twelve on the left and twelve on the right (Coote and Morton 44).

Planned to extend for six months, the exhibition was so successful that it ran for six years. This is the exhibition that brought the African collection of the Pitt Rivers Museum to world attention; and as Jeremy Coote says, it had "a direct effect on the life-histories of the objects contained within it" (51). Some objects, included in the illustrations of the exhibition catalogue, went on to be displayed in other exhibitions at other museums or to appear in other publications. But the casket was not pictured in the "Art from the Guinea Coast" catalogue; and the only description of its decoration was that it was "grotesque."[18]

This may seem an incongruous choice of word for an object that earlier commentators had figured as "pretty" and "dainty," although in European art history the grotesque in fact refers to an aesthetic category that is characterised by incongruity, combining ugliness with ornament. (It is precisely this incongruity that Ling Roth struggled to encompass in his description of the casket's decoration as both "harmonious" and "bizarre.") Still, in its application to African art, the grotesque was a quality of primitivism. It showed a lack of discipline. More specifically, "the type of the grotesque," as Wyatt MacGaffey writes, was fetishism, which, "for Enlightenment thinkers from De Brosses to Hegel . . . was the antithesis of civilization; it was the product of merely random impulses and violated the elementary Cartesian distinction between animate and inanimate beings" (138). As Sidney Littlefield Kasfir reminds us, "The popular reading of religion in West Africa generally was to denigrate it as fetishism" (68). The term originated with Charles de Brosses's *Du culte des dieux fétiches*,

---

[17] For a idea of the museum's non-permanent exhibition programmes (1965–1993), see Kay White, "'Why Do We Do It?' Temporary Exhibitions at the Pitt Rivers Museum," MA dissertation, Leicester University, 1993.

[18] Bernard Fagg, "Art from the Guinea Coast," catalogue.

published in 1760, and subsequently (as Rosalind C. Morris and Daniel H. Leonard put it) was "sutured into the Enlightenment project," for which "it functioned as the signifier of a constitutive alterity" (Morris and Leonard viii).

It was Africa—the idea, as opposed to the reality—that served as the "doubled scene of Reason's birth in Enlightenment discourse: the site from which it emerged as departure but also the place to which its return was fearfully anticipated" (Morris and Leonard viii). This meant that fetishism was "tethered to notions of Africanity" (Morris and Leonard viii). In the mid-nineteenth century, MacGaffey tells us: "The romantic reaction against the academy and the classical ideal brought about a reevaluation of emotion as against reason, and therefore of the primitive" (138). But even as "primitive" objects edged their way into European consciousness as "art of a sort" (MacGaffee 138) they retained their determined status as the dark image of European "civilisation." In this context, after the Sacking of Benin, the Bini (Edo) became perhaps the most powerful exemplar of West African fetishism, conjoining supernatural and political power in the figure of their Oba. Ling Roth included a whole chapter about "Fetish and Kindred Observances" in *Great Benin* (Ling Roth *Great Benin* 48–84). But he had to admit that he had no idea of "the uses of the casket" Ling Roth *Great Benin* 224).

Fagg—unlike Ling Roth—must have at least known that the grotesque in ceremonial contexts often functions to intensify the emotional experience. Nonetheless, to the best of my knowledge, the first person outside of Africa to ever comment on the purpose of the casket was Paula Girshick Ben-Amos, a good fifteen years after the Pitt Rivers exhibition. In her book, *The Art of Benin*, she says that vessels like this are used during the annual ceremony of *Ugie Erha Oba* to honour the ancestors and to emphasise the Oba's own mystical authority and right to rule (103ff). During this ceremony, Barbara Plankensteiner observes, the members of the herbalists' guild, Ewaise, would bring a vessel such as this to the Oba filled with "medicine," and he would tap its lid four times while they prayed for him to remain securely on the throne.[19] This was part of the greeting ceremony known as *Otue* that takes place on the first day of *Ugie Erha Oba*, when, as Kate Ezra says, the Oba received homage from his chiefs and title-holders, each in order of his rank: "They greet him and receive gifts of kola nuts and palm wine in return, thus dramatically showing their acceptance of his superiority and of their own rank in the Benin sociopolitical hierarchy" (19). Of course, none of this information was available to Ling Roth in the late

---

[19] Plankensteiner, *Benin Kings and Rituals* 428.

1890s. In his discussion of the casket's ornamentation, while he had observed such details as the human face on the lid, with the snakes radiating out from it and sliding down the sides of the vessel, he could not explain them, which is why he thought them "bizarre." He must have realised how omnipresent they were in the royal arts of Benin—they appear in the text of *Great Benin* no less than forty times—and he knew that they were "fetish figures." But he could not know what they meant to the Edo. Fagg surely must have known when he was curating the "Art from the Guinea Coast" Exhibition. His brother, William, who was at that time the deputy keeper of ethnography at the British Museum, was well on his way to becoming a world authority on African sculpture, focusing particularly on Benin. The British Museum had acquired its casket in 1954 as a donation from the Wellcome Institute for the History of Medicine. So its "medical" purpose—as a ritual vessel of the herbalists' guild—must have been known. In *The Art of Benin*, Ben-Amos Girshick credits the anthropologist Robert Bradbury's 1973 volume *Benin Studies* for the information she provides about the ritual use of the casket. But he had gathered that information in the field as early as 1958. Today the curator's commentary on the vessel held by the British Museum record that the human face on the lid is most likely "the generalised image of an ancestor."[20] Further, "the snakes descending from the top of the vessel may be pythons, messengers of Olokun, god of the sea, sent to the settled land to protect the king." This draws directly from Ben-Amos:

> The python is considered as the "playmate" and messenger of Olokun, sent to warn neglectful devotees to change their ways. . . . Prior to the destruction of Benin City by the British army expedition in 1897, a large brass casting of a python decorated the frontal turret of the palace, emphasising the correspondence between King of the Dry Land (the Oba) and King of the Sea (Olokun). (247)

Ben-Amos Girshick was the first to date the Pitt Rivers casket—on iconographic grounds—to the eighteenth century.[21] This might give us a

---

[20] https://www.britishmuseum.org/research/collection_online/collection_object_detai ls.aspx?objectId=615204&partId=1&ethname=6698&termA=6698-1-2&page=7, accessed 11 September 2019.

[21] As Jim Ross observes, "Eighteenth-century art abounds with ritual containers of many forms, an indication that kings took full advantage of the capacities of objects to hold and store power." http://raai.library.yale.edu/site/index.php?globalnav=image_detail&image_id=596 7, accessed 11 September 2019.

clue as to why Bernard Fagg had so little to say about it in the catalogue for the "Art from the Guinea Coast" exhibition. His brother, William, denigrated the bronzes of the Late Period in Benin's artistic evolution as "decadent" (Fagg, *Nigerian Images* 37–38). Unlike the works of the highest flowering— the Middle Period, from the mid-sixteenth century to the seventeenth century—they were (as he saw it it) more prone to the "tasteless proliferation of flamboyant baroque decoration" (38).[22]

As far as I can tell, the Pitt Rivers casket has only once been borrowed for display by another museum—almost forty years after the "Art from the Guinea Coast" exhibition. The occasion was the Victoria and Albert Museum's exhibition "Inventing New Britain: The Victorian Vision," to commemorate the 2001 centenary of the death of Queen Victoria. This exhibition aimed to celebrate the achievements of the Victorian period— from the popularisation of holidays at the seaside to the adoption of football as a national sport and the invention of heated curling tongs—all the key elements in the making of modern Britain (MacKenzie). It is pertinent obviously to ask what role the Edo casket played in this celebration. In what way can it be seen to have assisted in the making of new Britain? How did it participate in the development of "the modern, motorised, bourgeois culture based on industrial and biological productivity" that constitutes Britain even today? (Conrad) The answer to these questions is perhaps provided by Peter Conrad's review of the exhibition in *The Guardian*:

> Britain's imperial primacy required the subjugation of other cultures and the dishonouring of their gods. The exhibition makes amends by gathering together some of these toppled totems—a disarmed samurai in gleaming armour, plump fertility deities from Africa and a slavish "Jolly Nigger" money-box from the USA. At the exit, a digest of Victorian films concludes with a car overtaking a staid horse and buggy, then speeding towards us to crush the camera. The title of this prophetic snippet is *How It Feels To Be Run Over*; this is what progress feels like if you have been briskly declared obsolete. (N.p.)

In summary, the exhibition suggested, the Victorian period promoted the ghoulish worship of death.

In 1897 the Benin Empire was declared obsolete in the most dramatic fashion. The Edo people of course have never accepted this obsolescence and are today demanding the restoration of their kingdom. The cultural

---

[22] For a detailed consideration of degenerationist theories of African art, see Lawal (193–216); Wood (115–37).

corollary of that political crusade is their repatriation movement to have the Benin bronzes and other cultural treasures returned.

Outside Africa, and beyond the specialised European discourses of cultural theory and art terminology, the secular imagination tends to forget the stimulative power of the grotesque, regarding it simply as ugly and repulsive. Add a touch of racial bias to that memory loss and it is easy to arrive at the notion that the grotesque in Africa is unconscious—in other words, that horror there has been normalised—which was one of Britain's justifications for invading Benin City in the first place: it was a city flowing with the blood of sacrifice and torture. Thus, from the British perspective, the founding of the Southern Nigeria Protectorate was a restorative measure aimed at denaturing an indigenous culture of grotesquerie. As Oyekan Owomoyela writes: "Africa was the land of the grotesque—grotesque creatures with grotesque features, grotesque mentalities and grotesque habits" and practices (78). In this context, while Bernard Fagg's description of the casket as "grotesque" may have been anthropologically correct in 1965, it was politically naïve even then. As Milton Allimadi, the publisher of *Black Star News* in the United States, has shown, the independence movements that swept across Africa in the early 1960s, sometimes violently, were reported in the *New York Times* by two-time Pulitzer Prize–winning journalist Homer Bigart, who regularly described them as "barbaric," "savage," and "grotesque" (n.p.). It would be interesting to know whether, in the 1970s and 1980s, when other museums began to follow through more substantively on the Pitt Rivers Museum's fledgling efforts to forge culturally appropriate methods of African display, the more authentically grotesque and confronting objects began to disappear from view. In any case, we know that with the increasing sophistication and more sharply critical museum studies of the 1990s, museum curators began to feel more and more nervous about charges of neocolonial stereotyping and even racism. While the casket in the Pitt Rivers Museum remains on permanent display, the British Museum's casket has disappeared from view (Coote and Morton 2). Objects are not free agents. The violence of the 1897 British punitive expedition not only robbed the Edo of their material heritage. It also robbed the objects involved of their indigenous agency, transforming them into diasporic objects, and forcing them to perform different roles in different contexts according to different agendas. As the agendas changed, so did the object's performances. But as that discourse developed and was taken up by European artists and critics it rapidly distanced itself from the indigenous art that inspired it. African "primitivism" came to be seen as "cultural," whereas European "primitivism" was consciously "aesthetic." Cubism, Fauvism and expressionism drew upon African art to a different end. By 1959, as Kingsley Widmer wrote, it had become patently obvious—from "even a cursory examination of some of the best-known artists who [had] employed primitive materials and/or techniques in the contemporary period"—that their work was disassociated "from primitive cultural and historical associations" (345).

To some degree the effects of the epistemic violence committed against the Benin objects are now being addressed, not only by the increasingly sophisticated museum display of African material culture but also through the progress of the Benin Dialogue Group toward establishing a new Benin Royal Museum in Nigeria where the looted artworks might soon be reunited.[23] For object biographies such as this one that hopefully will mean that the life of the subject, currently occluded by the colonialism experience and its aftermath, will finally be restored to full visibility.

References

Allimadi, Milton. "Inventing Africa," *Fair* (September 2003). Web. https://fair.org/extra/inventing-africa/11 September 2019.

Allman, R. (1897). "With the Punitive Expedition to Benin City." Web. 28 August 2019.

Ben-Amos, Paula. "Men and Animals in Benin Art," *Man*, n.s., 11:2 (June 1976), 243–52. Web. 5 May 2018.

Balfour, Henry. "Report of the Curator of the Pitt Rivers Museum for the Year 1900." Web. 30 July 2019.

—. "The Origin of Decorative Art as Illustrated by the Art of Modern Savages," *Midland Naturalist*, XIII. May 1890.

Bennett, Tony. *The Birth of the Museum: History, Theory, Politics*. Abington: Routledge, 2013.

Birkett, Deborah. "Networking West Africa," *African Affairs*, 87 (1988), 115–19.

Bradbury, R. E. *Benin Studies*. Oxford: Oxford University Press, 1973.

Conrad, Peter. "Victorian Values Revisited," *Guardian*, 8 April 2001. Web.

---

[23] The membership of the Benin Dialogue Group includes representatives from the Royal Court of Benin, the Nigerian government, and museum directors and curators from Germany, Britain, the Netherlands, Austria, and Sweden. In September 2019, the British architect David Adjaye who was born in Tanzania to Ghanaian parents (and who designed the Smithsonian Institution's acclaimed National Museum of African American History and Culture), was commissioned to undertake a feasibility study for the new Benin Royal Museum in Nigeria.

Coombes, Annie E. *Reinventing Africa: Museums, Material Culture, and Popular Imagination in Late Victorian and Edwardian England.* New Haven: Yale University Press, 1997.

Coote, Jeremy, and Edwards, Elizabeth. "Images of Benin at the Pitt Rivers Museum," *African Arts*, 30:4 (Autumn 1997), 26–35. Web. 8 October 2019.

Coote, Jeremy, and Morton, Chris. "A Glimpse of the Guinea Coast: Regarding an African Exhibition at the Pitt Rivers Museum," *Journal of Museum Ethnography*, 12 (2000), 39–56. Web. 4 October 2019.

Davidson, Basil. *Africa in Modern History: The Search for a New Society.* Harmondsworth: Penguin, 1978.

Duerden, Dennis. "The 'Discovery' of the African Mask," *Research in African Literatures*, 31:4 (2000), 29–47.

Ediagbonya, Michael. "A Study of the Portuguese-Benin Trade Relations: Ughoton as a Benin Port (1485–1506)," *International Journal of Humanities and Cultural Studies*, 2:2 (September 2015), 206–21. Web. 4 March 2019.

Ezra, Kate. *Royal Art of Benin: The Perls Collection in the Metropolitan Museum of Art.* New York: Metropolitan Museum of Art, 1992.

Fage, J. D., "When the African Society Was Founded, Who Were the Africanists?" *African Affairs*, 94 (1995), 369–82.

Fagg, Bernard. Introduction to *Art from the Guinea Coast*, Pitt Rivers Museum Illustrated Catalogue No. 1. Oxford: Pitt Rivers Museum. Web. 3 March 2018.

Fagg, William. "Benin: The Sack that Never Was," in *Images of Power: Art of the Royal Court of Benin*, Flora and Shea Kaplan, eds. New York: Museum Studies Program New York U, 1981, 20–21. Web. 2 September 2019.

—. *Nigerian Images.* London: Lund Humphries, 1963.

Gosden, Chris, and Marshall, Yvonne. "The Cultural Biography of Objects," *World Archaeology*, 31:2 (1999), 169–78.

Griffin, Helga. "Roth, Henry Ling (1855–1925)," *Australian Dictionary of Biography*. Web. 31 July 2019.

Hill, Kate, ed. *Museums and Biographies: Stories, Objects, Identities.* Woodbridge: Boydell Press, 2012.

Husemann, Manuela. "Golf in the City of Blood: The Translation of the Benin Bronzes in 19th Century Britain and Germany." Polyvocia: SOAS Journal of Graduate Research 5 (2013): 3–24.

Jones, Jonathan, "Spoils of War," *Guardian*, 12 September 2003. Web.

Joy, Jody. "Reinvigorating Object Biography: Reproducing the Drama of Object Lives," *World Archaeology*, 41:4 (2009), 540–56.

Kasfir, Sidney Littlefield. *African Art and the Colonial Encounter: Inventing a Global Commodity*. Bloomington: Indiana University Press, 2007.

Kingdon, Zachary. *Ethnographic Collecting and African Agency in Early Colonial West Africa: A Study of Trans-Imperial Cultural Flows*. New York: Bloomsbury Visual Arts, 2019.

Kingsley, Mary. *Travels in West Africa, Congo Français, Corisco and Cameroons* (1897). London: Cambridge University Press, 2010 (reprint).

Koloss, Hans-Joachim, ed. *Africa Art and Culture: Ethnological Museum, Berlin*. New York: Prestel, 2002.

Kopytoff, Ivor. "The Cultural Biography of Things: Commoditization as Process," in *The Social Life of Things. Commodities in Cultural Perspective*, Arjun Appadurai, ed. Cambridge: Cambridge University Press, 1986, 64–91. Print.

Landow, George P. "Ruskin and the Aesthetic Movement: Inspiration and Strawhorse." Web. 28 August 2019.

Lawal, Babatunde. "The Present State of Art Historical Research in Nigeria: Problems and Possibilities," *Journal of African History*, 18:2 (1977), 193–216. Web. 1 August 2019.

Luschan, Felix von. "Alterhümer von Benin," *Verhandlungen der Berliner anthropologischen Gesellschaft*. March 1898. 146–62.

MacGaffey, Wyatt. "Astonishment and Stickiness in Kongo Art: A Theoretical Advance," *RES: Anthropology and Aesthetics* 39 (2001), 137–50. Print.

MacKenzie, John M, ed. *The Victorian Vision: Inventing New Britain*. London: V&A Publications, 2001.

McDougall, Russell, and Davidson, Iain, eds. *The Roth Family, Anthropology, and Colonial Administration*. Left Coast Press, 2008. Print.

McDougall, Russell. "The Making of *Great Benin*: Felix Norman Roth and Henry Ling Roth." *The Roth Family, Anthropology and Colonial Administration*. Ed. McDougall and Davidson Left Coast, 2016, 73–92. Print.

—. Review of Philip Jones, *Ochre and Rust: Artefacts and Encounters on Australian Frontiers*. Adelaide: Wakefield Press, 2007, *Transnational Literature*, 3:1, November 2010. Web. 6 September 2019.

Morris, Rosalind, and Leonard, Daniel. *The Returns of Fetishism: Charles de Brosses and the Afterlives of an Idea*. Chicago: University of Chicago Press, 2017. Print.

Owomoyela, Oyekan. "With Friends like These . . . A Critique of Pervasive Anti-Africanisms in Current African Studies Epistemology and

Methodology," *African Studies Review*, 37:3 (December 1994), 77–101. Print.

Penny, H. Glenn. *Objects of Culture: Ethnology and Ethnographic Museums in Imperial Germany.* Chapel Hill: University of North Carolina Press, 2003. Print.

Röschenthaler, Ute. "Of Objects and Contexts Biographies of Ethnographica," *Journal des Africanistes*, 69:1 (1999), 81–103. Web. 5 August 2019.

Ross, James J. Archive of African Images: "Pitt Rivers Museum, Oxford; Bequest of Mary H. Kingsley; Collected by Ms. Kingsley or by Felix Norman Roth (Collection at time of publication)." Web. 1 August 2019.

Roth, Henry Ling. "Primitive Art from Benin," *Studio: An Illustrated Magazine of Fine and Applied Art*, December 1898.

—. *Great Benin; Its Customs, Arts, and Horrors.* Halifax: F. King and Sons, 1903.

—. "Notes on Benin Art," *Reliquary and Illustrated Archæologist. A Quarterly Journal and Review Devoted to the Study of Early Pagan and Christian Antiquities of Great Britain*, 4:3 (July 1898), 161–72.

—. "Stray Articles from Benin," *Internationales Archives für Ethnographie*, 13 (1900), 194–97.

—. "Primitive Art from Benin," *Studio: An Illustrated Magazine for Fine and Applied Art*, 15 (1898), 179.

—. "Examples of Metal Work from Benin," *Halifax Naturalist* 3:4 (1898), 32–38.

Schamberger, Karen, et al., and the *Australian Journeys* Gallery Development Team (National Museum of Australia), "Living in a Material World: Object Biography and Transnational Lives," in *Transnational Ties. Australian Lives in the World.* Desley Deacon, Penny Russell, and Angela Woollacott, eds. Canberra: Australian National University Press, 2008, 275–98. Web. 19 September 2019.

The Works of John Ruskin; Volume XVI: Joy for Ever*; Two Paths; with Letters on Oxford Museum and Various Addresses 1856–1860.* Eds. E. T. Cook and Alexander Wedderburn, eds. London: George Allen (1903–12).

Widmer, Kingsley. "The Primitivistic Aesthetic: D. H. Lawrence," *Journal of Aesthetics and Art Criticism*, 17:3 (March 1959), 344–53. Web. 1 August 2019.

Wood, Paul. "Display, Restitution and World Art History: The Case of the 'Benin Bronzes,'" *Visual Culture in Britain*, 13:1 (2012), 115–37. Web. 1 August 2019.

LOCATING LATIN AMERICAN MATTERS THROUGH FRANCISCO DE GOYA'S *LINDA MAESTRA**

INDRANI MUKHERJEE

While the entire history of Latin America has comprised the defeat of the objects of the continent to the design of coloniality at large, today it has become increasingly conscious of the geopolitics of this materiality. Why have language and culture always enjoyed their own agency and historicity while matter has figured as passive and immutable? This essay will look at select books and bodies (matter) from Latin America to argue how and to what extent Francisco de Goya's *Linda maestra* articulates and transgresses the borders of any givenness of knowledge (culture) in terms of the national, the global, or any other privileged siting of these books and bodies. This proposed reading (through the Goyan image as a metaphor of our own materiality) will also address our embodied performativity as readers of these books and bodies contaminated by our own immediate realities and worldviews.[1] What is the relationship between the materiality of these books and bodies, and an epistemology of a Latin American literature read in Spanish from India? That Latin American matter is not simply passive and malleable for easy consumption is contested by its historical narratives in literature and culture. Hence, this essay will highlight situations of how the books and bodies of Latin America have often induced a counter-narrative of violence and have survived burning, bans, or even exile. It will also look at reading Latin American literature in Spanish from India as a

---

* A shorter version of this essay with a slightly different perspective was presented at the XX International Conference of the Forum on Contemporary Theory: The Humanities across Cultures, held from 17 to 20 December 2017 at Gopalpur-on-Sea, Odisha, India.
[1] Readership will mainly dwell on direct reading of selected Latin American texts though eventually it will also refer to reading translations. This ambiguity prevails because the broader picture is about the embodied materiality of the location of this readership.

performative that locates the reader in a potentially dangerous space vulnerable to violence, death, or even exile.

While knowing has been mainly a Western phalogocentric privilege, the KNOWER had left himself out of his own preview of knowing as he considered himself transparent. He was thus the sole evaluator of all knowledge that he made, which was fundamentally Christian or secular/Renaissance or Enlightenment knowledge based supposedly on the rational mind. There was a fallacy in this as all knowledge systems that fell outside were marked as mythic, folkloric, magic, superstitious, ghostly, and savage. However, if the phallus and the written word were the tools of dominant hegemonic narratives, then Goya's *Linda maestra*'s broom and body are a very interesting counter-discourse. A reading with the prohibitive body knowledge of an old celestinesque hag is informed by a refusal to become the passive object of knowledge or the known. The take-off position of her body riding her broom is significant as it gives her the agency to bypass her drudgery and her circumstances to "teach" the young rider she takes with her. The knower-knowing assume agendas that transgress dominant normativity to take stock of the world that she had exited long back. The exile, displacement, and unbelonging of the nineteenth-century witch have continued to be relevant to this day. She is the material border that continuously pushes the hegemonic centre of power as she seems threatening, foreboding, and unscrupulous. She articulates the liminal heterotopias of conflictual spatiality that subvert the grammars of space-time-matter in order to politicise the most trivial questions of subjectivity or agency of sub-national, minor-gendered identities. She plays with nomadic contours to transgress any givenness of knowledge for passive consumption.

It is in this sense that I propose to use Goya's figure of the old hag to represent or perform a relocating of knowledge as she is called the *linda maestra* or "pretty teacher." This figure comes from a collection of dark paintings, where Goya articulates how the death of the rational mind produces monsters. Critics have pointed out that these dark paintings represent Goya's problems with or his endorsement of Enlightenment or perhaps Spain's own dark withdrawal into the violent dogmatism of the Counter-Reformation. More concretely, it also articulates Goya's own problems with the "conflicting demands of patrons, by his loyalty to the Spanish elite and *pueblo* alike, and by the shattering of previously secure divisions between public art and private desires" (Crow 78). Such controversy notwithstanding, this ambiguity is precisely why the *Linda maestra* has come to be useful for our purpose. Calling an ugly, bony, and naked old hag of a witch riding her broom a "linda maestra" definitely identifies her as a dislocated site of knowledge in a very significant manner. Essentially what she articulates is the breakdown of a centric monolith of a discourse called Enlightenment and Romanticism into a materially multipolar and contesting one. Indian readers of Latin American literature in Spanish position ourselves in this ideal embodied pluriversalism of a liminal space between two languages and cultures. We transgress these two realms of cultures trough translation and transduction, burdened by an ethics of highly political reading as performative.

To understand what this act entails, let us refer to Walter Mignolo's understanding of the issue of knowledge in terms of coloniality of power as he reads Anibal Quijano and Enrique Dussel among many others. He proposed border thinking as another way of thinking that breaks into hybrid zones of knowledge ensuring that the inherent violence of monolithic "civilised" narratives and practices of humanism remained exposed. As resistance to such violence, he gives the example of young Nahuatl translators who are trans/cribbing-lating their oral narratives into purposefully ungrammatical Spanish as an example of epistemic disobedience to the coloniality of power.[2] Epistemic disobedience couldn't perhaps be visually better represented than by the highly scandalous *Linda maestra* image. The woman's body and her broom become tools of manipulation, control, and agency for the most colonised subjects.

Mignolo has in the context of geopolitics of knowledge and decoloniality made issue of the lack of privilege of the Latin American critic who can only be so and no more, though European or North American critics become unquestioned masters of their opinions and their knowledge of Hispanism (Mignolo 2009). Given this situation, what could be said about reading Latin American literature as a foreign language literature in India? They are caught in the dualism of understanding as a native Hispanist/Western expert, which would preclude any use of their Indian baggage. At the same time, they continuously negotiate through translation and transduction any understanding at all. They run the risk very often of reducing themselves to the status of mere informers or interlocutors who should deliver from within a Hispanic habitus. They are conscious of their lack of privilege and pedigree appertaining to intellectuals from the West. Thinking through the geopolitics of knowledge production in this sense enables actionable critical thinking in unique ways. The zero point hubris therefore becomes problematic as we belong to neither of the worlds. Need our reading be the same as that of native Hispanics or Western experts? Can we work towards an epistemic delinking as we read Latin America critically? What would be the purpose of a unique reading? Mignolo argues

---

[2] See Mignolo, *Double Translation*, 2003.

that decolonial practices would involve a "definitive rejection of 'being told' from the epistemic privileges of the zero point what 'we' are, what our ranking is in relation to the ideal of humanitas and what we have to do to be recognized as such" (Mignolo 2009, 3). However, as Indian readers reading in Spanish, we are not part of that "we" to which Mignolo refers. How can we address this situation without being conscious of a heightened sense of alienation and distress? Translation becomes that zone that we continue to struggle against as the discrepancy between language and truth (culture and "matter") continuously fight against each other in our act of reading.

At the same time, can we look at ourselves through Latin America? Our geopolitics of knowledge, therefore, finds the Goyan witch to be an adequate trope for articulating our lack of privilege and "situatedness"; it is a feminised and embodied space of contestation and struggle as it potentiates a critical under/stand/ing of the materiality of the world and its perception in so many different ways. Knowledge is never assumed by her (us) as a given as she (we) manoeuvre(s), manipulate(s), and maraud(s) to traverse into areas of illegitimacy, ungrammaticality, and the abnormal, allowing visibility into our own ways of thinking to tinker with our rendition of the same. Comparative literature lends itself very comfortably to sit upon as our magical broom that traverses prohibited domains.

Even as we ride this broom of comparative literature, we are aware that perhaps we are also slipping into the only "permitted" slot from where to speak or from where we are even allowed a hearing. Indian Hispanists struggle hard to wriggle themselves out of any such designer templates of Western theories as they labour through the birth of their decolonial thinking via epistemic disobedience. Why should and how can we justify our use of the *Linda maestra* to argue about Indian Hispanism? As they are hybrid bodies, is that why? There is also the fact that the character of the classical Spanish witch called La Celestina, can be traced back to its North African and Asian roots. She has been the most suppressed classic in Spanish literary history, and one of the least known outside Hispanic letters (González Echeverría 1). Goya's invocation of the witches in his dark paintings in the eighteenth century is very significant in this sense. Nevertheless, any claim of Indian Hispanism as a precarity around which to organise ourselves risks a possible danger of falling into a slot of a certain identity habitus that could privilege one (us) over other fellow colleagues (them) without really empowering either. Thus, if we try to become the doorkeeper to this new hubris of democratic belonging with global Latin Americanists, we would be once again redoing coloniality. Our struggle, therefore, has to constantly be informed by this contradiction. It is in recognition of multiple points of power that our efforts towards a democratisation of knowledges can be somewhat achievable at all.

Books and Bodies used in Colonial Latin America

Latin American postcolonialists have shown that modernity was activated exactly when America was "discovered" and the "project of modernity" continues to be an ongoing process even today. Such a project, they argue, consists in submitting the entire global materiality to the control of knowledge systems through taxonomical order and violence. European humanism/modernity is premised on this violence as it implicates "exclusions from its imaginary the hybridity, multiplicity, ambiguity, and contingency of different forms of life" (Castro-Gomez and Martin).

The tools of domination were also things like books, bodies, and "myths" of the conquistadores who used them all to destroy indigenous political, economic, and human material dispensations and practices. Books and bodies were deployed by the missionaries and the conquistadores in order to delete, deform, and delegitimise all indigenous "texts" and bodies. Cartography, anthropology, and other sciences had achieved incredible triumphs over the inhospitable terrains on the continent and the bodies of Amerindian and African slaves (without their consent or knowledge) while biologists were making great "discoveries" of flora and fauna. America was the Hegelian land of the future as it awaited colonisation and "redemption" from its darkness and savagery.

Yet, what we argue about here is the fact that alternate "modernities" have always contested the monolithic grammaticality of a single modernity, both materially and epistemologically. Here given below is a Nahuatl poem by an unknown poet after the fall of Tenochtitlan, the capital city of the Aztecs in Mexico. It was translated later on into Spanish. The gory details of the destruction of the city are shocking because the books written by the Spanish conquistadores don't tell this story at all. Material remains of the conquest of Mexico by Hernán Cortés as elaborated here speak for themselves and for us. Moreover what is problematic in terms of the canon is that this is Nahuatl poetry. Canonical Latin American literature is normally considered as the literature written in Spanish, just as Spanish literature hides/deletes any Arabic and Hebrew literatures that emerged from Spain. This poem works like a historical archive that captures the plight of the Mexican peoples after the fall of the great city.

AFTER THE DEFEAT
(By an anonymous Nahuatl poet)

And all this happened to us.
We saw it,
We admired it.
With this mournful and sad luck
We found ourselves in anguish.

On the roads lay broken darts,
The hairs were scattered.
Unroofed were the houses,
Blood stained, its walls.
Worms swarm through the streets and the plazas
And the walls splashed with brains.
Scarlet the waters, as if dyed,
And when we drink them,
It is as if we drank saltpetre water.

We struck the walls of adobe,
And it was our lot just to find a net of holes.
The shields became his shelter,
But even with shields their solitude could not be sustained.

We have eaten sticks of colour,
We have chewed SALT GRASS,
Stones of adobe, lizards.
Mice, ground dust, worms.

We ate the meat barely,
When the fire was set.
When the meat was cooked,
From there they snatched it,
From the fire itself, they ate it.
We got a price.
Price for the young man, the priest,
The child and the maid.
Enough: the poor were worth
Only two handfuls of corn,
Only ten fly cakes;[3]
They were just our price
Twenty pies of salty grass.

---

[3] A kind of corn cake.

Gold, jade, rich rugs,
Quetzal plumage,
All that was so precious,
Yet in no way were they valued. (My translation)

Guaman Poma de Ayala's book *The First New Chronicle and Good Government* is another classic example of the period of colonisation. The book, however, was never published. Material destruction of indigenous texts had become the basis of the Spanish Renaissance as ideology and practice. It's impossible to track all of them as they were burnt. Some survived through translation and some others, through hidden memories of oral narratives. This effort of a Peruvian Indian to actually be published following European codes of publication is an amazing attempt at resistance. Guaman Poma de Ayala not only writes the history of his peoples, but also denounces the brutality of the conquistadores. Modernity in the plural thus threatens the processes of violence through tracking the remnants of dehumanising war (as in the Nahuatl poem above) or by writing books, like the one by Guaman Poma de Ayala. Alternate modernities had to use the coloniser's tools in order to bypass them or overcome them. They couldn't possibly confront the roadroller except on their terms: a Nahuatl poem to archive prohibited history and a translated book to avenge so many books burnt. Both texts were hidden ones, lurking between anonymity and unpublished status, respectively.

Bodies of Resistance

The *encomienda* system of labour was put in place in Latin America to exploit the indigenous peoples. Private owners of farmlands or mines had their own encomienda where the condition of the indigenous peoples was horrendous. Many of them died due to overwork, abuse, and disease; as their population decreased, black slaves were brought from Africa. When the conditions worsened, the Jesuits took charge of these affairs and they built huge encomienda where they trained the Indian peoples to do work as per their own requirement or the requirement of anyone who needed their labour. These unique enclosures of Indians were called "reductions" and protected them from physical abuse, abduction, and further displacement. Here large communities of Indians who were displaced were herded into policed spaces and were looked after in terms of health and hygiene, monogamous marriage, and family planning.[4] These Indian peoples were so loyal and dependent on their Jesuit priests that when the Jesuits were expelled in the eighteenth century, the whole system broke down and the Indians were once again vulnerable to abuse. The story of the black people was completely different. They were displaced and their bodies marked with seals, whip lashes, and other physical abuse. They had no protection of any kind from anywhere.[5]

Working with Canonised Bodies/Books

Our syllabi usually deal with the most canonised works, such as those of letters of discovery, conquest, and colonisation, Sor Juana de la Cruz, Domingo F. Sarmiento, José Martí, Rubén Darío, social realist texts, Horacio Quiroga, Miguel Ángel Asturias, Jorge Luis Borges, Gabriela Mistral, Pablo Neruda, César Vallejo, Juan Rulfo, Gabriel García Márquez and the boom novels, Manuel Puig, some female novelists, short-story writers, and finally the testimonial literature.

Here it is important to look at nineteenth-century Latin America. As nations were carved out after the exit of the Spanish crown, strong debates on race and nation-building sprung up throughout the continent. The most important book was Domingo Faustino Sarmiento's *Civilization and Barbarism*. It justifies genetically whitening out the Argentine population through miscegenation. This was implemented through massive immigration of Italians, Germans, and English peoples, as it was believed that such mixing out of the genes of people of colour would take Argentina to prosperity and development. (We could call this a genetic cartography through the bodies of people of colour). However this manifestation of an openly racist agenda where the coloured is racially marked as an object of knowledge and bodily control has been contested as the very bodies of people of colour have often refused to submit to miscegenation; moreover a

---

[4] For more on this see my paper "Syncretisms amidst Indigenous Peoples in Goa/South India and Paraguay/South America." In Ignacio Arellano and Carlos Mata Induráin, eds., *San Francisco Javier y la empresa misionera jesuita*: *Asimilaciones entre culturas*, 155–65, accessed 7 June 2018. http://dadun.unav.edu/bitstream/10171/27924/1/14_Mukherjee.pdf.

[5] My paper co-authored with Sanghita Sen, "The Kalaripayattu and the Capoeira as Masculine Performances: From Bodies of Resistance to Neoliberal Tourism Bodies," explores responses of black bodies through surreptitious martial art moves under colonisation. See *Longing and Belonging / Désir et Appartenance*, Massimo Fusillo, Brigitte Le Juez, and Beatrice Seligardi, eds. *Between*, 7:13 (2017), http://www.betweenjournal.it/.

white-majority Argentina has not been able to overcome its "third worldly" status any better than the other countries of Latin America.

The geo-politics of knowledge goes hand in hand with the geo-politics of knowing. Who and when, why and where is knowledge generated (rather than produced, like cars or mobile phones)? Asking these questions means shifting the attention from the enunciated to the enunciation. And by so doing, turning Descartes's dictum inside out: rather than assuming that thinking comes before being, one assumes instead that it is a racially marked body in a geo-historical marked space that feels the urge or gets the call to speak, to articulate, in whatever semiotic system, the urge that makes of living organisms "human" beings (Mignolo 2009 2). The monolith of European centrality in knowledge production is contested as other books and bodies defy any sacredness of a monolith highlighting pluriversalism, instead of universalism.

The Twentieth Century Canon

Of these "texts,"[6] I shall dwell here, for the purpose of brevity, on the most famous ones, of Jorge Luis Borges, Juan Rulfo and Gabriel García Márquez. Reading any text implies interpretation/translation anyway. The implications of reading a text such as that of Rulfo become doubly problematic, as it is so deeply entangled in its local history, unlike, for example, those of Borges or García Márquez. Rulfo's text also poses a major problem with its ghostly and elusive language of deformed spaces and times. When we enter the field of comparative literature, it is clear that it is not our aim to deconstruct such Eurocentrism, but rather to respond to situations closer to our local histories of conflicts of social class, sexual genres, and political discourses such as neoliberalism. It consists of a practice that transcends any linguistic, nationalistic, and generic frontier to pluralise an imagined and desired horizontality of the study of culture without hierarchy. It turns out that any deal with the pedagogical question of a literature in a foreign language refers to comparability, which invokes or embarks an act of interpretation/translation. Hence, interpretation becomes problematic, since there is the potential danger of reducing the text to mere content, domesticated and lame (Susan Sontag).

The book, however, enables dead voices to speak, remember, and dream so that they have the ability to make us nervous, to push us to rethink and

---

[6] The word *texts* here is used with some ambiguity in its relationality with books, poems, or narrative. It acknowledges Roland Barthes's "Death of the Author" as much as it admits Michel Foucault's "What Is an Author?"

repair the murmurs, whistles, and shadows of the ghosts lurking in the infernal spaces of their texts. So how can we do justice to a work of literature like that of Rulfo when we read it in India to teach? I am referring not only to a question of methodology but also to the epistemological problem that it is almost impossible to avoid falling into the trap of surrendering to an interpretation that in the end may result in another difficult monologue stagnating communication, or simply to create another text for it. The Rulfian text carries a whole Catholic ethic entangled in a sub-history of the Mexican Revolution, that of the Cristeros in rural Mexico. We find ourselves taking advantage of the complex spatial thinking of Henry Lefebvre and the Aleph of Jorge Luis Borges, who considers spaces not only as data but also as a production, a production based on a performative of simultaneity of a socio-political context.[7] We are both bodily present and absent at the same time, like the linda maestra!

Yet we end up suffering a great political anguish of how to transmit this vision beyond the constructed text of slippery words. This is presented as the most difficult pedagogical challenge because it is impossible to transcend the role of the said landscape. It is smooth and still rough, suffocating and still open, complicit and even inhospitable. It not only serves as a background but also plays with the characters that cross it, including the readers. Should the translation/interpretation that we make serve an objective proposal of an illusory ideal of the target language/culture or is it that we surrender to a more playful and intimate urgency of hybridity? Why should it matter how Indian Hispanists work with Latin American texts?

But reading in India makes it possible for us to approach it from outside the canon on the pretext that we are foreigners. Or does it? Thus such a step takes us to the no-space that we produce by placing ourselves in the Borgesian Aleph. So how can justice be done to the work of literature as it is taught/read? It is almost impossible to avoid falling into the trap of surrendering to an interpretation that finally tames the text. That is where we can empathise with the linda maestra who inhabits prohibited hybrid zones and deploys witchcraft in order to break in everywhere. This is an enabling and empowering situation of a south–south communication by clearly avoiding Western prescriptions of what literature is or how it can be read. We "translate" literally and metaphorically with our embodied presence in a very problematic hybrid space.

---

[7] The Aleph in Borges is a space from where one can see everything everywhere at the same time.

For a class exercise in which students are asked to search for other images of the said infernal landscape, they come with the blue paintings of Picasso, the photographs of Rulfo, the dark paintings of Goya (even Van Gogh or Tagore sometimes), extracts from the hell of Dante, and even children's literature or videos of ghosts. I do not suggest in any way that this methodological exercise solves our pedagogical or epistemological anxieties. But it suggests a way of overcoming, at least partially, the potential danger of reducing the text to mere content. The text, however, makes us nervous, pushing us to rethink and repair the murmurs, whistles, and shadows of the ghosts lurking in the infernal spaces of their texts.

Reading Gabriel García Márquez in India

Gabriel García Márquez is another cup of Hispanic American tea that poses a real challenge. Our reading, however, happens in Spanish as we work from departments of Hispanic studies. Our approach to *One Hundred Years of Solitude* is burdened with Hispanic baggage, especially that of the Spanish Baroque. The story of Macondo and the Buendias is notable in this sense as it evokes the epic ghosts of Cervantes's *Don Quixote*, Tirso de Molina's *Don Juan*, and the unique Latin American epic poetry of *La Araucana* by Alonso de Ercilla and the early chroniclers of the Americas. These ghosts, thereafter, take us towards understanding our own histories of yester-years and of today in very unique ways. Colonisation is often passed off as something that is common to us and to them.[8]

This version of colonisation can be traced to post-1492 Catholic Spain's experiences with the Inquisitorial invisible "Orient" in the metropolis and is thus unique. It involved Castilianisation, miscegenation, and Christianisation, which meant that the same processes of the gagging of multi-lateral translations into a unidirectional one continued throughout Latin American histories. Entire civilisations of indigenous peoples were "managed" such that any difference was converted into capitalistic value and at the same time into an epistemological one favouring Occidentalisation (Quijano 184–85).

Such New World myths and its protectionist agenda is read into the utopia-like foundation of Macondo in *One Hundred Years of Solitude* where

---

[8] See Quijano 181–224. In this essay, Quijano describes the coloniality of power as a concept of global capital and racial categorisation that informs Eurocentric perspectives from conquest to modernity. Quijano highlights three main components: 1. Belief in a historical evolution of modes of production, leading to the pinnacle of capitalism. 2. The belief that these modes are developmentally sequential and homogeneous systems that don't overlap each other. 3. The belief that modernity is a historical evolution justifying control of Europe over non-Europe.

Aureliano Buendia builds twenty houses on a river bank so that all the houses receive the same amount of sunshine and water. This was not simply an evocation of a nostalgic utopia for us. Nor does it reek of the romanticism of the Malgudi.[9] The Buendias who founded Macondo were an incestuous exiled couple. There was no myth of the Dorado that perhaps articulates García Márquez's rejection of the agenda of the foundational narratives of Latin America in Domingo Sarmiento's proposal of a racial social engineering (and an aesthetic one of nation-building) to genetically whiten out American people of colour through miscegenation. This aspect was something that Indian readers of García Márquez in translation have often ingested fantastically as the notion of the magical in his narratives. Here again one has to negotiate a border epistemological space between Indians reading García Márquez and Indian Hispanists' readings of García Márquez. Indian readers read him as an example of the postcolonial literature of resistance and/or as an example of world literature. The image of linda maestra as depicting her own unbelonging within Spain and Spain's own marginality within Europe becomes an interesting analogy compared with García Márquez as treated here.

No wonder then that many Latin American critics have maintained that the term "postcolonial" imported from India is inappropriate in the context of Latin America and that concepts like "*Transculturation Antropofagia*," "*Nepantlismo*," "contact zone," and "in-between-ness" are more appropriate (Gordon Brotherstone 23–42.) Many Latin American critics also deplore the commercial packaging of Latin American writing with magical realism. Yet García Márquez has argued in favour of such labelling not only through his own literary texts but also through such essays as "Fantasia y creación artística en América Latina y el Caribe" (1979). Dismissing the use of fantasy in the conversion of a man into a large insect by Kafka or that deployed by Walt Disney as essential to their artistic creations, he maintains that actually for the Latin American writer there is no such scope; on the contrary, he says that Latin American writers are challenged with having to translate the dimension of their realities into a credible one. Thereafter he traces the experiences of the conquistadores and the chroniclers of the Americas, the dictators and the heroes, and all the literatures that followed them. He contends that there has always been a real issue with respect to the insufficiency of the Spanish language to depict that reality. The magical real therefore represents a struggle of material reality with language, not unlike the use of the idiom of craziness by Cervantes in *Don Quixote*. Such a struggle with language has to be read against one of the most violent

---

[9] The Malgudi of R. K. Narayanan's *Malgudi Days.*

political histories in the world involving dictatorial regimes across the nineteenth and twentieth centuries, the Cuban Revolution, American imperialism, and neoliberalism.

Later trends in Latin America therefore, have had to reckon with shifting the paradigms of literatures of resistance such as those by García Márquez to others, such as the testimonial "writings" of Rigoberta Menchú that are a result of socio-political movements; or to Gloria Anzaldúa, whose real condition of unbelonging translate into border literature. Such writings become problematic for any claim of nationhood, an aspect that would put in crisis any disciplined literature. García Márquez thereafter moves away from writing a total novel competing with the real and the imaginary, and delves instead into reporting, chronicling, or simply writing seemingly marginal fictions, thus treading into the realm of the undisciplined. These are direct and crisp and very brief narratives. They are not allegorical, nor ideologically charged, nor inspiring. His last book, *Memories of my Melancholy Whores* (originally published in 2004), seems like a completely other world. One can't really say that there is anything typically Colombian *or* Latin American about it! It is true that it still fits in with the rejection of nineteenth-century agendas of romance myths of civilisation and barbarism. But there is nothing magical or national about it!

Earlier Borges had been hounded with questions of national literature. Borges, who faced harassment from Latin American provincialists many times over the course of his life, devoted a text to confronting these notions. He wrote, "the idea that a literature must define itself in terms of its national traits is a relatively new concept; also new and arbitrary is the idea that writers must seek themes from their own countries." Both these ideas survive in the notion of García Márquez's influence (Garcia Vasquez).[10]

Certain more contemporary Latin American writers such as the group Crack from Mexico and Roberto Bolaño from Chile have also made a point of *not* submitting to designs of "national literatures." The above-mentioned Crack Mexicans state in their Manifesto, ". . . every novelist discovers his own pedigree and flouts it proudly. The Crack novels, as children of champion parents and grandparents, challenge all kinds of risks."[11] In the case of Roberto Bolaño, there are ongoing debates only now after his death about how to include him in Chilean "national" literature. Bolaño had no patience for claims of national identity. "Books are the only homeland of the writer, books that may sit on shelves or in the memory," he said (Bolaño).

---

[10] Borges's text referred to here is "The Argentine Writer and Tradition." See his *Selected Non-Fictions.*
[11] This is my translation from Volpi 2010.

Reading García Márquez in India today perhaps continues to serve as an example of problematic belongingness. García Márquez is, without doubt, a brilliant storyteller. For us though, García Márquez becomes a window which sensitises us to read our realities through it. García Márquez has given us a "language" and an idiom for articulating the most violent, bizarre, and trying realities of our everyday lives. Such realities are scripted with full knowledge of the consequences involving social engineering and the new political alliances of global new-liberal and fascistic forces that have till recently remained controlled and contained by our liberal secularism and socialism as inscribed in our constitution. But that is beginning to be short lived. In our classes, García Márquez really does induce our students to relate the text with their own Indian experiences. "Love in the times of Hindutva" was the provocative response of one student! This slogan is really catching on since it appeared in the *Hindu* on 15 February 2015! While JNU students were protesting on the streets of Delhi, students of Delhi University and Ambedkar University were found ranting mockingly with garlands and wedding garbs before the offices of the Hindu Mahasabha, an organisation notorious for moral policing and harassment of couples found together on Valentine's Day, often forcing them to marry each other in order to ensure "morality" in society. The students, by protesting in wedding attire and holding garlands, intended to provoke the Mahasabha members into harassing them and forcing them to marry. This was meant as an act of rebellion. The students were all bundled off into police vans, thereafter.

Macondo however is a city of mirrors and one is also reminded of the glitz of Indian megacities with Macondo's glamorous night sky as well as its ghettoes, its trade union activism suppressed by police or false propaganda, and the land reform acts and farmers' suicides that stir up the United Fruit Company affair. The spate of riots and resilient survivors "chronicle" deaths foretold and like Miguel Littin, film-makers such as those behind *Parzania* or documentaries like *En Dino Muzaffarnagar*, recreate narratives that purport to speak truth to power. Activists, journalists, and intellectuals are harassed and any critical voice is very easily trivialised and criminalised. They either have to face the wrath of the state or write "clandestinely" using language of greater ambiguity. These are books of reconciliation with their immediate Indian realities. Our own realities seem like the enactment of García Márquez's scripts of "magical realism"! Life turns out to be a copy of fiction!

Thus, at this juncture any apprehension at viewing García Márquez as a magical realist perhaps runs the risk of falling into a prescriptive Euro-centric pit of so-called "marginal third world literature." Comparative literature itself, which rejects area studies, is also continuously challenged by its own *submission* to European/North American academia's seemingly condescending designs to hear it out as a third world voice! Is a south–south dialogic relationship possible at all on its own terms and conditions? Neo-colonialism and neo-liberalism continue to justify "global" frames of reference and yet can we provincialise the "global"? Ought we to? How can Indian comparatists and Indian Hispanists face this challenge and yet speak "truth" to power in order to cross or break permissible thresholds?

Perhaps some scholars at departments of history or cultural studies might have had to read this book. The point to be noted is that of alternate historiography or perhaps of the question of writing any history at all. But in Spanish the word *historia* means both story and history! For the Indian reader of García Márquez, her position is fraught with risks like a witch mounted on her broom. Fiction actually brings us down to our immediate realities. She has to negotiate the text and its spill over in tactical ways such that conflict and acrimony is minimised as our present times also reek of rising tendencies of intolerance and jingoistic nationalism. These books tell historical stories about chauvinistic nationalism, such as the Chilean case, and also about its exact other, which is the world of crime as in the Colombian case. These texts bring to the fore the terrible violence that is the result of the competing machismo of fascistic nationalistic discourse and the violent criminality of the drug mafia. This is also the case for an Indian writer who has found in García Márquez a baroque pen that helps her/him to map its most absurd experiences. What has also been the most attractive feature for Indian writers is the uniqueness of the way the Boom writers belong as a group. García Márquez was known to have given away a large share of his new earnings for the ideological cause without his wife's knowledge. His friendship with Pablo Neruda and Fidel Castro were his most important links with anything to do with India. India really did not leave any footsteps in García Márquez's writing.[12] Instead, what a wonderful spectacle the García Márquezian texts have been for us all!

---

[12] To explore further the Colombian writer's connection with India when he actually visited India in 1983 accompanying Castro to participate in the Non-Aligned Movement summit held in New Delhi, see Gerald Martin 444–45. Also see the following press releases: Nina Martyris. "A Gandhi, a Gypsy and a Rushdie: García Márquez's India Connect," Forbes India, 9 April 2014. Web. 2 June 2015. Nina Martyris. "Gabriel García Márquez's India Connection: Sanskrit, Indira, Rushdie and Solitude," Forbes India, 14 August 2015. Web. 2 June 2015. "Gabriel García Márquez and Fidel Castro: A Controversial Friendship," *IndiaTimes*, 18 April 2014. Web. 2 June 2015.

Did García Márquez himself wriggle out of his typecasting as a magical-realist third-world writer? This of course is a rhetorical question. Though many have criticised him for hobnobbing with political power, there can be no denying that he and his books have suffered bans and exile. His 1996 outburst calling to writers to intentionally flaunt and deploy the ungrammaticality of Spanish resulted in a great scandal at the Spanish Royal Academy of Language.

In 1996, García Márquez settled an old score in Colombian history, heading a small revolution against the dictatorship of dictionaries. To the horror of the Royal Spanish Academy and its American counterparts gathered in Zacatecas, Mexico, the celebrated author—lord and master of "Spain's eternal presence in the language"—declared himself in favour of the abolition of spelling. The snub was the final victory of liberal Colombian radicalism over conservative grammatical hegemony (Krauze).

For the Indian Hispanist this is doubly problematic since s/he has to cope with ungrammaticality and wrong orthography in a Spanish department. For comparatist writers and bloggers from this part of the world, reading García Márquez has become synonymous with an intellectual labour that is akin to traversing a dialogic heteroglossia. The cruel assassination of Rajib Haider and Avijit Roy in Bangladesh by fundamentalists and the harassment of Indian writers and creative artists in their own country have shown that there is no magic remaining in the creative faculties. An Indian writer of Tamil literature, Perumal Murugan, recently declared himself dead when some fundamentalists banned his book. Avijit Roy, according to one tweet, was reading *Love in the Time of Cholera* on 18 March 2014![13] Peruval Murugan also has admitted his indebtedness to García Márquez. I wonder how we would have received García Márquez in our own country today, had he been alive; though surely his ghost will keep reappearing in our safe laboratories like Melquiades's did. Are we all not actually reliving the solitude that the gypsy once envisioned for a single continent? Macondo has stretched its borders much beyond its own limits and has gone transnational. The more we indulge in t/his text, the more we may see how reality has become a reflection of fiction.

---

[13] See http://www.goodreads.com/user/show/25034185-avijit-roy, accessed 31 May 2015. Avijit's readings included *Schindler's List* and Anne Frank's *Diary* among various others.

References

Adorno, Rolena. *Writing and Resistance in Colonial Peru*. University of Texas Press, Austin/Institute of Latin American Studies, 2000.

Castro-Gomez, Santiago, and Desiree A. Martin. "The Social Sciences, Epistemic Violence, and the Problem of the 'Invention of the Other.'" *Nepantla: Views from South* 2.3 (2002), 269–85.

Crow, Thomas. "The Tensions of Enlightenment: Goya." In *Stephen Eisenman*, ed., *Nineteenth Century Art: A Critical History*, 78–97.

Eberstadt, Fernanda. "The Anti-Orientalist," *New York Times*, 16 April 2006. Accessed 1 August 2017, http://www.nytimes.com/2006/04/16/magazine/the-antiorientalist.html.

González Echevarría, Roberto. *Celestina's Brood: Continuities of the Barroque in Spanish and Latin American Literature*. Durham, NC: Duke University Press, 1992.

Lugones, Maria. "Heterosexualism and the Colonial/Modern Gender System," *Hypatia*, 22.1 (Winter 2000), 186–209.

Mignolo, Walter. "Epistemic Disobedience, Independent Thought and De-colonial Freedom." *Theory, Culture and Society*, 26, 7–8 (2009), 1–23.

Mignolo, Walter. "Transculturation and Colonial Difference. Double Translation." https://idus.us.es/xmlui/bitstream/handle/11441/33514/Transculturacion%20y%20la%20diferencia%20colonial.pdf?sequence=1. Accessed 27 July 2017.

No Signs and Graffiti in Contemporary Medellín: Significant Paradoxes in the Time of Peace

Juan Ignacio Muñoz Zapata, Édison Lopera Pérez, and Álvaro Sánchez Giraldo

In this essay, we reflect on the relationship between graffiti and the discourse performed by urban norms and the peace settlement in Colombia. Taking as a starting point the paradox of negation statements in signs (visual authorising prohibitions) and events (democratic refusals to "peace" that are violated by the state in order to install "peace"), we outline a brief history of graffiti in Colombia and Medellín, confronting the urban ordonnances, judgments on graffitists and their practice, and finally, the peace agreement document signed by the Colombian government and the guerrilla FARC. We follow a semiotic/deconstructionist analysis of the materiality of certain urban manifestations, comparing them with the abstraction and emptiness of discourses and symbols of peace. Graffiti expresses the post-conflict scenario more clearly than discourses on peace, through their subversive logic.

The Paradox of "No" Signs: Graffiti and Peace

A notice (shown in Figure 1) appeared on the backdoor of a private Catholic secondary school in Medellín, Colombia, during the first semester of 2017. Stuck on with Scotchtape during a rainy season, it did not stay up long. What amazed passers-by who had the opportunity to see it was the evident paradox between what is forbidden and what is allowed in a spatial distribution—the door and its columns versus the grey and peripheral wall. This spatial configuration does not exclude the prohibition on the "free writing zone": neither offensive images or writings (containing sexual images or coarse language) nor political statements can be displayed. Paradoxically, the sentence includes a pictorial term in an abstract acceptation—*tinte*—which can be translated as "hue," "hint," "tinge," or "touch." A weak and ephemeral piece of paper, probably written by a staff member from the religious school and printed by a secretary, it functions as a subversive method of expression in order to protect an immaculate green metallic door and alleviate the social discourse that can be caustic for the indoor teaching and learning community.

Figure 1. The notice can be translated as: "To all graffitists: you are urged not to paint on the door and its columns. You can use the wall for your graffiti, provided that they do not have an offensive or political hue. Thank you." (Photo taken by the authors.)

This piece of paper is the site of a top-down/inward to bottom-up/outward negotiation between the official normative discourse and a shapeless emergence of other voices. The grey wall becomes a mural, a way of using "art projects in order to take control of urban surfaces used by graffitists while rallying public opposition to graffiti expression" (quoted in Moreau and Alderman 109). The aestheticisation of graffiti as a controlled art in terms of its spatiality and its contents, surviving thus as street art and murals of apparently inoffensive coloured tags in confined and interstitial urban spaces such as non-residential segments of avenues and streets, bridges or metro facilities, would be the only condition of "decriminalisation" and tolerance. The notice in Figure 1 works as a more solid prohibitive sign such as "No Skateboarding," "No Pets Allowed," "No Walking on the Grass," or "No Loitering" (Moreau and Alderman 110). Public space is constructed with the materialisation of normative ordonnances and assumptions based on common sense (quoted in Moreau and Alderman) and these manifestations are considered to be "pollution," "disease," or "danger" against the beauty of urban landscape and private and public property.

The comparison enables us to understand the current process of peace in Colombia through a "battle" or "war" between prohibition signs and graffiti in Medellín in terms of iconography and discursivity. After more than sixty years of war, Colombia is facing a possible change in its history due to the agreement the government and FARC, one of the prevailing guerrilla groups in the country, signed in 2016, despite a plebiscite won by a small margin by peace-process detractors. Public opinion is divided over with the resultant turmoil mirroring the historical identity of the nation, the current stirring in Latin American geopolitics, and the nightmares that both right- and left-wing representatives and supporters project in their discourses. In Medellín—an extremely well-known city because of its historical records of violence and drug trafficking—the "no" vote was double that of the "yes" vote, as Table 1 shows. Likewise, the "no" vote outnumbered the "yes" vote in percentage in Bogotá, the capital of Colombia.

CITY	YES FOR PEACE TREATY VOTE	NO FOR PEACE TREATY VOTE
Bogotá	56.07% (1.423.612 votes)	43.92% (1.114.933 votes)
Medellín	37.02% (253.548 votes)	62.97% (431.173 votes)

Table 1. The Results of the plebiscite for the endorsement of the peace agreement in Bogotá and Medellín. Source: *El Tiempo* (October 2016).

On 3 October 2016, the world woke up to the news of another Brexit—only, this time, it was in South America. Comparisons are odious, but they help us understand events. Contemporary democracies utilise a logic different from nation-state projects, as much in a First World country as in a developing one. A referendum with the question "Should the United Kingdom remain a member of the European Union or leave the European Union?" or a plebiscite asking for endorsement for the peace agreement might bring a majoritarian negative decision, declining such possibilities of peace. Governments are forced to assume the consequences. In the case of Colombia, the "no vote," whose sponsors are suspected of engaging in fraudulent propaganda, insisted upon a revision of the final agreement that the government and the FARC representatives signed on 24 November 2016. The symbolic failure after the first signature on 26 September was overwritten with a final revision—like a tag appearing on a prohibition sign, or the most revolutionary political message in aerosol being removed from a wall. Signs are the temporary materialisation of changing events and contradictory unchanging human nature.

Signs are paradoxical, being the point at which opposite elements—the signified and the signifier in the Saussurean semiotic model, the abstract value and the devalued metal of a coin, culture, and economy, the soul and the flesh in a dualistic religion, materiality and semantic spirituality—intersect. Signs imply their own negation: an element is defined by its negation within a closed system. Even the sign "no" is an affirmation of a negation: we (do not) want peace; we (do not) want to stay. In this sense, graffiti defines clean walls in cities and their prohibition is an invitation to show up; referenda and plebiscites are questions to "no" answers that turn out to be "yes" decisions for states. Acceptance of graffiti means an aesthetical domestication of its *raison d'être*; however, the political message can find other means of codification such as colours, textures, allegorical drawings, and the unnoticed figuration of millions of underdogs.

Graffiti exists because prohibition offers erasure, which is an overwriting. Rather than the consubstantial act of signification in the Saussurean linguistic sign, graffiti has sheer material semiosis in this *sous rature* or overwriting. Following Derrida's and Eco's (mis)interpretation of Peirce's texts, a paradox that has its "charms," semiosis is "the endless process of signs interpreting signs, within which only is there meaning" (Short 45). As the semiotic counterpart of philosophical deconstruction, this means that we are always pursuing meaning in an endless chain of signs. But, instead of desiring a signified sought by totalitarians, those who need a "reassuring end to the reference from sign to sign" (quoted in Short 46), graffiti has a semiosis with an anchored political meaning—if this meaning is not explicit and socially extended, graffiti transforms into tags. Instead of a list of meanings that multiply in the paradigmatic axis, graffiti capsulises signifiers and engraves them on a few metres of brick, condensing in this point the syntagmatic axis—if they offer meaning elsewhere, they are allegorical murals and sophisticated street art. Prohibitions, such as we observe in Figures 2 and 3, transform graffiti into urban palimpsestic signs whose semiosis is encrypted by layers of overwriting.

Figure 2. Official billboard from the Mayoralty of Medellín: "We all are Medellín. Behave yourself." (Photo taken by authors.)

Figure 3. "This wall is the property of the City of Medellín." (Photo taken by authors.)

Obviously, in these images, we do not have graffiti, but tags, signatures with a restricted meaning for the vast majority. However, the fact they are overwritten in official signs renders them paradoxical signs, no-signs. The imperative watchword *portate bien* ("behave yourself," "be wise") is an invitation to transgression and engaging in "bad behaviour." The public property of the city acquires materiality only when it is violated by a minority. If the piece of paper on the school backdoor as shown in Figure 1 provides a semantic and spatial delimitation to graffitist practices, Figures 2 and 3 anchor the meaning of abstract words such as *civility* and *property* in their negation. We can draw "happy people holding hands" or "another brick on the wall" in order to illustrate the ideas of civility or propriety, but as semiosis and deconstruction argue, we will grasp more signs ad infinitum. Regarding peace, talking about symbols, a white dove carrying an olive stick is nothing else but a drawing of a white bird with something green in its beak, or what we want it to be. We decide its meaning. It also applies to a definition of graffiti or peace. We can comprehend the former through a brief history of its arrival in Colombia.

A Brief History of Graffiti and Its Arrival in Colombia

The social phenomenon of graffiti has been configured today as an action that generates the possibility of free expression. Since its beginning in caves and ancient civilisations, lines and strokes were not only symbols for ideas but also representations of what was happening in a specific context (quoted in Ramírez 5). Through this mode, the inhabitants locate themselves in the space they inhabit and develop certain approaches to everyday events. Individuals who are confronted by oppressive situations thus obtain a space to express their political stance. In this regard, Herrera and Olaya state that graffiti can be: "a narrative emerging from visual worlds that are created in the cities where politics are less discussed than muted" (54). Thus, a silent request paints the streets with the potential to depict the social conditions of individuals who are opposed to the system. This makes others, especially youngsters, imitate the modes of transmitting messages that were used in New York during the 1960s, when a young man wrote his name and the street number: "Taki 183." After that, teenagers began imprinting their signatures in different parts of the city (quoted in Powers 139). Even if this act turned out to be vandalism, they motivated other people to follow their example and take decisions for their own empowerment against the logic of common sense and normative urban patterns. As a significant act, there is more than a signature or a message on the wall, since a cultural conflict underlies the act: the population must accept graffiti and street art as social and cultural expressions or label them as criminal acts to be eradicated.

In a similar mode, graffiti developed in Colombia against a political background, in the beginning of the 1980s, a period that was "highlighted by [an] unstable political scene, an increase of violent acts, the rise of traffic drugs cartels" (Mendoza 19). Besides, illegal armed groups such as the guerrillas and the paramilitary got stronger at the same time as social movements involving minorities and unions were knocked into shape all over the country. Students and communal leaders perceived the walls as channels for spreading their message and ideology. But it was also a mechanism that subversive and illegal groups used for displaying threats, territorial signposting, and for misappropriation of lands in rural regions and small towns. Intimidation of minorities, homosexuals, or political adversaries could appear early in the morning in a strategic place—the façade of a house, a church, a school, a hospital, a police station. Sometimes the perpetrators of those visual acts of terrorism were anonymous; sometimes, they left their signature.

In the urban sphere, state universities were the first canvases for politicised and satirical messages that rejected the increase of violence due to national ideological differences and displayed a penchant for left-wing agendas in a Cold War world. Liévano, known by the pen name Kesheva, wrote in *El Tiempo* in 1984 that the president Belisario Betancurt Cuartas asked the population to draw doves, the symbol of peace, on the walls of cities. That was a motivation for graffitists to move from the university walls and bathrooms to bourgeois, Catholic, self-righteous Colombian cities. Thereafter, many corners of the country became spaces for registering discontent, with the larger public as the intended audience. However, the spread of graffiti also led to a proliferation of prohibition signs hampering the free expression of graffiti.

With the release of movies such as *Electric Boogaloo* (1984) by Sam Firstenberg or *Beat Street* (1984) by Stan Lathan, depicting New York, graffiti gained popularity in several cities, among which was Medellín, the second most populous in the country. However, little by little, it tuned into a more artistic form that was less explicitly political in its content—a more pleasing and subtler street art. Youngsters understood graffiti as a source of hip hop culture, which was welcomed in the outskirts and peripheral neighbourhoods. Hip hop schools were established and there was a change of mindset among young people who, seeing no opportunities for their life projects and pushed to delinquency, entertained the idea of using graffiti as an alternative.

From the latter half of the 1980s through the 1990s and 2000s, violence in the city reached its peak with innumerable homicides, kidnapping, and extortion cases registered. This made graffiti a risky activity. Numak, one of the first graffitists in Medellín, commented in an interview for *Cartel Urbano Magazine*: "many people were scared of going out and painting in the streets because the local authority for a long time was not the police, but, for instance, paramilitary groups named Convivir" (n.p.). He also explained that "the owners of the *comunas* [suburban districts] ruled and did not allow artists to write on the walls" (n.p.). Despite the violent acts they faced, graffitists did not stop their work, thanks to the hip hop schools, the community commitment, and the work of directors of cultural affairs. Currently, in Medellín, graffiti is considered a tool for strengthening the resilience of its population and rebuilding the city symbolically. Nowadays, two important activities involving graffiti take place in the city. One of them is Graffitour, an initiative that began after the assassination of Comuna 13 leaders in August 2017. The group Casa Kolacho has transformed the place into a comfortable landscape for expressing artistic and political ideologies through graffiti. The second activity is Pictopia, an international festival of urban visual art that began in 2013. Both are attempts to attract the attention of outsiders and to overwrite the dismal past with a new narrative.

Visual Arts, Graffiti, and Police Ordinances in Medellín

Medellín has stood out in the fields of visual and plastic arts with names such as Fernando Botero (b.1932), the most famous Colombian figurative artist and sculptor, and Débora Arango (1907–2005), one of the first female painters in Colombia, dominating the artistic scene. We use the case of Botero to explain a social and aesthetic judgement regarding graffiti. A series of sculptures of Fernando Botero's particular rounded human and animal figures are exhibited outdoors in public squares and his paintings can be found in the Museo de Antioquia. No one can deny the value of his work and its importance to official culture. However, the appearance of a tag on one of his sculptures (see Figure 4), not in Medellín, but in Milan, Italy, pushed the artist to assert that "graffiti are not art; they are a misfortune for humankind, they have ruined a lot of beauties [in] the world" (EFE, n.p.). This kind of judgement is not exclusively the preserve of people in the field of art. Laypeople have also expressed similar opinions regarding graffiti.

Figure 4. Botero's sculpture in Milan, Italy, which was vandalised with a pro-feminist "w" in the area of the female genitalia (Source: EFE, July 2007).

Perceptions of graffiti are controversial. Some state that it is an act of vandalism, generally associated with youth subcultures. However, according to Hurtado Galeano,

> . . . young people from Medellín do not give up in their pursuit for recognition seeking to widen our narrow political sphere where there are only political habits anchored in patronage, corruption, militarism, bossism, authorism, machismo, indiscriminate devastation of living beings. (112)

Young people from Medellín "pretend" to articulate political ideologies through artistic projects. They perceive the city as a space where they are able to show their messages on the walls in order to make citizens more aware of what is happening in the region or the country. In the same article, Galeano affirms that

> . . . that same overwhelming reality emerges when we think about strong and radical strategies that exclude multiple groups from political community, a separation leading to the complete wipe-out of the other. Young people from Medellín belong to this map of diverse life-forms and subaltern cultural identities in an ongoing strive against hegemonic culture. (112)

In Medellín, graffiti art is a cultural tool that links social imaginaries that people want to represent on the streets (González 26). This can be observed around many places in the city. For instance, close to San Vicente Hospital and on the columns of Hospital Metro Station, the graffiti alludes to all kinds of messages and purposes. Proximity with the metro utilities has caused some problems. In 2016 and 2017, some wagons were found painted (Figure 5), inviting controversy: Francisco Torres, the manager of the Medellín Metro infrastructure, announced that the company would proceed to clean up the wagons and denounced the incident: "We report this act drawing on material evidence left by the vandals, such as aerosol bottles and others elements. Besides, we reiterate that we will intensify security measures in order to avoid the repetition of an act like that" (Velásquez, "Nuevamente el metro" n.p.).

Figure 5. Picture taken on 6 March 2016 (Source: Velásquez, 2017).

On the basis of these cases, one can highlight several issues about the legitimacy of graffiti. Is it an act of vandalism per se in the contemporary normative world of blurred public and private spaces? During the furore over the metro incident, Jeihhco, a graffitist, painted an imitation of Botero's signature on a wagon, asking offended people on Instagram if that could be taken as art or vandalism (Noticias Caracol, "¿Qué decían?"). If it is art, where can it be produced? If there is a place to do it, should it be restricted to be just a domesticated form of minor art encompassed in decorative urban murals? These questions should be considered in view of ordinances such as the Police National Code of 2016, which forbade graffiti:

Article 140: Behaviors against the care and integrity of the public space.
    3. To alter, remove, damage or destroy urban or rural amenities such as

traffic lights, road signs, public telephones, hydrants, transport stations, lanterns or lighting components, benches or garbage containers. ("Congreso de Colombia" 80)

Playing or not with the semantic scope of each verb—alter, remove, damage, destroy—and the implication of graffiti over amenities, one can infer, regarding the questions raised above, that if all manifestations of graffiti are considered acts of vandalism and the culprits must pay a fine, then there is a direct prohibition of any kind of political expression coming from the othered sections of the society.

Another problematic situation emerges when prohibition signs and graffiti are encountered. The sense of graffiti for those who practice it and for those who see no sense in this form of expression are radically opposed to each other. For graffitists, graffiti completely loses its essence, its meaning, when its execution and exhibition need an opinion and/or authorisation from a third party. Graffiti, in most cases, has the major objective of stirring up controversy, either by the symbolic message it contains or by appearing in places that are culturally considered unfit for this kind of act. In short, an act of rebellion. As Aldo Civico puts in an opinion column for the newspaper *El Espectador*: "graffiti art is essentially a political act of transgression and a ritual of empowerment. It is born to annoy, provoke and annoy 'right thinking.' Graffiti art is not for you to like, but to make you uncomfortable" ("Que viva," n.p.). Besides, urban artists are aware of contradictory discourses: "while appreciating art and condemning vandalism is done with the intention of being inclusive, in fact, at a deeper level, this distinction reveals a stigmatizing attitude" (Cívico 12). This stigmatisation can be seen in a publication in *El Colombiano*, where Federico Gutiérrez, the mayor of Medelin, states: "most citizens reject a fact that was vandalism. [. . .] We have had groups of graffitists who respect the norms" (n.p.).

Coercive norms combine with preconceptions and social representations regarding graffiti. Botero condemns an overwriting of femininity on his sculpture as vandalism. The "W," which stands for "Women" is a signature, just like various elements in Figures 2 and 3, which stand for civility and property. Such elements in graffiti intensify an abstract idea, an intensification that reveals ambiguities and paradoxes in the social order. Indeed, producing these paradoxes, although they remain unconscious in practical everyday life, is part of the social learning where consensus, treaties, and meanings are anchored. For example, the adult and mature population consider it necessary to have rules that regulate the practice of graffiti. However, this claim for regulation is more a matter of morality as a social construct than it is a form of visual aesthetics. "La pared y la muralla son el papel del canalla" (the wall is the rogue's sheet) is a popular saying that

Colombian children have to listen to at home and in the classroom. But, at the same time, children are urged to write in order to acquire literacy. The point is that young children have to learn the difference between the wall and the sheet, or the white/chalk board and a doorway. He or she can become literate only if the practice of writing takes place on "acceptable" sites in "acceptable" modes. Offensive statements and political hues or *tintes* must be avoided at all costs. If he or she fails to do so, the state will tag them "illiterate rogues" who must be "brought under control."

Definitions and Decisions: Post-Conflict Medellín and Graffiti

Since 2012, under the mandate of President Juan Manuel Santos, who was the Nobel Peace Prize Laureate in 2016, the Havana peace dialogues between delegates of the Colombian government and members of the guerrilla group FARC-EP have attempted to bring the fifty-six-year-old armed conflict to an end (Presidencia de la República 1). The outcome of this process was the cessation of the war in 2017, despite opposition from a significant section of the political class and a detractor branch of the FARC, the continuation of subversive activities by ELN, another Marxist guerrilla group, and the reappearance of right-wing self-defence groups. The introduction to the document of the Final Agreement argues that Colombia has been witness to the confrontation between the two groups for many years, with civilians being the most affected:

> Finishing the armed confrontation will mean, in the first place, the end of the enormous suffering that has caused the conflict. There are millions of Colombians who have been forced to displacement, hundreds of thousands of deaths, tens of thousands of disappeared people of all kinds, not to mention the large number of populations that have been affected in one way or another across the territory, including women, children and adolescents, peasants, indigenous, Afro-Colombian, Creole communities, Romani people, political parties, social and trade union movements, economic guilds, inter alias. We do not want one more victim in Colombia. (6)

This is an indication of how much the peace agreement between FARC-EP and the Colombian government will benefit the country if all constraints are eased.

The document draws on an inclusive and multicultural model, in which the word "peace" is defined as a "universal right" and mentioned 557 times over 310 pages. This universal right, once achieved, will be "stable" and "durable" (54). Through loose definitions formulated without philosophical discussions, parties involved in the negotiation envisaged a utopian state in order to achieve certain goals including rural reforms, political participation guarantees, a bilateral ceasefire, the eradication of illicit drug production and consumption, reparations for victims, and the implementation of the agreement. Again, paradoxically, we are faced with a deconstructive situation. Since the meaning of peace is unachievable, it is impossible to define it in concrete terms. The materiality of peace comes from its abstraction and shows up in terms of commitments, which are promises, future signs, indexes, rituals, theatricality.

The theatricality of peace symbols could be observed, for instance, during the visit of Pope Francis I in 2017. National public channels broadcast his five-day visit during which he travelled around several cities and sites, promoting a discourse of reconciliation and supporting the pro-peace agreement agenda. One of the most significant scenes took place on 8 September in Villavicencio, when he prayed in front of a crucifix with no arms, no legs, and no cross behind: the Christ of Bojayá. In the Pope's words, this national and catholic icon: "has a strong symbolic and spiritual value. [. . .] He does not have arms and His body is no longer there, but He keeps His face and with it, He looks at and loves us. A broken and amputated Christ, for us is 'more Christ' indeed" (*Descontamina Colombia*, n.p.). Like a semiotician, he points out a strong significance where there is only absence or mutilation. On the contrary, symbols of peace, such as the painted white dove or those mentioned above, will not be allowed if they mean something other than the absence of peace. If graffiti is a condensation of signifiers with an anchored signified given by prohibition, "peace"/"*paz*" is a word, more related paradoxically and phonologically to "pathos"—the pain of this dismembered *ecce homo* of Bojayá—whose meaning is impossible to track.

Charles Webel states that peace, "like many theoretical terms, is difficult to define. But also like 'happiness,' 'harmony,' 'love,' 'justice,' and 'freedom,' *we often recognize it by its absence*" (6). A negative definition of peace is "absence of war and other forms of large scale violent human conflict" (7), while a positive definition refers to the presence of "quietness." In addition to this distinction between negative peace (–peace) and positive peace (+peace), there is also inner peace, interpersonal peace, and social peace, blending psychoanalytical, psychological, and sociological topologies, often separated by disciplines. There is another peace that Webel sketches— "divine peace" (8), a theological peace whose intervention can be considered as a miracle when evil is removed from history, at least for a specific period. But instead of a providential peace guiding events in human life, or a Kantian perpetual peace, Webel interrogates whether it is better to pursue an "imperfect peace" (12), which is far away from the "durable" and "stable" peace conceived by the Colombian agreement.

Figure 6. Graffiti by artist Worm compared with the original National Coat of Arms. (Picture taken by the authors.)

Imperfect peace, according to a negative definition, should assume absence as the removal of something: evil, war, conflict. But imperfection does not imply a search for opposing concepts. Graffiti could perform this idea better. In Figure 6, the graffitist Worm leaves his signature on the Colombian flag and replaces the "O" with the National Coat of Arms. The original shield has cornucopias and another symbols of abundance in the middle. Worm erases them and moves the condor from its central position to the left of his signature tag. Emptiness is a kind of peace that overwrites the symbolic but not effectively real richness displayed in national symbols. Another possibility would be adding something in order to embrace a positive peace. During the signing of the agreement, people who watched the event on television could see a Colombian flag with four colours waving for a few seconds. Besides the yellow, blue, and red stripes, a white one had been added above. Someone had proposed the new flag for the time of peace. The proposal implies a decision based on the arbitrary definition of what a white stripe means in terms of a positive and perfect peace. But, for an imperfect peace, the addition could be a new meaning, a new sign, a new infinite chain of signifiers, such as that in Figure 7, in which "love" is the answer, decision, and definition that everybody, including totalitarian regimes and urban semiotic deconstructionists, looks for in the midst of uncertainty.

Figure 7. "Peace is Love. Farc-EP," while a policeman reads it. Picture taken in San Diego, Department of Cesar. (Source: *El Heraldo*, 2017.)

Conclusion: Painting an Angel for the Future

In the moment that we are un-/re-/overwriting the article that you are reading now, the 2018 Colombian presidential elections approach. Conventional media and social networks propagate misinformation and polarisation among the public. They have created narratives of fear such as the imminent danger of Colombia becoming another Venezuela, that is to say, a communist dictatorship, if a left-wing/pro-peace candidate assumes the presidency in August 2018. Expropriation, taxation, suppression of freedom, famine, and devastation are seen as potential threats. On the other side of the spectrum, the figure of the senator Álvaro Uribe Vélez, who served as the president between 2002 and 2010, continues to inspire affection and indulgence in a section of the population, despite the twenty-eight cases for which he is under investigation by the Supreme Court of Justice. It is interesting to note that these cases include allegations of his involvement in sabotaging the peace process, in the disappearance of peasants and human rights activists, and for engaging in institutional murders and slander (RCN Radio). As Corral Garzón states: "Colombia struggles today between two alternatives: Civilization and Barbarity" ("Lo que le espera a Colombia", n.p.).

But, according to Garzón, the biggest challenge for Colombians, beyond the political conundrum and the prediction of economic difficulties, is overcoming the pessimism that has come to characterise the country. Quoting Daniel Pécault, he writes:

> trauma which came firstly from violence, after drug trafficking and, finally the armed conflict, has ended any idea of progress in Colombia. Besides, each one of these episodes involved a more significant collapse of any national symbolism due to the fragmentation of legal and illegal local powers. (56)

Thus, the symbolism of peace and its materialisation in history are in the shadow of a cultural metanarrative of pessimism and atavism. Not coincidentally, Corral Garzón alludes to the famed *Angelus Novus* (1920), a painting by Paul Klee that Walter Benjamin had bought and depicted as the "angel of history" (249):

> His face is turned toward the past. Where we perceive a chain of events, he sees one single catastrophe which keeps piling wreckage upon wreckage and hurls it in front of his feet. [. . .] A storm is blowing from Paradise; it has got caught in his wings with such violence that the angel can no longer close them. The storm irresistibly propels him into the future to which his back is turned, while the pile of debris before him grows skyward. This storm is what we call progress. (249)

The impossibility of conceiving a future and transforming the past into opportunities is, in a nutshell, the prohibition sign that Colombians have posted on the smudgy wall of their present.

The *Angelus Novus* could appear today as a graffito in any street in Medellín or Bogotá. In fact, the original painting, a figure composed of shapes, coloured in a scale of yellow and brown on a background similar to that of a dirty and porous wall, has much more in common with contemporary urban art than the abstract art of the European intelligentsia. A *flâneur* could take a stroll around the Comuna 13, musing on the "no-signs" resulting from prohibitions, and overwritten tags, murals, and graffiti. S/he could speculate on the disappearance of the cornucopias in a coat of arms or the legs and arms in a crucifix, and the appearance of "W" instead of a seashell on a pubis, "love" as a new meaning for peace, and anonymous or collective signatures as negations of property and civility. Rather than a semiotic and deconstructionist inquiry, her/his speculation would be a train of thoughts spanning the city, like the Medellín Metro, which is neither underground nor hidden from the outsider's eye. Not allegorising a perfect peace or anchoring in the past, the Angelus Novus would look inside herself/himself for the layers and colours of bricks, the colours of hundreds of buildings and houses engraved on the mountains, where thousands of youngsters, graffitists among them, desire to write their history beyond a pessimistic hue or "*tinte*."

References

Barrios, Miguel. "Farc pintan grafitis alusivos a la paz en Media Luna, Cesar." *El Heraldo*. 8 July 2016. https://www.elheraldo.co/cesar/farc-pintan-grafitis-alusivos-la-paz-en-media-luna-cesar-270101. Accessed 5 March 2018.

Benjamin, Walter. "Theses on the Philosophy of History" *Illuminations*. New York: Schocken Books, 1969.

Cívico, Aldo. "Que viva el graffiti." *El Espectador*. 8 March 2016. https://www.elespectador.com/opinion/opinion/que-viva-el-grafiti-columna-620959. Accessed 5 March 2018.

Cárdenas, Santiago. "No se puede confundir arte con Vandalismo: Federico Gutiérrez." *El Colombiano*. 7 March 2016. www.elcolombiano.com/antioquia/grafiti-en-el-metro-es-vandalismo-alcalde-federico-gutierrez-DA3714630. Accessed 5 March 2018.

Congreso de Colombia. "Capítulo II del cuidado e integridad del espacio público, Artículo 140." *Código Nacional de Policía y Convivencia*. 2016. https://www.policia.gov.co/sites/default/files/ley-1801-codigo-nacional-policia-convivencia.pdf . Accessed 5 March 2018.

Corral Garzón, Hernando. "Lo que le espera a Colombia en 2018: entre luces y sombras." *El Tiempo*. January 2018. http://www.eltiempo.com/elecciones-colombia-2018/presidenciales/lo-que-viene-en-paz-y-economia-para-colombia-en-2018-169344 Accessed 4 March 2018.

Descontamina Colombia. "Papa Francisco puso tragedia y dolor de víctimas a los pies del Cristo de Bojaya."

http://www.accioncontraminas.gov.co/prensa/2017/Paginas/170908-Papa-Francisco-puso-tragedia-y-dolor-de-victimas-a-los-pies-del-Cristo-de-Bojaya.aspx. Accessed 21 April 2019.

EFE. "Botero indignado por ataque a escultura en Milán: 'Graffitis no son arte.'" http://www.emol.com/noticias/magazine/2007/07/13/262519/botero-indignado-por-ataque-a-escultura-en-milan-graffitis-no-son-arte.html Accessed 4 March 2018.

El Tiempo. "Las capitales quedaron divididas tras votación," October, 2016. http://www.eltiempo.com/multimedia/especiales/votacion-y-resultados-plebiscito-por-la-paz-en-colombia-2016/16697643/1/index.html. Accessed 4 March 2018.

El Tiempo. "Grafitis: escrituras, pinturas y rayones sobre las paredes de Bogotá," 12 January 2016. http://www.eltiempo.com/archivo/documento/CMS-16479462. Accessed 5 March 2018.

Herrera, Marta, and Vladimir Olaya. *Ciudades tatuadas: arte callejero, política y memorias visuales*. Bogotá: Universidad Central. 2011.

Hurtado, Deicy. *Los jóvenes de Medellín ¿ciudadanos apáticos?* Bogotá: Nómadas. 2010.

Mendoza, Stella. *El conflicto armado en los graffitis de Bogotá*. Universidad de Palermo. 2013

Moreau, Terri, and Derek H. Alderman. "Graffiti Hurts and the Eradication of Alternative Landscape Expression." *Geographical Review*. 101 (1), 2011, 106–24.

Noticias Caracol. "¿Qué decían los polémicos grafitis del Metro de Medellín?" March 2016. https://noticias.caracoltv.com/Medellín/guerra-de-trinos-por-grafiti-en-el-metro-de-Medellín. Accessed 4 March 2018.

Presidencia de la República. "Preámbulo." *Acuerdo final para la terminación del conflicto y la construcción de una paz estable y duradera*. 24 August 2016. http://www.altocomisionadoparalapaz.gov.co/procesos-y-conversaciones/Documentos%20compartidos/24-11-2016NuevoAcuerdoFinal.pdf. Accessed 5 March 2018.

Police National and Coexistence. "Artículo 140. Comportamientos contrarios al ciudadano e integridad del espacio público." 29 July 2016. https://www.policia.gov.co/sites/default/files/ley-1801-codigo-nacional-policia-convivencia.pdf . Accessed 5 March 2018.

Powers, Lynn. "Whatever Happened to the Graffiti Art Movement?" *Journal of Popular Culture*, Spring 1996: 29.

Ramírez, Alejandro. *Medellín entre rayas de colores: Construcción de una cultura del Graffiti en la ciudad de Medellín*. Medellín: Universidad de Medellín. 2017.

RCN Radio. "Corte Suprema adelanta 28 procesos contra Álvaro Uribe." February 2018. https://www.rcnradio.com/judicial/corte-suprema-adelanta-28-procesos-contra-alvaro-uribe Accessed 4 March 2018.

Short, Thomas L. *Peirce's Theory of Signs*. Cambridge: Cambridge University Press, 2007.

Vanegas, Catalina. "La cultura de Medellín en las comunas." *Cartel Urbano*. 9 August 2016. http://cartelurbano.com/arte/la-cultura-de-Medellín-en-las-comunas. Accessed 5 March 2018.

Velázquez, Juan. "Nuevamente el metro de Medellín fue pintado con un grafiti." *El Colombiano*. 18 March 2017. http://www.elcolombiano.com/antioquia/seguridad/nuevamente-el-metro-de-Medellín-fue- pintado-con-un-graffiti-LD6173805. Accessed 5 March 2018.

WHEN A HOUSE IS MORE THAN A HOME: THE LIBERATORY LIFE OF OBJECTS IN A POST-APARTHEID FUTURE

JENNIFER YVETTE TERRELL

> All people shall have the right to live where they choose, to be decently housed, and to bring up their families in comfort and security; Unused housing space to be made available to the people.
>
> —Freedom Charter[1]

In 1955 the Congress of the People met in Kliptown, Soweto, and adopted the Freedom Charter, a declaration that merged political, civil, and socio-economic demands such as land, employment, education, and housing into a singular vision for a post-apartheid future. The declaration privileged a vision of liberation grounded in the material necessities of everyday life in contrast to a vision of freedom and equality based on a common humanity as outlined in the Universal Declaration of Human Rights. While the charter is one of the founding documents of South Africa's new republic, the discernible shift in economic policy from one that sought economic growth through poverty alleviation with government-led social programs that addressed material inequalities (the Reconstruction and Development Programme, RDP) to one that privileged fiscal austerity, deficit reduction, and the curtailment of social programs to spur growth (Growth, Employment and Redistribution Programme, GEAR) overshadowed the liberatory potential of distributing objects. One of the few programs to survive this shift was government subsidised housing, colloquially known as RDP housing. This program was designed to alleviate extreme poverty by distributing a physical structure rather than simply guaranteeing access to housing, which would have resulted in even greater variations in the actual delivery of structures (Huchzermeyer 2001; Padayachee 2005). While the charter offered individuals a portal through which to imagine a

---

[1] Congress Alliance, *Freedom Charter*, Collection Number AD1137—Federation of South Africa.

better future, the reality of providing housing to the dispossessed has proven insurmountable, calling into question the meaning of liberation.

The Union of South Africa enacted its audacious claims of racial difference by confiscating land, which prevented the original inhabitants from realising the material benefits associated with the transformation of land into property. This also initiated a reorganisation of space and time that defined where different races could exist and how they were governed; together these actions initiated dispossession (Hall 2014; Mamdani 1996; Walker 2008). In 1948, the National Party enacted apartheid and furthered dispossession with the creation of a racial classification system that was initially sustained and then reproduced through a distinct deployment of infrastructure. Ultimately this led to the state's disavowal of blacks by declaring them citizens of internal homelands and aliens in white South Africa. These actions encouraged government officials to infiltrate intimate spaces and shape the social reproduction of communities, i.e., ". . . the terrain on which the everyday routines of social existence are ordered and institutionalized" (Wilkinson 1998, 216). Non-whites often experienced the dehumanisation of apartheid in the home; the house is the physical site where families were forced apart and government agents appropriated property, policed intimate relationships, and dismantled mixed-race and black urban neighbourhoods. Thus a central objective of the post-apartheid government is to provide the basic necessities of the built environment required for a dignified life, as suggested by the constitutional right for housing and water (RSA 1996; Pieterse 2017). When the government provides a house in the hopes of reconciling historical trauma and contemporary need, it equates material objects with justice for the people qua citizens. However, to make a house viable it must also provide the requisite infrastructure and social services to a collection of houses—housing—and manage the people qua a population to ensure that contemporary desires do not compromise future survival. The distinction between a house and housing signals the complexity of postcoloniality and the conundrum of translating liberation from a political relationality between former oppressors and the oppressed to the objects that undo the de-humanisation and dependence associated with subjugation.

Liberation from colonialism and apartheid is often articulated in terms of former subjects becoming dignified humans; yet dignity is often realised and assessed on the basis of an ability to acquire objects that meet a minimum threshold and facilitate the realisation of equality (Ackerman 2012; Sen 2000). When objects are tasked with reconciling historical injustices, contemporary needs, and future survival, there is a need to consider the social and political relationships they mediate in conjunction with the contingencies associated with their material lifecycles, which can either wreak havoc or instil harmony within the built environment. On the basis of Arjun Appadurai's concept of the "social life of objects" and Jane Bennett's concept of "vital materialism," I suggest that objects, when viewed from the Tricontinent, possess a liberatory life that emerges from the struggles to acquire the object and subsequently the interplay between an object's function and circulation (Appadurai 1986; Bennett 2010). This life signals the potential for new modes of being that were initially contingent upon the legal transformation ushered in by independence, but have since stalled given the persistence of material inequalities. The struggle to gain an RDP house and make decisions about its future signal a reanimation of the revolutionary struggle to realise liberation and new modes of being on the basis of the needs of the historically dispossessed rather than the desires of the historically privileged. The discipline of anthropology has advanced our understanding of a house as the primary locus of domesticity and self-creation; however, when a house is provided as a consequence of political struggles and regulated by socio-economic policy, I suggest, it emerges as a discrete object with use-values that are fundamentally political (Cieraad 1999; Miller 2001). I draw on three sources—apartheid and contemporary legislation, historical and contemporary newspapers, and my ethnographic research in eMasangweni, a rural location in KwaZulu-Natal[2]—that reveal the "thingness" of a house and articulate the tension between providing citizens with a house and housing the dispossessed.

Recovering the Tricontinental: From Historical Injustice to Everyday Liberation

The Tricontinental initiated the possibility of an international proletarian revolution centred on anti-imperial movements and transcontinental solidarity, rather than such movements being an appendage to the Cold War. However, the politics of alignment in Africa, Asia, and Latin America oriented political struggles for national sovereignty and self-determination towards the ideological struggles between the United States and Soviet Union rather than the desires of local citizens. While historical calls for liberation assumed that self-determination and territorial independence would resolve the material and immaterial consequences of the symbiotic processes of industrialisation and colonisation, it became clear that a

---

[2] My ethnographic research in eMasangweni began in late Winter 2008 and I have made four additional trips to the location, most recently in July 2017.

universal solution predicated on freedom *or* equality could not resolve the incessant dehumanisation associated with ethnic, racial, class, and gender differences (Mignolo 2011). Today, countries from the Tricontinent are confronted with two distinct political dilemmas regarding liberation. First, how to resolve historical injustices with contemporary needs, given that capitalist processes of production continue to rely on exploited labour, sustained in part by epistemic violence that dehumanises labourers and justifies their subjugation. Second, how to resolve contemporary desires with future survival given the reality of dwindling resources and the socio-environmental impact of extractive industries (Charkrabarty 2015; Mignolo 2014). Here, I begin to sketch these dilemmas by discussing the politico-legal context of the housing question from the perspective of relevant legislation and historical and contemporary newspapers.

Beginning in the 1910s the Union of South Africa consolidated piecemeal acts of land appropriation from the previous century and established the blueprint from which successive leaders would further extract labour and property from non-whites. Key legislation included the Native Land Act of 1913, which circumscribed where blacks could own property and effectively transferred 87% of the land to whites and left the remaining 13% to blacks; the Native Affairs Act of 1920, which established a system of tribal leaders in rural areas; and the Urban Areas Act of 1923, which designated land for black labourers near cities in an effort to restrict their migration into city centres. Apartheid augmented historical acts of material dispossession with more repressive acts of segregation that transformed the state's rationale from the maintenance of colonial privilege to the extension of white supremacy (Hall 2014; Meierhenrich 2008; Walker 2008). Legislation reflected this shift by further extracting blacks from the nation itself. The Population Registration Act of 1950 registered all inhabitants by their race and ethnicity, which facilitated subsequent legislation that further spatialised the state's racial hierarchy. The Prohibition of Mixed Marriages Act of 1949 and 1968 and the Immorality Act of 1957 policed marriages and sexual relationships between whites and non-whites, as they could undermine the myth of racial purity and disrupt the racial classification system. The Group Areas Act of 1950, 1957, and 1966 and the Reservation of Separate Amenities Act of 1953 and 1960 established segregation in residential and commercial districts and in the use of public services. Housing policy often reflected the rationale of the aforementioned laws and was typically executed by local authorities. Interest in the design and quality of blacks' homes only became of concern when authorities were addressing public health scares or trying to increase the residential capacity of townships. Metropolitan housing policies worked in tandem with housing practices for mining and agricultural laborers in single-sex hostels at work sites and their wives and children in the rural areas. This allowed for the suppression of industrial wages, as women and children's welfare was supposedly assured in communal areas in the rural parts of the country. Consequently, local officers from the Department of Black Affairs typically addressed housing for blacks in rural areas; and made decisions on the basis of their prerogative rather than on specific legislation (Meierhenrich 2008; Wilkinson 1998; Wolpe 1972).

The ultimate act of dispossession was the creation of the homeland system with the Black Authority Act of 1951, the Black Self-Government Act of 1959, and finally the Black Citizenship Act of 1970. The homelands were, theoretically, meant to reflect the myth of a spatially contained African nation at an ethnic group's site of origin; however, these areas were constructed, contemporaneously, by appropriating white- and black-owned property and evicting blacks from land they occupied in order to create strategic, contiguous locations near labour-intensive industries and beyond major urban centres. However not all the homelands became contiguous areas; for example, in Natal some black communities were dispersed among white communities (known as blackspots) and collectively they constituted the homeland of KwaZulu. In the late 1960s and early 1970s Lawrence Morgan for the provincial newspaper the *Natal Mercury* and Stanley Uys for the national newspaper the *Sunday Times,* often reported on the "African Question," namely how to engender modern black communities and make their transition to "independent states" easier. Morgan and Uys offered critical assessments on the government's progress of removing blackspots and offered insights on the deplorable housing conditions for black communities. But the deplorable conditions were not a consequence of cultural differences. Rather it was a continuation of dispossession as even the minimal benefits associated with tenant farming or labour agreements for farmworkers were deemed a threat.[3] In "Tents are Home to 4 Women and 41 Children," in the *Rand Daily Mail*, the authors report on Linah Ntombela, Gladys Sangwini, Elsie Buthelezi, an unnamed woman, and forty-one children who were evicted from a white-owned farm after it was sold; they refused to move into the township of Mpungamphlope. Mrs. Buthelezi explains why they would not move, "We are a farming people. We don't know life in the township. We are used to having our cattle . . . and growing our crops. We cannot change our lives" (Wellman et al. 1970). Yet the authors describe their valiant resistance as "futile" and "pointless,"

---

[3] See John Aitchison, *Collection on Blackspots, Forced Removals and Resettlement at the Alan Paton Centre and Struggle Archives*, University of KwaZulu-Natal-Pietermaritzburg, accessed 24 May 2017.

suggesting the inevitability of their move into Mpungamphlope. The article includes two photos by Clifford Ranako, the first shows two of the women and three children in front of two tents and the other is a wide-angle shot of the children carrying firewood in front of three tents. The pictures are striking because of what they show and do not show, i.e., a concrete house, suggesting the women were too stubborn to realise the ostensible benefits of civilisation. The life they refused to relinquish was not based on historical Zulu practices, rather it was a life based on an ability to provide for themselves from their limited means rather than being compelled to live on a rented plot in an overcrowded location and forced to purchase consumer food products. The tragedy was being subjugated to the socio-economic vagaries of racialised capitalism.

After the democratic transition, the Department of Human Settlements was tasked with alleviating decades of material dispossession and physical displacement by helping citizens acquire decent housing. The Housing Act of 1997 established a comprehensive program that develops the legal framework to create sustainable communities, which includes the procedures by which to enact, finance, and implement housing policy and the relationship among the national, provincial, and local housing officials. The department oversees a range of programs and subsidies that help citizens by providing infrastructure to informal settlements, improvements to existing shelters, subsidised loans to purchase a house, and finally the chance to own a house, i.e., the RDP house (RSA 1997). The RDP program provides "beneficiaries with a fully built house that is provided free of charge by the Government." Beneficiaries must comply with a set of stipulations including being a minimum age of twenty-one; married, cohabiting with a partner, or single with financial dependents; a maximum monthly household income of 3,500 ZAR; a first time government subsidy recipient; and a first time homeowner. The 2001 Amendment of Housing Act 1997 declares that a house cannot be sold during the first eight years of occupancy (DHS 2018; RSA 2001). The RDP house is viewed as an asset, and by offering the title deed at a later date, the government attempts to cultivate an owner's investment in their property and help them realise that wealth comes from diligently making home improvements and routine investments. However, due to a housing shortage and a desire by beneficiaries to realise immediate financial returns, an informal RDP housing market has emerged as beneficiaries sell their houses, rent out rooms, or use houses for businesses. There have been discussions about imposing further restrictions on and taking punitive action against those who violate the moratorium, including using biometric data to verify home ownership or bringing criminal charges against beneficiaries; however, such actions have yet to be implemented

(Gqirana 2015; Property24 2014; Zungu 2015). The qualifications for ownership and subsequent regulations on housing are meant to prevent future homelessness and can be interpreted as techniques to balance citizens' claims from the government and balance claims among citizens.

The informal RDP housing market is emerging alongside other housing challenges: increased evictions of squatters and communities living in redevelopment zones, increased migration to cities, and sub-standard housing construction—all of which have inspired protests and riots. When these actions are documented with photographic images, they readily invoke apartheid. In "Metros Pay Millions to 'Red Ants,'" Sihle Manda highlights the emergent practice of privatising evictions and firms making "big money" from suspect evictions. The legality of privatised evictions is suspect when there is a failure to present a court order, when government officials are not present, and when employees steal from and brutalise evictees. However, while an eviction is happening it is difficult for residents to hold these companies accountable or to seek redress later. The article is accompanied by three images: a phalanx of employees awaiting their deployment to the eviction site; the words "pray now" spray-painted onto a building; and women and children sleeping in the cold with their belongings underneath the N2 motorway in Johannesburg (Manda 2017). These and other media images of half-finished structures, derelict buildings, political rallies, and violence against protestors are stark reminders that *any* government can use the provision of infrastructure and brutality to enact a particular socio-political order. They also remind us of the ongoing revolutionary struggle to realise a central claim of the Freedom Charter, as enshrined in South Africa's iconic constitution—the right to housing.

Four Walls and a Floor: From Everyday Liberation to Future Survival

The life of an object brings to the fore the interactions that emerge from unique exchanges and culminate in its circulation. Arjun Appadurai famously designates such an object as a commodity and stresses that an object's most important social feature is its potential to be exchanged (Appadurai 13). I utilise this definition as the foundation for an object's liberatory life, albeit the motivations for exchange are political rather than social. There is always the potential to exchange an RDP house. While money is often considered the primary motivator, the desire to sell, rent, or repurpose a house is about what one can *do* with that money today to realise a particular future. Grace Ndlazi,[4] from eMasangweni, turned her RDP house into a chicken coop. Even though the house is an upgrade from her current home, she felt she would benefit more from a "capital" upgrade to her business since she still had a functional shelter.

RDP housing in rural areas differs from urban areas in that the structure is typically built in a beneficiary's yard, which is secured by customary property rights. Repurposing the house for a business can be construed as a violation of RDP housing regulations, and in eMasangweni rumours circulated that if one misused a house it could affect other family members who were trying to get on the RDP housing list. Even though prohibitions against repurposing a house are not explicitly stated, they do go against the spirit of the law and could cause problems later. But such repurposing also signals a willingness to exploit lacuna within the law in an effort to make one's life viable according to immediate needs rather than politicians' agendas. Repurposing also suggests a creative response to an object's form and its creator's intentions, a diversion that can free Mrs. Ndlazi from financial dependence on family or on social welfare grants. However, if a majority of beneficiaries were to repurpose their house for a business, such diversions call into question whether government policy is calibrated to the needs of its constituents or to historical objectives that, while still important, are no longer sufficient for a post-apartheid world (ibid. 17–29). Diversions offer insights that surpass immediate policy design and efficacy, and signal an emergent concern in political theory regarding the relationship between authority, law, and objects and who decides how objects should be used. One approach to this relationship is Jane Bennett's vital materialism.

A house is the locus of home—intertwining emotions, memories, and intersubjective attachments with the textured walls, glass windows, roof, and the land it occupies in a demarcated place. However the psychic investment we place in the idea of home often obscures a house's immediate materiality, function, and evolution. These factors affect an object's meanings, associated practices, and the motivations that determine its future circulation. In *Vibrant Matter*, Bennett suggests that objects possess a vitality that is grounded in thing-power, a power that ". . . gestures toward the strange ability of ordinary, man-made items to exceed their status as objects and to manifest traces of independence or aliveness, constituting the outside of our own experience" (xvi). Vitality is the foundation of Bennett's vital materialism, in which the quasi-autonomy of inanimate matter, i.e., non-human actants, should be considered when reflecting on how our world is reproduced. We routinely engage with objects from the built environment

---

[4] Name has been changed.

that have effects beyond our control, especially in terms of their maintenance or disintegration; and one component of an RDP house that has varied consequences is concrete.

Concrete is a vital element of the built environment and was first used in ancient Mediterranean civilisations for functions such as shelter and cooking, which proved essential for the domestication of nomadic communities. Use of concrete in modern times, however, has both enhanced and damaged the environment; for example, it has greatly enhanced the health of occupants, especially for those previously living in structures with dirt floors that made them susceptible to disease. Also, paved concrete roads can greatly enhance a community's viability as they facilitate transportation and enhance property values. Yet the *mass* production of concrete contributes 5 per cent annually to global carbon dioxide emissions and its consumption in building construction is often irreversible—once the concrete is laid, the land cannot be used for other purposes for the foreseeable future (Crow 2008; Kenny 2012). eMasangweni is witnessing drastic changes to the built environment since the arrival of RDP housing. Given that yards often house multiple generations and there is a one-RDP-house-per-yard restriction, new land is being cleared to accommodate the spatial expansion of extended families. Also in the last three years, the government has begun installing concrete sanitation infrastructure, which should enhance current water delivery and sanitation systems within the next decade. Consequently, RDP housing is overlaying a new infrastructure network onto a historical one, which will change the density and dynamics of the community and relationships to decaying concrete structures, as they still serve as personal and communal artefacts with evolving meanings and practices. I observed practices in relation to both new RDP houses and older concrete houses that both protect and beautify the home, such as laying vinyl tarps on the floor, placing a sealant on the walls to prevent erosion, or painting the house and additional structures in the yard to signify personal taste or pride in their home. Community members also recycle old concrete structures, such as breaking foundations into chunks and using them in mud houses or as fences; and if such practices are sustained during the infrastructure expansion, they could benefit the community's long-term sustainability. The other materials in a house are also treated with care and repurposed when deemed "waste"; and while the abstract conception of environmental degradation is not a prominent concern, there is always the desire to gain the most from any object. Such concerns demonstrate Bennett's vitality and should be cultivated both practically and theoretically—practically, in terms of repurposing materials due to a lack of resources, and theoretically, in terms of fully understanding the link between an object's function and the political and ethical values it embodies—values that are contingent upon one's socio-economic status. By considering the life of an RDP house after the initial exchange between the government and beneficiaries, there is an opportunity to consider how the house's circulation along expected and diversionary paths is the foundation for contemporary and future liberation.

Although it will be decades before we fully grasp the environmental impact of eroding RDP houses, especially given the number of houses built on cleared land, their questionable quality, and intensifying weather patterns, my observations, suggest that individual community members respect the precarious nature of their housing structures. They are fully aware that there is little chance they will receive another government house, so they must preserve what they have now. Such respect is based on more than monetary calculations regarding its future commodity phase or candidacy; it is also based on the sincere hope they have escaped the arbitrary nature of an illiberal politico-legal regime and that a predictable daily life can emerge.

It is easy to fathom the respect an individual might have for a single object; but the long-term vitality of similar objects reveals an assemblage, which is more perplexing. An assemblage is a collection of similar objects that are interconnected via networks that make it viable—networks such as infrastructure, real-estate markets, and service delivery districts that make a house part of a housing scheme. A housing scheme is meant to provide a seamless transition to sustainable, efficient communities. In practice, however, an assemblage is also a confederation ". . . able to function despite the persistent presence of energies that confound them from within" (Bennett 24). Assemblages within vital materialism privilege the contingencies that compel human actants and activate non-human actants into actions and decisions at critical moments, which in the moment appear reasonable, given limited information and available choices, but in retrospect, appear naïve, corrupt, or delusional. Given the antagonisms associated with housing, decisions such as renting or buying a RDP house in the informal market, squatting in derelict buildings, or becoming a radical housing activist despite personal and professional risks informs what people are doing. Housing as an assemblage engenders an entity that is reproduced by residents despite being a site of contestation whose ramifications reverberate across space and time. Ponte City Tower is an instructive example for RDP housing.

The structure, located in central Johannesburg, is a round apartment block with fifty-four floors and a central atrium; when built in 1975 it served as the modernist linchpin for the racialised utopia envisioned by grand apartheid. It is located in Berea on the border with Hillbrow, which began as a bohemian neighbourhood where whites and non-whites commingled in manners similar to racially mixed enclaves in Australia, the United Kingdom, and the United States. This space was tolerated, provided the community's lifestyles were contained within the neighbourhood's borders. The building's design reflected apartheid in that only whites were allowed to legally live in flats and black service workers were permitted to live on the premises, albeit in smaller flats located in the building's interior, designed to obstruct views into the apartments of the whites. But as apartheid faltered in the 1980s, everyday actions to survive subverted the laws designed to impede racial integration. Landlords began to rent to coloured people and Indians, under the pretence that they could not identify their race, or they rented to them under false European names. Also, as whites fled to the outermost suburbs, public services such as sanitation were curtailed and neighbourhoods became derelict, at which point, landlords willingly rented flats to blacks. Over time Ponte's modernist design coupled with the building's neglect made it easier to traffic illicit drugs and sex, and for illegal black occupants from the homelands and neighbouring countries to remain. Today the building is undergoing revitalisation and the most obvious signal is the return of the whites to the area, especially as Berea and Hillbrow are primed for economic redevelopment. Finally, given its brutalist architecture, size, and history, the structure has become an ideal site for the visual arts—film, advertising, and music videos—to connote dystopian futures (Brown 2017; Marinic 2017). This aesthetic life helps renew the structure, as it is likely that usage fees and international attention will enhance future returns on capital investments in the building and the surrounding neighbourhoods.

Ponte City Tower and RDP housing are the consequences of architectural design geared towards a political purpose. The Tower was to be a cosmopolitan hub that eschewed the realities of apartheid in the hopes of attracting high-skilled white migrant laborers in an effort to maintain white supremacy, while RDP housing signals the new republic's ability to realise, albeit partially, demands from the Freedom Charter. Yet the life of a structure often extends beyond its immediate vicinity as images, public discourse, legislation, and academic research about a structure also critique the temporal context from which it emerged. The commodification of Ponte City Tower's aesthetic and dystopian past in visual and discursive artefacts resuscitates a negative aspect of law, namely its potential to legitimate illiberal and unethical practices. However, the structure's current biography and the revitalisation of notorious neighbourhoods are integrated into discourses about the Rainbow Nation and the promise of renewal; they signal the potential of the law to correct itself once its foundation is proven immoral. Despite obvious differences between an apartment and a house, an apartment block or a neighbourhood, both function as a shelter object and an assemblage, respectively, and encounter similar concerns regarding the lifecycle of the structure and the social networks they create. The life of Ponte City Tower is instructive for the liberatory life of RDP housing as it demonstrates the power of subversive acts in relation to objects. The structure endured, in part, because of landlords' and occupants' willingness to subvert the law and the permanence of materials that can be rehabilitated. Such subversion signals a practical autonomy that allowed individuals to craft a life on their own terms despite the political will to create law-abiding citizens within the apartheid logic of a racialised utopia. Beneficiaries' subversion of RDP restrictions echoes this subversion, albeit the differing political contexts make subversive acts in Ponte City Tower appear necessary, whereas today's actions appear self-interested and corrupt. The subversion of law often occurs in conjunction with the diversion of objects, of repurposing consumer products and objects from the built environment as a means to enhance everyday life; but over time, they signal a direct challenge to authority. An RDP house provides a unique vantage point from which to examine this conundrum, as it is an object that is imbued with abstract political meaning. But it is how people use and circulate it in their everyday life, even if they subvert the laws that brought it into being, which will determine its liberatory life and legacy.

Vitality captures a more dynamic meaning of objects and our relationships to them in that it examines the practices associated with objects and how such practices enhance everyday life; it is these practices that help translate abstract liberation into a practical meaning of human dignity. As those practices move beyond an individual home and to the larger community, the socio-political mobilisations to make places liveable demonstrate a continuation of Fanon's revolutionary struggle as suggested by Drucilla Cornell. The Fanonian struggle to be human is not the recognition from the former coloniser to the colonised; rather, it is the recognition that comes from the struggles among the former colonised to realise the goals articulated during political struggles for liberation, and the routine organising work that is required to maintain achievements and create new goals (Cornell 2014; More 2014). The relationships we forge with objects necessarily entail relationships to each other. Yet in vital materialism, objects no longer mediate social relationships and signal abstract intersubjective connections; rather, they offer opportunities to consider the mobilisations required to effectively confront the contingencies of the built environment and ensure survival.

One of the greatest obstacles faced when addressing postcolonial justice is the realisation that the past can never be undone and that counterfactuals and political imaginaries that explore Africa's interrupted modernity ultimately only serve as political critique. While such counterfactuals amplify a desire for the wealth and objects associated with a life that could have been, there is a need to think more creatively about the objects that are within reach now. The RDP house existed prior to its actual creation in that the lack of decent housing for non-whites, coupled with the strident political claim codified in the Freedom Charter and the constitution cultivated the promise of homes for the dispossessed. But the failure to deliver houses to all who need one and to deliver an expansive built environment, suggests a distinctive failure of the post-apartheid state. However, when we consider how people use their RDP houses, especially when they subvert expectations of it, there is a chance to move beyond questions of national liberation and policy implementation and focus on the distinctive practice and meaning-making of liberation in everyday life. It is in the everyday that we can fully grasp an object's vitality and an assemblage's contingencies—and the practices to maximise its longevity, which would offer a distinct avenue to translate abstract liberation into a practical meaning of human dignity.

If liberation requires, in part, objects such as a house, there is a need to think about their lifecycles and how our maintenance and disposal of such objects signal (dis)respect for their vitality. It is this (dis)respect that will ultimately have a greater impact on the ability of citizens to remake their lives and to realise that stopping the perpetual displacement and marginalisation of populations will require a reformulation of our relationships to objects and a keen awareness of the socio-political consequences of their production and consumption.

References

Ackerman, Laurie. *Human Dignity: Lodestar for Equality in South Africa*, Juta and Company. 2012.

Appadurai, Arjun. "Introduction: Commodities and the Politics of Value." *The Social Life of Things: Commodities and Cultural Perspective*, edited by Arjun Appadurai, Cambridge University Press, 1986, 3–63.

Bennett, Jane. *Vibrant Matter: A Political Ecology of Things*. Duke University Press, 2010.

"Biometrics in Allocation of RDP Houses." *Property 24,* 10 July 2014, property24.com/articles/biometrics-in-allocation-of-rdp-houses/20171.

Brown, Ryan Lenora. "The South African Building That Came to Symbolize the Apocalypse." *Atlantic*, 21 February 2017, theatlantic.com/entertainment/archive/2017/02/the-south-african-building-that-came-to-symbolize-the-apocalypse/517056/.

Cieraad, Irene, ed. *At Home: An Anthropology of Domestic Space*. Syracuse University Press, 1999.

Chakrabarty, Dipesh. "The Human Condition in the Anthropocene." Tanner Lecture Series, 2015, tannerlectures.utah.edu/Chakrabarty%20manuscript.pdf.

Cornell, Drucilla. "Fanon Today." *The Meanings of Rights: The Philosophy and Social Theory of Human Rights*, ed. Costas Douzinas and Conor Gearty, Cambridge University Press, 2014, 121–36.

Crow, James Mitchell. "The Concrete Conundrum." *Chemistry World,* 27 February 2008, www.chemistryworld.com/feature/the-concrete-conundrum/3004823.article.

Gqirana, Thulani. "Govt Seeks to Discipline Those Selling RDP Houses." *Mail & Guardian*, 8 June 2015, mg.co.za/article/2015-06-08-govt-seeks-to-discipline-those-selling-rdp houses/.

Hall, Ruth. "The Legacies of the Natives Land Act of 1913." *Scriptura,* 113.1, 2014: 1–13.

Huchzermeyer, Marie. "Housing for the Poor? Negotiated Housing Policy in South Africa." *Habitat International*, 25.3, 2001: 303–31.

Kenny, Charles. "Paving Paradise." *Foreign Policy*, 3 January 2012, foreignpolicy.com/2012/01/03/paving-paradise

Mamdani, Mahmood. *Citizen and Subject: Contemporary Africa and the Legacy of Late Colonialism.* Princeton University Press, 1996.

Manda, Shile. "Metros Pay Millions to 'Red Ants'." *Mail & Guardian,* 15–22 June 2017, 8.

Marinic, Gregory. "Adapted Utopia: The Rise, Fall and Reemergence of Ponte City." *The African Metropolis: Struggles over Urban Space, Citizenship and Rights to the City*, ed. Toyin Falola and Bisola Falola, Routledge 2018, chap. 4.

Meierhenrich, Jens. *The Legacies of Law: Long-Run Consequence of Legal Development in South Africa 1650–2000.* Cambridge University Press, 2008.

Miller, Daniel, ed. *Home Possessions: Material Culture behind Closed Doors*. Berg, 2001.

Mignolo, Walter. *The Darker Side of Western Modernity: Global Futures Decolonial Options.* Duke University Press, 2011.

—. "From 'Human Rights' to 'Life Rights.'" *The Meanings of Rights: The Philosophy and Social Theory of Human Rights*, edited by Costas Douzinas and Conor Gearty, Cambridge University Press, 2014, pp. 161–80.

More, Mabogo Percy. "Locating Frantz Fanon in Post-Apartheid South Africa." *Journal of Asian and African Studies*, 52.4, 2014: 127–41.

Padayachee, Vishnu. "The South African Economy, 1994–2004." *Social Research* 72.3, 2005: 549–80.

Pieterse, Marius. *Rights-Based Litigation, Urban Governance and Social Justice in South Africa: The Right to Joburg*. Routledge, 2017.

Republic of South Africa. *Constitution of the Republic of South Africa*, No. 108 of 1996.

—. *Housing Act*, No. 107 of 1997.

—. 2001 Amendment of Housing 1997. Act No. 4 of 2001.

National Department of Human Settlements, www.dhs.gov.za, February 2018.

Sen, Amartya. *Development as Freedom*. Anchor, 2000.

Walker, Cherryl. *Landmarked: Land Claims and Land Restitution in South Africa*. Jacana and Ohio University Press, 2008.

Welllman, Peter Langa Skosana, Martin Mahlaba, and Clifford Ranako. "Tents are Home to 4 Women and 41 Children," *Rand Daily Mail* 23 July 1970. Folder PC 14/5/2/2 John Aitchinson Collection, Struggle Archives at the Alan Paton Center, University of KwaZul-Natal, Pietermaritzburg, Accessed 24 May 2017.

Wilkinson, Peter. "Housing Policy in South Africa." *Habitat International*, 22.3, 1998: 215–29.

Wolpe, Harold. "Capitalism and Cheap-Labour Power in South Africa: From Segregation to Apartheid." *Economy & Society* 1.4, 1972: 421–56.

Zungu, Lungani. "Don't Abuse RDP Housing, Warns Sisulu." *IOL News,* 23 August 2015, iol.co.za/news/politics/dont-abuse-rdp-housing-warns-sisulu-1904234.

"Matter Out of Place": The Ontologies of Waste in Teju Cole's *Every Day Is for the Thief*

Minu Susan Koshy

Waste is conceived of as an element that no longer possesses utility value in the socio-economic order in which it is located, having exceeded its "utility time," gradually turning into an object of abjection. Waste denotes not just objects or dirt but also human beings who are considered "trash"— unproductive and/or "polluting." Rather than the features of the "wasted" object or person in itself, it is the saturation of its role in the existing system that confers the status of "trash" on it, reducing it to a "discardable" item or human being of no value in the period in which it exists. It inevitably exudes a sense of "impurity" and "disgust," making it imperative for the individuals in proximity—either emotionally or physically—to it, to seek modes of disposing of it. Waste is definitely an object to be avoided and ejected from the social network in order to preserve the "purity" of the existing systems and render them "liveable" and "cultured," or so it seems. Structuring waste or bringing it under control through "healthy disposal," "recycling," and "reuse" has for long been considered symbolic of "culture" in both the developed and the developing worlds. Urban and rural waste management, the recycling of everything from plastic waste to metro tickets printed on paper, and reusing items have become fashion statements showcasing the "sophistication" and "social commitment" of individuals and institutions, turning these activities into fashionable trends.

Human beings have always felt the need to "tame" waste—whether animate, as in the case of colonisation, the Holocaust, and genocides, or inanimate, as in the case of human excreta, dirt, and urban waste, in order to preserve the "pristine" image of a "civilised society." Thus, our approach to waste is based on two major premises—one, that waste denotes impurity and abjection, and two, that waste needs to be tamed. The essay attempts to explore the depiction of waste—both animate and inanimate—in Teju Cole's *Every Day Is for the Thief*, with emphasis on how certain areas, objects, and people are "wasted" and reduced to objects of abjection by the forces that seek to "cleanse" the globe and tame what they deem "waste." The modes in which objects or beings are projected as "waste," the ideologies underlying the "abjectification" of waste, and the politics behind "taming" waste would be scrutinised in the context of Nigeria, as represented in Cole's work.

In *Every Day Is for the Thief*, the narrator's entry into Nigeria is marked by the disdain he feels for the country as is evident from his description of the airport, where "disembarkation, passport control, and baggage claim eat up more than an hour of time" (Cole 10). For the narrator, who has been away from Nigeria for decades, the country is one that does not value time, one that "wastes" time. Time here becomes a precious commodity that, when wasted, turns into a marker of "inefficiency" (Cole 10). Throughout the novel, we observe the narrator engaging in comparisons between Nigeria and the United States, with the latter always triumphing in his estimate. One of the factors that he emphasises is the way time is always "wasted" in the African country, whether due to traffic jams or bureaucratic red tape or the activities of goons. Time wasted here indicates the general "lethargy" and "complacence" of the Nigerians—factors that are frowned upon in "civilised" societies.

"Garbage is . . . the mountain of indistinguishable stuff that is in its own way affirmed by a resolute dismissal: it is *refuse-d* (not accepted, denied, banished). Garbage is . . . the lowly that has sunk to the depth of a value system . . ." (Scanlan 14). The novel contains frequent references to garbage as a contaminating factor, disrupting the smooth functioning of the body of the city. The narrator is disturbed when his "bags finally arrive, damp and streaked with dirt" (10). "Dirt," an element that revolts us and elicits the sole response of disgust, features as a prominent motif in the novel. "Cultured" human beings are expected to avoid dirt at all costs in order to remain sophisticated, dirt being the symbol of a general lack of hygiene and disorder. As Mary Douglas remarks in her pathbreaking work *Purity and Danger: An Analysis of the Concepts of Pollution and Taboo* (2002), "Dirt is essentially disorder . . . matter out of place" (44). For the narrator, the dirt on the bag functions as an indicator of the disorder that characterises daily life in Nigeria as observed by him as a *flâneur*, where people, objects, and events occupy spaces that do not really "belong" to them, thus becoming "waste" in the eyes of the narrator. This is best exemplified by the manner in which he perceives all bureaucrats in Nigeria as corrupt, demanding bribes for carrying out their duties. By taking what is not legitimately theirs, they become part of the general "waste" that is Nigeria, making it a space barren of all productivity and justice.

The work is a prolonged attempt at portraying Nigeria as a wasted country, of no worth to the global market system or to itself as is evident from the exclusive focus directed to the lack of facilities in the country. There are repeated references to power cuts and traffic congestion that disrupt the rhythms of the narrator's daily life, prompting him to leave the country for good.

> . . . there is also the question of my tolerance for the environment. Am I ready for all the rage Nigeria can bring out of me? . . . The hardest thing to deal with, after weeks of constant power cuts, is the noise of the generators. . . . When they all come on, I can feel my mind fraying. . . . This is but one issue out of many. Combined with traffic congestion which is a serious problem in Lagos, and considering the thousand natural shocks to which the average Nigerian is subject—the police, the armed robbers, the public officials, the government, the total absence of social services, the poor distribution of amenities—the environment is anything but tranquil. (66–67)

An entity is transformed into waste when it cannot compete with similar entities at a given historical point in terms of utility value. Nigeria is unable to provide the same facilities to its inhabitants as other countries—specifically, developed countries—do and hence becomes trash. Here, it is significant to note that the narrator's perception of Nigeria does not arise from a neutral or objective vantage point; rather, he observes it through the eyes of the neo-colonialist nurtured within the American value system. There are frequent comparisons between the two locales where America is always privileged as a city with less waste and more "sophistication," as is evident from the narrator's description of his experience at the National Museum. Lamenting the meagre collection, the lack of documentation and upkeep, he writes:

> My recent experience of Nigerian art at the Meteropolitan Museum in New York was excellent. The same had been true at the British Museum, as well as at the Museum fur Volkerkunde in Berlin. A clean environment, careful lighting, and, above all, outstanding documentation that set the works in the proper cultural context. What each of those places had done was create a desire in me to see this astonishing art at its best, to see it in its own home. The West had sharpened my appetite for ancient African art. (74)

The country as "wasted" arises here mainly due to its lack of facilities "as compared to" the West. Neocolonial strategies of establishing dominance can be observed at work here, designating the developing world as "trash."

The narrator as *flâneur* finds pleasure in exoticising the "lost" homeland, travelling by crowded buses and visiting local markets, his detest for which he makes evident throughout the text. The exoticisation here involves a making-conspicuous of all that is "waste" existing in the country, turning it into a grotesque "spectacle." The narrator, who believes himself to be a Western subject, as he reiterates through his references to "my light complexion making me a target" (38) and his close identification with Western belief systems, insists on exploring the city in a danfo arguing that "being there on the danfo, being there on the streets, is the whole point of the exercise" (34), emphasising his "desire to know that life [of the city]" (35). As an "alien," "anglicised" subject, he finds the city exotic by virtue of the crowds, the "waste" and "the thick of that assault to the senses that is the Ojodu-Berger Bus Terminus" (35). He elaborates upon the crowds at the bus stop, the "exotic" sight of danfos stuffed with passengers and the "cries of touts" (35), together turning the place into a detestable locale—a site to be avoided owing to the lack of hygiene and safety. The narrator's attempt at projecting the country as a wasted one reaches its zenith in his description of the market, which is portrayed as an exotic locale.

> I move through the warren of shops, which, like a souk, is cool and overstuffed, delighting in its own tacky variety, spilling seamlessly into the cavernous indoor shop. Piles of bright plastic buckets line the entrance, and behind them, the cloth merchants—these ones are women, *alhajas*—swaddled in laces and looking out with listless gazes. (58)

The Western gaze deems the market a colourful melange where "wasted" lives are lived. For the narrator, the market presents a contrast to the malls that dominate America, where each item is meticulously catalogued and stored in specific places without the least trace of disorder (which by itself, is taken as a mark of the lack of cleanliness, translated as "dirtiness"). The Nigerian market is unorganised and there is a constant negotiation with space, which presumably is for the optimum utilisation of space (thereby avoiding "waste"), but ultimately results in creating "waste" through the location of objects outside their designated spaces. The author emphasises the "tackiness" of the objects in the market, pointing to how the Western gaze perceives the Nigerian market as a locale where "sub-standard" items, which are considered trash in the West, are sold as objects of utility value. Thus, what is "waste" in the West is "valuable" in Nigeria, thus reinforcing already existing hierarchies that privilege the West. The designation of an object as waste thus possesses the ability to highlight and entrench hierarchies, especially in a highly consumerised global order.

Susan Signe Morrison, in *The Literature of Waste* (2015), argues that certain individuals are considered as "wasted humans" (102) who can be disposed of, because they are "disposable." Wasted humans are "those who are unemployed or redundant. They are unnecessary: they have been disposed of *because of being disposable*. The wasted . . . can turn up anywhere and threaten the pristine borders of our constructed inviolability" (102). This becomes conspicuous in the case of the Nigerians involved in the "advance fee fraud" (Cole 25). Unemployed men and youths often resort to fraudulent practices such as scams using the internet in order to earn money. These "wasted" humans are considered threats to the civilised social order, threatening legal borders laid down to ensure security for the elite few. The narrator describes a man he observes in an internet café, involved in the scam, as "chairman of nothing" (27). The modes in which unemployed people, who are often forced to resort to fraudulent activities due to a lack of financial resources, are dismissed as human waste, without agency or even an identity, become conspicuous in the narrator's attitude.

The instance of the child who is killed by the people for stealing portrays how, even within Nigeria, certain sections of society are perceived of as disposable bodies, the disposability being exacerbated by their non-normativity. "The politics of disgust, manifested in the refusal of another person's full humanity" (Nussbaum xiii) becomes evident here.

> The boy is eleven, but he has eaten poorly all his life and looks much younger. He is crying. Someone told me to do it, he says. . . . The tire is flung around the boy . . . he is doused with petrol. From the distance, two traffic officers watch. . . . The fire catches with a loud gust . . . the boy dances furiously. . . . The crowd, chattering and sighing, momentarily sated, melts away. The man with the digicam lowers his machine. He, too, disappears. The air smells of rubber, meat and exhaust. (61)

The lack of financial resources forces the child to associate with mafia dons who exploit him to make profits. The helplessness of the child, which arises from his poverty and lack of cultural capital, makes him a "disposable" body, which can be punished in any way the mob deems fit. The child is transformed into a "*homo sacer*" or "sacred man" (Agamben 71), who "the people have judged on account of a crime. It is not permitted to sacrifice this man, yet he who kills him will not be condemned for homicide" (Agamben 71). The child's murder is witnessed by the state as represented by the traffic officers who passively watch the spectacle, thereby pointing to how the *homo sacer* is perceived as waste that should be disciplined either by the rules of the state or by the brute force of the mob. The citizens here function as the ideological state apparatus, functioning to discipline "wasted bodies" that might otherwise threaten the sovereignty of the state.

Bodily waste has been considered an object inspiring disgust, and for centuries the attribution of properties associated with such waste to "othered" human beings and cultures has been a strategy to further dehumanise them, with the mainstream being taught to express "disgust" towards the waste and as a corollary, to the othered human subjects. Martha Nussbaum, in *From Disgust to Humanity* (1984), asserts that the disgust "expresses a universal human discomfort with bodily reality, but then uses that discomfort to target and subordinate vulnerable minorities" (119). Properties of disgust such as "sliminess, bad smell, stickiness, decay, foulness" (Nussbaum 347) have been attributed to targeted minorities in order to project them as threats to the "clean" normative social order, thus furthering their alienation. This is evident in *Every Day* when the narrator repeatedly speaks with contempt of the "tout's body odour" (43) and the sweat emanating from the bodies around him. The disgust he expresses is also his attempt at asserting his superiority over the people of Lagos, with the odour and sweat functioning as "evidence" of their "dirtiness" and thus of the lack of sophistication. The one who emits "waste" is also to be treated as "trash" since they are wasted human beings who should not be allowed into the "clean" mainstream. Here, the narrator speaks from a privileged vantage point that his class status endows him with. Hence, it becomes interesting to note that all the people he dismisses as "dirty" or "fraudulent" are lower middle-class subjects, pointing to how class hierarchy functions in designating some subjects as waste. Recounting his experience in the city, the narrator uses a condescending tone while talking of the lower-class subjects whom he considers as potential "oppressors":

> . . . there is much sorrow in the way that difficult economic circumstances wear people down, eroding them, preying on their weaknesses, until they do things that they themselves find hateful, until they are shadows of their best selves. . . . when you step out into the city, your oppressor is most likely your fellow citizen, his ethics eroded by years of suffering and life at the cusp of desperation. (69)

There is a clear correlation made between economic hardship and lack of ethics, pointing to the perception of lower-class subjects as "trash" who degrade the country through "things they themselves find hateful" (69), through their "lack of cleanliness" and "fraudulence." The fellow citizen is seen not through the lens of a shared national identity or sense of community, but through the lens of class status and resultant prejudices.

Waste features as a prominent motif in the novel, functioning to designate individuals, communities, and even nations as non-functioning entities, capable solely of emitting and being "trash." The body of the city is depicted as a body constituted by various kinds of "filth"—in the form of objects or human beings who do not fit in within the normative paradigms of existence. In *Every Day Is for the Thief*, we observe a systematic attempt at depicting Africa as a "wasted" country, almost always functioning as a foil to the "clean," "sophisticated" West where the narrator believes he "belongs." The waste in Lagos is employed as a metaphor for the entire nation and the narrator highlights it repeatedly while justifying his decision to leave "this damned country" (96), damned by virtue of its location at a "wasted" space and by centuries of having been "trash" for the colonising West. Just as in the case of the European "civilising mission," which aimed at civilising African cultures by bringing "waste" under control, the narrator highlights the "waste" that the country and its people are and how it needs to be "tamed." Dirt and garbage become metaphors for a "ruined" country to which the narrator never wants to return. Waste, as "matter out of place" renders the nation non-functional for the narrator, eliciting the sole response of "disgust" from its citizens and outsiders alike. The attempt to portray the former colony as a locale impossible to redeem finds fulfilment in the waste that characterises it.

References

Ammons, A. R. *Garbage*. New York: W. W. Norton, 2002. Print.

Brown, Bill. "Thing Theory." *Critical Inquiry* 28.1 (Autumn 2001): 1–22. JSTOR. Web. 2 September 2014.

Cole, Teju. *Every Day Is For The Thief*. London: Faber and Faber, 2014. Print.

Douglas, Mary. *Purity and Danger: An Analysis of the Concepts of Pollution and Taboo*. London: Routledge, 2002. Print.

Kristeva, Julia. *Powers of Horror: An Essay on Abjection*. Trans. Leon S. Roudiez. New York: Colombia University Press, 1982.

Morrison, Susan Signe. *The Literature of Waste*. New York: Palgrave Macmillan, 2015. Print.

Scanlan, John. *On Garbage*. London: Reaktion Books, 2005. Print.

DECENTRING THE CENTRE: EXAMINING THE MATERIALITY OF CONNAUGHT PLACE

ARUNDHATHI AND SARAH ZIA

Delhi, the capital city of India, is a city older than its contemporary visual and material form probably allows one to imagine. A city with a population of over eleven million, it is ever growing, looking forward to the future, but unable to shed its past. The title of William Dalrymple's acclaimed book *City of Djinns* is perhaps a paean to Delhi's rich historical past, the remnants of which are scattered across the city, forcing inhabitants to look back every now and then, in order to confront "what was" and the significance of "what was" in the present moment. For one hundred years Delhi has been the capital of India, and there are many archaeological wonders belonging to different historical periods scattered primarily across the northern and southern parts of the city. While Mughal architecture probably dominates the set, buildings of the British period are not far behind. In the scale of time, as well as in physical grandeur, the buildings commissioned by the British are very close to those of contemporary times. Dalrymple observes:

> New Delhi was not new at all. Its broad avenues encompassed a groaning necropolis, a graveyard of dynasties. . . . But where Delhi was unique was that, scattered all around the city, there were human ruins too. Somehow different areas of Delhi seemed to have preserved intact different centuries, even different millennia. (8)

The British decided to designate Delhi as the national capital in place of Calcutta in the year 1911. Edward Lutyens was commissioned with designing various parts of this new city, and a good part of central Delhi is still known as Lutyens's Delhi. Of the many buildings that Lutyens designed, perhaps none is more imposing than what is today known as Rashtrapati Bhawan or the President's Palace, originally conceived as the Viceroy's house, built atop the Raisina Hills, at the end of what is presently known as Rajpath, then Kingsway. William Dalrymple (85) says that "authoritarian regimes tend to leave the most solid souvenirs; art has a strange way of thriving under autocracy. Only the vanity of an Empire . . . assured of its own superiority . . . could have produced Lutyens's Delhi (85).

Connaught Place: A Brief History

While much has been said and written about Lutyens' Delhi, both in terms of architecture and its historical significance, little has been said about the nearby arcade, which was also commissioned to rival some of the finest arcades in the world. Connaught Place was designed by the architect Robert Tor Russel, who, in the words of Sam Miller, ". . . was given some of the lesser buildings in New Delhi to design" (8). CP, as the place is popularly known, was ready by the 1930s, soon after which the British were to leave India. As Miller notes, "the inspiration for the double-storyed curving colonnades of CP, the architectural historians tell us, was Bath's Royal Crescent and Circus, or even a decapitated, inside-out version of the Colosseum" (8).

Noted historian R. V. Smith (who we interviewed for the purpose of this essay), mentioned that Connaught Place was constructed as a rival to Piccadilly Circus, in order to replicate the finer parts of England for British citizens far from home. In a fascinating oral account, Smith recounted for us the history of Connaught Place, and how it was conceived from a wilderness area.

The land on which CP now stands was part of a vast wilderness, which was originally under the ownership of the Scindias. It was this wilderness that helped many soldiers escape the violence during the 1857 Mutiny, and when Delhi needed space to expand, it was decided to do away with this wilderness and the surrounding villages, people from which were forced to move to other areas such as Masihgarh (Smith, personal interview).

While Connaught Place has often been understood as the concentric circles and the arcades that make them, the British had well-thought-out plans for the periphery of this central arcade. Places of religious worship are to be found at the edge of the final concentric circle, notably a church, a gurudwara, a temple, and a mosque. Land for the Sacred Heart Cathedral was originally allotted in Delhi cantonment but later, it was decided to shift this iconic structure to the outskirts of Connaught Place.

This brief account of the history of Connaught Place from its non-being to its inception is testimony to the changing materiality of the place. In its existence as "a jungle of babool trees" (Smith, personal interview), it was a symbol of untamed nature, which needed to be "civilised." It was this vision of civilising that guided the British to design a space for themselves that reminded them of their home. As Smith recounted, "nostalgia made the British build Connaught Place" (Smith, personal interview).

While construction is one aspect of how a space is perceived, another crucial aspect to the understanding of space is the everyday actions that constitute how a space is used. Materiality is physically and symbolically affected by everyday actions.

> The materiality of a place is the outcome of contests about the way it should be used; it is materialized and built power. Encountering the place, one feels and interacts with the power that is molded into the concrete materiality. In the place, the pavement guides the walker, the closed door stops the movement, and the uncomfortable bench discomforts the one who tries to rest. Materiality is more than the dead product of human labor and culture . . . it is an active participant (or "actant") in social relations. (Frers and Lars 2)

Connaught Place was designed as a district for pleasure and consumption. In contrast to an Indian "bazar," it was conceived as not just a shopping arcade but a place for the British to "let their hair down and enjoy" (Smith, personal interview). Young British men would bring their girlfriends to dance above the Regal cinema, some would visit Connaught Place for drinks and a game of billiards, while many others would flock to the Regal cinema to watch the latest English films. In the childhood memories contained in his book *Looking for the Rainbow*, author Ruskin Bond recalls that the cinema halls in Connaught Place showed the latest Hollywood films and there were bookshops and restaurants to be frequented.

Smith adds that Connaught Place was originally envisioned as a market-place-cum-residential area, with residences on the first floors of the shops. He mentions that Karol Bagh and Lodi Colony were the only residential colonies those days, and Connaught Place was built as a market catering to the needs of the government offices nearby. It was, in many ways, an exclusive space, and many things were available only in Connaught Place and nowhere else. Smith cites the example of Christmas trees, which could be bought only on Janpath. He adds that Connaught Place had a free atmosphere, where young men and women could walk holding hands, with nobody batting an eyelid. This was the reason why many young British officers residing at the Civil Lines would visit Connaught Place with their girlfriends for drinks, dancing, and strolling.

The accounts of Bond and Smith essentially point to what can be loosely termed a colonial lifestyle, and activities that were meant to recreate English life in an Indian space. The supremacy of British rule was not just the result of state power and authority, but was established through an active control of space by controlling the activities that defined the purpose of the space. Connaught Place was one such space that was set up to be a marker for "superior" British subjects, showcasing their culture. Different aspects such as food, cinema, and easy access to drinks together painted a picture of the liberated British (wo)man, as opposed to her/his Indian counterpart, who was pushed to the periphery, both literally and symbolically. However, this breezy colonial dream was a short-lived one, as the Second World War was shortly followed by the culmination of the freedom struggle in 1947, when India won independence from British rule.

The British left India, but left behind their materiality, mainly in the form of architectural structures. Connaught Place was one such colonial inheritance among many others, which the people of India readily took over. India witnessed Partition in the wake of Independence, and this led to a major shift in the demographics of parts of northern India, including Delhi. Partition saw many Muslims fleeing Delhi and the influx of Punjabis from the other side of the border, who saw opportunities for growth in a marketplace like Connaught Place, and set up shops, businesses, and dhabas.

Bigger changes were ushered in during the 1990s, after the liberalisation of the economy. As India opened its doors to foreign investment, new goods and services flooded the markets and Connaught Place was not spared. Eateries and stores selling branded clothing were established and, very soon, the residential facilities on the first floor of the shops were vacated and replaced by more eateries and shops.

As one of the storeowners we spoke to remarked, "CP used to be a high street, but now it has become an eatery hub." This shift in consumption patterns, from luxury or retail goods to the consumption of food, merits more nuanced analysis. A survey carried out by us for this research paper focused on the question of people's purpose for visiting CP. While some of them cited eating out exclusively, most reported visiting CP for "just hanging out." This "hanging out" would inevitably be followed by eating at any one of the popular restaurants, or consumption of alcohol at one of the many pubs. However, very few respondents actually went to CP for shopping, and even those who did visited peripheral areas such as Palika Bazar (the underground marketplace notorious for selling fake electronic items, pornographic films, and rip-offs of international brands) and the street market on Janpath.

Despite this, international clothing brands have opened stores in Connaught Place over the years. Often, international brands wishing to enter the Delhi-NCR market choose CP to launch their flagship stores in this region. Cases in point include Xiaomi (News18.com), Brioche Doree (FE Online), One Plus (IndiaToday Tech), and Starbucks (Tandon), among others. National and international brands such as UCB, H&M, Nike, and Adidas have stores in CP; but the majority of people rarely, if ever, visit these shops. Most of our survey respondents admitted that they would rather visit such stores in a mall than shop at the outlets in CP. Many of them do not visit stores in Connaught Place while they are "hanging out" because they do not leave the metro station when visiting CP. The Delhi Metro is a transport phenomenon that has changed CP both physically and symbolically for the average Delhi inhabitant. A closer examination of its effect on the materiality of Connaught Place is necessary for understanding the linkages between transport, space, and materiality.

Transport and Materiality

Rajiv Chowk is the name of the metro station that services Connaught Place. However, the only external markers of its existence are in the form of signboards or stairways, escalators, and lifts leading downwards, strewn across the circumference of the inner circle surrounding the Central Park. This has led to the creation of the Rajiv Chowk/CP duality, with Rajiv Chowk being seen as the underground contemporary of the over-ground CP.

If CP is seen as the quintessential colonial arcade with white pillars, Rajiv Chowk is different materially and functionally. A structure of steel, glass, and concrete, Rajiv Chowk is a living symbol of the passage of time. Rush hour sees the arrival and departure of trains in quick succession, with passengers swarming in and out of automated doors in hordes. This moving mass of human bodies cares for nothing but time, as passengers rush from one platform to another, interchanging between different lines. While Connaught Place was envisioned as a symbol of British victory over colonial space, Rajiv Chowk can be seen as an attempt to reclaim some of that space, by establishing control over time. Being located underground, it may appear as if time has been subordinated to space; however, the attempt is to control time by capturing space. This highlights how means of transport play a significant role in transforming the physical and symbolic materiality of a place. In its initial years, CP was accessible primarily by tonga[1] and tempo traveller. With the passage of time, cars became a popular means of accessing the place. As of today, choked with buildings and cars, CP suffers from an acute lack of parking space, as articulated by shoppers, shop-owners, and the media. As a response to the growing need for efficient transportation services and in a bid to reduce the use of private vehicles, the government introduced the Delhi Metro in 2002. Rajiv Chowk was

---

[1] A horse-drawn carriage.

envisioned as a central interchange station, and in order not to disturb the heritage buildings in and around this area, it was decided to build the station underground.

Sam Miller, who witnessed the construction of the metro station at Rajiv Chowk, shares an account of the digging up of the Central Park in order to build the station deep under the earth. He says that "it is a landscaped lid covering a deep hole: an entirely artificial creation perched on the roof of the subterranean Metro station" (Miller 16). The importance of the metro can be gauged from the fact that nearly 84 per cent of our survey respondents claimed that they use the metro to reach CP. However, the metro is not just a means of transportation. As mentioned before, it has transformed the materiality of CP by expanding the reach of the place into underground space. In doing so, it has reclaimed nature and brought it under the control of technology, an ideology that originally supported the introduction of railways in India by the British.

Seen this way, the introduction of the metro (which, incidentally, is foreign technology), mirrors the introduction of the railways in India, which were seen as an essential component of the "civilising mission" of the British. The only difference is that introducing the metro has been the decision of Indians themselves and not that of any foreign powers.

A visit to the premises of Rajiv Chowk Metro Station will make one question whether there is any difference between the exterior and the interior of the station. With a total of four platforms (two on the first level and two on the second), the station has a small food court that houses both indigenous and international food brands like Keventers and Burger King, whose outlets can be seen in CP too. The food court near the automated fare collection and exit gates caters to both commuters and casual diners. In a way, the leisurely experience at CP is recreated in a space with clearly marked entry/exit points, which is otherwise designated for fast movement of bodies and trains to ensure efficiency. What is the logic behind locating the same outlets both above- and belowground?

The answer was found in the responses of our survey participants, nearly 60 per cent of whom claimed that they had "hung out" at Rajiv Chowk without actually exiting the metro station. The station has added a layer of materiality not only in steel, concrete, and glass, but also by providing the same options that are available overground for consumption. In doing so, it has taken away the "charm" of Connaught Place, as articulated by old-timers. This is an example of the influence of technology not only on the materiality of space, but also on its influence on the sociality and culture of a particular space. As Tim Dant observes:

> . . . it is through the direct interactions between individuals and material
> objects that the culture is mediated: the objects have embedded within the
> materiality of their design and manufacture a series of cultural values that
> shape the practices of body and of mind, by which those objects are used.
> (Dant 3)

The transition from the use of tongas to cars to the metro is a telling remark
on the conglomeration of different materialities in a single space. While
both tongas and cars are somewhat personalised means of transport, the
metro is a means of "mass" transportation. The construction of a metro
station in CP has opened it up and provided access to people who might not
otherwise have ever visited it. In doing so, it has led to radical changes in
the embodied practices of visitors.

The Duality of the Consumption Experience

While skylines contribute to a city's visual identity, markets and shopping
streets can shape a city's material identity, as they not only represent the
economic status of the locale or population, but also determine how social
relations within a community are produced and play a key role in
manufacturing place identities (Felder and Pignolo 97). Despite being made
of bricks and mortar, they show that places can be dynamic in the sense that
their relevance or position in the cityscape can change depending on how
they are consumed. They also represent a duality, wherein brick and mortar
structures may remain unchanged, while the role of the streets in shaping
the city may be dynamic, just like the status of those using these spaces for
upward mobility. Further, it is argued that shopping streets mark the meeting
place of individual taste and preferences in a collective environment, which
is about not only who one is but also who all are "here" (Felder and Pignolo
97). In his analysis of Indian malls, Sanjay Srivastava argues that malls have
found favour with the spending class in India because they came with an
assurance of a certain "crowd." One of his interviewees suggested that she
preferred high-end malls because "you don't have to put up with the dirt"
(Srivastava 51). Juxtapose this with the consistent reports of betel leaf stains
dotting the arcades in the face of cleanliness campaigns at CP. Often,
cleanliness is a mechanism to exclude a certain social group from a place,
as is evident from the following shopkeeper's statement: "Street vendors
without licences are setting up shops. Besides lowering hygiene standards,
this has restricted space for pedestrians to walk. The entire market has been
cluttered by hawkers selling food and tobacco" (Vatsa).
    It is interesting to note that if one visits CP, one can actually have a range
of snacks including a drink and a dessert for under Rs.100 (approximately

$2) from the street vendors. The circle's arcade is lined with elevated platform-like borders where people can sit if the weather is not too oppressive. One can have a complete outing including just "hanging out," eating, and relaxing, without having to actually enter the air-conditioned restaurants or showrooms. Consumers and visitors can "experience" CP without spending a single penny. Juxtapose this with the rent of an international sports-brand showroom that, a shopkeeper told us, comes to thirty lakh rupees a month. Thus, despite increasing footfall, shopkeepers lament the lack of sales and are particularly keen to entertain a certain group of consumers by advocating the beautification of the site as well as opposing pedestrianisation and car bans (Express News Service). Despite authorities claiming in court that CP is a no-vending zone, the arcades are lined with vendors selling nearly everything from snacks and jewellery to posters (Banka).

Given that it is possible for all social groups to access and experience CP, it becomes important to interrogate whether it qualifies as a high street. Almost every market in Delhi has a unique characteristic to it: for instance, Ghaffar Market is notorious as a grey market, Sarojini Nagar[2] is known as a venue for street shopping, while Khan Market is famous for its upscale status (PTI). Where does one then locate CP on the retail poshness map? For long, CP has been a symbol of nostalgia for those who grew up experiencing it in their childhoods or longing to experience what it once represented—colonial grandeur. But that was the case for the baby boomers and Generation X. Those born during or after the liberalisation of the Indian economy have had greater (often competing) avenues for spending, such as shopping streets, malls, and online stores. Further, they have greater capital as well as the means to spend it. It is also argued that upwardly mobile and affluent subjects are always able to take greater advantage of newer facilities (Williams et al. 204) and thus become "disadvantaged consumers" (cited in Williams et al. 205) who, due to lack of choice, may opt for "informal" sites. This complicates our understanding of both CP and its consumers, since even though CP is not a market for counterfeits, one need not spend a fortune to be a "consumer." It is possible that many who find it difficult to access malls (due to their inability to afford expensive purchases, and lack of mobility enablers like cars) may find it easier to access CP (due to the availability of the metro and the lack of urgency to shop); yet, those who frequent malls also frequent CP. Visitors to CP are thus not a social group that is easy to categorise.

According to the owner of a photography studio (a shop set up in the pre-independence era), the metro has made CP accessible to a different class of people who do not visit CP to shop. They have made it more crowded, and taken away the aura of CP as a "high street." At any given point of time, an observer can see that most people in CP walk in concentric circles. The act of walking, which has undertones of class-consciousness attached in the Indian context, can be seen as an act of defiance when viewed in a setting like CP. Those who walk do not necessarily shop, and when they do not indulge in the economy of conspicuous consumption, they threaten not just the business of the store owners, but also the so-called aesthetics and charm of the place, highlighting the inherent tensions in the power relations between different classes who jostle for space.

There are beneficiaries of space, just as there are those excluded from it, those "deprived of space"; this fact is ascribed to the "properties" of a space, to its "norms," although in reality something very different is at work (Lefebvre 289).

Many of our survey respondents also observed that CP has become more crowded over the years. Some even feel that is has become dirtier, compared with the cleaner metro station underneath. It seems as if the newer portion underneath (the one commissioned, designed, and operated by Indians) is striving to be known as better than its counterpart above, in a bid to erase the assumed superiority of the colonial powers that fashioned Connaught Place.

As of today, it is not uncommon to find pavement dwellers, beggars, and street vendors in the circles of CP. The owner of the photography studio says that it is the class of people who travel by metro who buy things from the street vendors. He laments the bygone days when CP was actually a "high street." Despite this lamentation, it is interesting to note that many international brands have opened stores in CP, the latest to join the bandwagon being H&M in 2016. One of our interviewees claimed that none of these brands actually made profits through the CP outlet, but nevertheless wished to have their presence on an erstwhile high street.

The paradox lies in the fact that 58 per cent of our survey respondents felt that CP could be considered a one-stop shopping location, but 56 per cent of them voiced a preference for shopping from the same brands at stores located in malls instead of CP.

The Periphery, the Core, and the Radial

The concept of "high streets" is a colonial one and there have been numerous debates about whether high streets are being eroded (Hubbard). Brands conventionally considered "high street" (such as Zara, Forever 21, and H&M) are finding favour among Indian consumers at prominent malls across Indian cities. The concept of the "high street" has been complicated by the case of CP. Today, apart from retail stores, CP is a hub of both global and local food chains—Starbucks, Subway, and Burger King co-exist with Saravana Bhavan and Depaul's. CP is also home to eateries such as Wenger's, which, apart from being a reminder of the colonial era, has only one branch in the city. In many ways, the postcolonial and post-globalisation exist in the same place through the same material existence—a shopping front located in the white colonial arcade. The sameness of post-globalisation cities is marked by conspicuous branding across areas. For instance, no matter what kind of building houses a Starbucks outlet, it will always be identified by the white characters in English (never in a local language) on a specific green background, and never by the building arcade. Thus, CP is a site where the "global" has replaced the "local" in some cases (as in the tragic instance of the Indian Coffee House that had been a venue for fierce political discussions in independent India, and lost its glory in the wake of market competitors [Jha]), and in other situations, a site where the "global" has embraced the "local," particularly through brick and mortar structures.

While shopping is one form of consumption associated with CP, another form, which is perhaps the most conspicuous, is the consumption of food. Many of our survey participants recalled their first experience of CP nostalgically as a visit to a restaurant with family or friends. One of them even recalled how "in those days, restaurants were to be found in CP only." With the proliferation of numerous food joints and multiple outlets of the same food brand/company, it is no surprise that CP has now become associated with restaurants and pubs. However, it is important to note that restaurants have now emerged in other parts of Delhi as well, depriving CP of its exclusive status as the only place with food outlets. This has led to a subtle and gradual shift in focus from the centre of the city to other areas, in an attempt to blur the boundaries between the core and the periphery. Restaurants had existed in CP from as early as the 1920s (Wenger's being an example), and newer ones (such as Kwality and The Embassy) were established in the 1940s.

The municipal authorities and real estate developers want to promote CP as a retail experience spanning sixty thousand square feet, in a format different from the shopping-mall experience. It then becomes interesting to see how this area will be mapped, and if retail will be the sole criteria to incorporate an adjacent area into the Connaught High Street. Currently, the Connaught Circus area is marked by three concentric arcades lined with shops. The radial opens across other peripheral streets, many of which are layered shopping streets with identities of their own such as Janpath (known for the Tibetan market) and Kharag Singh Marg (known for State Emporia).

The concentric circles do not mark the beginning or end of the retail experience; rather, they constitute the core due to its sheer size. Markets like Janpath may seem geographically peripheral; but they possess independent identities constituted by shopping sub-cultures of their own. The peripheries and the centre are bound together by the eateries and the resto-bars found in abundance across the radial roads as well as the circle.

We also examined how Connaught Place became a site for the consumption of nationalism and nationalistic fervour. When we asked our respondents about an image that comes to their minds when they think of CP, many of them mentioned the Indian national flag that stands in Central Park. This flag, which has been in CP since 2014, is one of the largest in the area, and towers over everything else as if symbolically marking the reclamation of the colonial arcade by the erstwhile colonised subjects. The visual spectacle of the flag is testimony to yet another form of consumption and can be subjected to further enquiry to understand how consumption can promote ideologies of nationalism, patriotism, and citizenship. The placement of the flag in Central Park can also be read as an attempt to establish CP as the core of the capital city, in order to clarify the boundaries between the core and the periphery.

Conclusion: Bringing It All Together

In the post-globalisation, postcolonial, and post-Independence context, CP is no longer the central district of the city in terms of housing offices and business districts. However, it continues to remain a central zone of consumption. Consumption occurs at multiple levels—in the form of consumption of goods (e.g., eating at restaurants and shopping at stores) and in the form of consumption of services (for instance, the use of the metro for travel). While the colonisers envisioned CP as a site for the consumption, dissemination, and maintenance of an essentially English culture, today it stands for consumption by the erstwhile colonised masses, who negotiate with both Indian and foreign goods and services. Whether or not it is the centre of consumption in the city is certainly debatable, as areas across Delhi compete with it by offering similar experiences of consumption. The change in its status as the epicentre of consumption is a marker of its duality, the source of which is its materiality. Despite the disruptions brought about by forces like globalisation and the embodied practices of citizens who frequent it, the materiality of CP has been static and dynamic simultaneously, owing to the CP/Rajiv Chowk duality.

The duality has a postcolonial, post-globalisation aura. The layers of its material existence (the arcades above, and the Rajiv Chowk station below the ground) have rendered it an uncertain entity in terms of its status as a "high street." The duality in nomenclature is reflective of multiple materialities, as well as an unease with the term "high street," which may not even be applicable to an area like Connaught Place with its fraught history, at both the material and the symbolic levels.

References

Appadurai, Arjun. *Modernity at Large: Cultural Dimensions of Globalization.* New York: University of Minnesota Press, 1996. Print.

Banka, Richa. "Delhi HC slaps Rs 5,000 fine on 14 CP vendors." *DNA India*, 4 October 2017, https://www.dnaindia.com/delhi/report-delhi-hc-slaps-rs-5000-fine-on-14-cp-vendors-2550148.

Bond, Ruskin. *Looking for the Rainbow: My Years with Daddy.* New York: Penguin Random House India, 2017. Print.

Dalrymple, William. *City of Djinns.* London: Harper Collins, 1993. Print.

Dant, Tim. *Materiality and Society.* New York: McGraw-Hill Education, 2004. Print.

Express News Service. "Car-Free Connaught Place to Take a Little Longer." *Indian Express*, 26 January 2017, https://indianexpress.com/article/cities/delhi/car-free-connaught-place-to-take-a-little-longer-pollution-ndmc-4491937/.

FE Online. "Haldiram's Brings French Bakery Brioche Doree to India, Opens First Store in Delhi." *Financial Express*, 10 February 2019, https://www.livemint.com/Industry/htH2AXiOnGlZthw9a2y1SM/Star bucks-opens-first-flagship-store-in-New-Delhi.html.

Felder, M., and L. Pignolo. "Shops as the Bricks and Mortar of Place Identity." In Ligia Ferro, Marta Smagacz-Poziemska, M. Victoria Gomez, Sebastian Kurtenbach, Patricia Pereira, and Juan Jose Villalon (eds). *Moving Cities: Contested Views on Urban Life.* Springer, 2017, 97–115. Print.

Frers, Lars, and Lars Meier. *Encountering Urban Places: Visual and Material Performances in the City.* London: Ashgate, 2007. Print.

Hubbard, Phil. *The Battle for the High Street: Retail Gentrification, Class and Disgust.* London: Palgrave Macmillan, 2017. Print.

India Today Tech. "OnePlus Experience Store in Delhi: Where T and Coffee Come Together." *India Today*, 19 December 2018, https://www.livemint.com/Industry/htH2AXiOnGlZthw9a2y1SM/Star bucks-opens-first-flagship-store-in-New-Delhi.html.

Jha, Martand. "Once the Hub of Intellectuals, This Famous Coffee House in Delhi Has Lost Its Flavour." *Youth Ki Awaaz.* 17 June 2016, https://www.youthkiawaaz.com/2016/06/indian-coffee-house-new-delhi/.

Lefebvre, Henri. *The Production of Space*. New York: Blackwell Publishers, 1991. Print.

Miller, Sam. *Delhi: Adventures in a Megacity*. New York: Penguin Books, 2008. Print.

News18.com. "Xiaomi Opens Mi Home in Connaught Place, Delhi; Adds 'Experience Zone' as a First for Global Products." *News18*, 9 May 2018, https://www.livemint.com/Industry/htH2AXiOnGlZthw9a2y1SM/Star bucks-opens-first-flagship-store-in-New-Delhi.html.

Smith, R V. "Connaught Place: Past and Present." Interview by Arundhathi and Sarah Zia, audio recording, 31 August 2017.

Soja, Edward W. *Postmodern Geographies: The Reassertion of Space in Critical Social Theory*. Verso, 1989.

Soofi, Mayank Austen. "Welcome to the Old CP." *Livemint*, 20 August 2016, https://www.livemint.com/Leisure/IJDezKOpIbvmdY3SAEgJfM/Welc ome-to-the-Old-CP.html.

Srivastava, Sanjay. "Shop Talk: Shopping Malls and Their Publics." In Nita Mathur (ed.). *Consumer Culture: Modernity and Identity*. Sage, 2014, 45–71.

Tandon, Suneera. "Starbucks Opens Flagship Store in New Delhi." *Livemint*, 7 February 2013, https://www.livemint.com/Industry/htH2AXiOnGlZthw9a2y1SM/Star bucks-opens-first-flagship-store-in-New-Delhi.html.

Urry, John. *Consuming Places*. London: Routledge, 1995. Print.

Vatsa, Aditi. "Swacch Bharat: It's Spit and Paan, not Spick and Span at Connaught Place." *Indian Express*, 28 September 2015, https://indianexpress.com/article/cities/delhi/swachh-bharat-its-spit-and-paan-not-spick-and-span-at-connaught-place/.

Williams, Peter, Phil Hubbard, David Clark, and Nigel Berkeley. "Consumption, Exclusion and Emotion: The Social Geographies of Shopping." *Social and Cultural Geography*, 2.2, 2001: 203–22.

GOALPORIA FOLKSONGS AS AN EPISTEMIC CULTURAL RESOURCE FOR UNDERSTANDING THE POSTCOLONIAL UNCANNY

NILAKSHI GOSWAMI

Folklorist Alan Dundes asserts: "Folklore is autobiographical ethnography—that is, it is a people's own description of themselves" (471). The statement verily underscores how the dialectic of folklores enables the study of another culture "from the inside out" while simultaneously serving as artefacts in tracing the intangible cultural heritage transmitted from one generation to the next. By delving into Goalporia Lokageet, or folksongs of Western Assam,[1] centring specifically on the works of folk-artist Pratima Baruah Pandey, the essay addresses how these folksongs function as manifestations of the process of exclusion of Koch Rajbonshis from the mainstream Assamese culture as well from the rest of the country. The essay also provides crucial sociological insights into the political manipulations by the British, resulting in the bifurcation of the community into Assamese and Bengali tribes. Focusing on the manner in which Pratima Pandey's Goalporia Lokageet are produced and disseminated, the essay reflects on these folk songs as key academic resources in recording the perceptions and dilemmas witnessed by this community. What are the manifold attitudes, concerns, contexts, and metaphors surrounding these folksongs? How do folksongs as epistemic resources capture the complexities of their daily lives? How do they serve as sociological documentations examining and interrogating the continuities and transformations in their community? How do Lokageet reflect on this indigenous community battling with the crisis of losing their language, culture, and civilisational roots? How do these folksongs, as epistemic cultural resources, enable one to capture the complexities of the cultural, linguistic, and social identity of the community?

---

[1] Before 1959, Goaporia Lokageet or folksongs were known as "Desi" songs or Bhaoyaiya songs that could be etymologically traced back to the rural songs sung by the buffalo keepers on "bhaoya" or grazing grounds.

How do they serve as historical documents unveiling the continuities and changes in the intimate cultural experience of the community?

Even before the coining of the term "folk culture" by William John Thomas in 1846, there already existed an ongoing study of folklores in late-eighteenth-century Germany. Induced by the Romantic nationalistic impulse, it was the Grimm brothers who brought together the *volkleider* or the folk songs, tales, sayings, and other idiomatic phrases that were still prevalent among the German peasantry. These remnants were considered by the Grimm brothers to be the survival of the past or "folk lives"—a study that later become highly influential in England.[2] This was followed by a series of analyses regarding old buildings and architecture, antique manuscripts and legal documents, ancient songs and customs, that later came to be labelled "popular antiquities." However, Thomas reframed this idea of "popular antiquities" with the Anglo-Saxon compounded word "folklore" in 1946. Ever since, the idea of "folklore" has been perceived as materials and resources assumed to have survived primarily among the rural peasantry, and, as such, mirrors their lives in the distant past. Dan Ben-Amos states:

> Folklore is the action that happens at that time. It is an artistic action. It involves creativity and esthetic response, both of which converge in the art forms themselves. Folklore in that sense is a social interaction via the art media and differs from other modes of speaking and gesturing. (10)

Indeed, folklores, as this essay intends to unravel, identify with the "folks" of the specific areas in which they are sung, and are a part of the oral culture that is verbally transmitted across the community. Since there is an innate relationship between folklore and culture, it becomes significant to note how culture is defined. While Edward Taylor, the founder of social anthropology, defines culture as a "complex whole which includes knowledge, belief, art, morals, law, custom and any other capabilities and habits acquired by men as member of society" (1), folklore, more specifically folk music in this context, could then be defined as a reaction to the geographical condition, linguistic position, and social interest on the basis of the commonality of livelihood.

---

[2] Alan Dunes discusses the pejorative association of the term "folklore" while tracing how while the Grimm brothers published their influential book on folklores, *Kinder- und Hausmärchen* (1812), Herder has already used terms such as *Volksled* (folk song), *Volksseele* (folk soul), and *Volksgalube* (folk belief). For further information of the historical overview of "folklore," refer to Alan Dunes, *Interpreting Folklore* (1980), 1–19.

By examining Goalporia Lokageet,[3] or the folksongs of Western Assam, while centring specifically on Pratima Baruah Pandey (1934–2002), a legendary folklorist who was also known as *hastirkanya* or daughter of the elephant, this essay intends to probe how they are reflections of the postcolonial history of Goalpara. The colonial history of Goalpara was a bystander to the political manipulations of the British Raj that resulted in the bifurcation of the densely populated Rajbonshi province into areas in Assam and Bengal. Koch Rajbonshis were one of the major tribes of the region.[4] India's attainment of independence on 15 August 1947 remained a paradoxical triumph for the Western Assamese community considering the politico-historical successions. Maharaja Jagadwipendra Narayan, the last king of Kochbehar from the Biswa Singha dynasty, had a meeting with the first prime minister of India, Pandit Jawaharlal Nehru, prior to the country's attainment of freedom expressing the possibility of annexing the state of Kochbehar with either Assam or Bengal while taking into consideration the wishes of the public—a reflection of the democratic temperament of the maharaja. However, contrary to its commitment to the maharaja, the Indian government declared the annexation of Kochbehar with Calcutta, against the desire of the people to have their state merge with Assam. Despite the efforts of the then chief minister, Mr. Gopinath Bordoloi, history was smeared by the regretful event of the anachronistic annexation to Bengal— a decision strongly influenced by the then governor general of Assam, Sir Akber Hyderi.[5]

Thus, considering this series of socio-historical developments, the densely populated Rajbonshi territories—inseparably associated in terms of their historical, cultural, geographical, and religious lineages and bondages— were now divided into two parts, namely Assam and Bengal, while gradually

---

[3] The epistemology of the word *lokageet* can be traced to the words *loka* in Sanskrit, meaning "world." In Hindu mythology, this world refers to cosmology, while in a mundane sense it refers to the public—both in general as well as *jati* or races. In fact, the word *loka* as inferred from *The Anglo Assamese Dictionary*, could be defined as "the mass of people, *mahunbikak, loka, praja.*" On the other hand, *geet* or *gaan* refers to song, or "a composition adapted for singing." Thus, together, the term *lokageet* could be deciphered as the race of tribe-specific song adapted for singing. In this context, the *Oxford English Dictionary* meaning of the word folksong could be literally situated in terms of "folksong" that is defined as "a song that originates in traditional popular culture or that is written in such a style" (713).
[4] Although a part of the Koch community referred to themselves as Rajbanshis, the term "Koch" was used as a comprehensive term referring to the old community of the Koch people.
[5] Cited in J. P. Rajkhowa, *General Chilarai and His Times*, Guwahati, 2003, 216–17.

losing their unity and harmony. While the Rajbonshis relegated to the Bengal region were now uprooted from their language as well as cultural and civilisational roots, the condition of the ones living in this newly formed state of Assam had degenerated as well, considering the series of sociological and political crisis they had to encounter. These Rajbonshis now living in Goalpara were defined by the mainstream Assamese people as *Goalporia Bengalis*—a derogatory misnomer. On the other hand, that which was annexed to Bengal, which later became Kochbehar, now became a territory subsumed under the inexpressible repression of Calcutta. It is within this postcolonial framework that one needs to analyse Pratima Pandey Baruah's Goalporia Lokageet, which has remained synonymous with the history of the growing cultural consciousness of the folk geo-cultural customs of the people of West Assam,[6] covering the nuances of all human relationships including the intimacy of married couples, the passion of youthful desires, the romance of young lovers, the distressing lives of mahouts, and the endless expanse of the wild landscape, among others.

Pratima Pandey's biographical details, more specifically, her expeditions into the jungles with her father from a tender age, remain significant in describing her close affinity with the intimate rhymes and rhythms of the rural folk. The carefree songs and audacious stories of the campers and the mahouts, the solitary tales of their lonely wives about their pain and pathos has painted the imagination of the folk artist ever since her childhood days. This romantic landscape brought out by the folk artist, in turn, has not merely functioned as a cultural platform of the songs that might otherwise have relapsed into oblivion but also rejuvenated the material objects of these indigenous communities consigned to the past. Her Lokageet are thus reflective of how culture is evinced in discrete forms engendered by human responses to diverse opportunities situated in distinctive socio-historical contexts. Moreover, in Golaporia Lokageet, it can be duly noted how the cultural system relies on the metaphors and symbolisms of the material life of the rural folk, in the process of excavating the postcolonial uncanny integrally entwined with the meanings, values, and norms shared by members of that community. Material life, in turn, can be seen to be shaped by the cultural imperatives as well.

In this vein, Pratima Pandey, one of the greatest folk artists, not only contributed to the revival of Goalporia Lokageet, saving it from impending oblivion, but herself became the subject of a vibrant contemporary folklore

---

[6] Using Goalporia Lokageet as an "epistemic resources" in understanding the geocultural crisis endured by the Rajbonshis can be placed within an already existent body of sociological research on folk music and folk culture, which has been identified as a reservoir of people's said and unsaid expressions.

of her times. Her life continues to remain a glaring illustration of the evolutionary process that Assamese identity has undergone.

As already stated, Pratima Pandey collected these folk songs at the time they were seemingly about to be extinguished from public memory. Taking into consideration the turbulent history, the ways in which an abrupt chapter was opened driving the Koch Rajbonshis to abandon their socio-cultural moorings and acquire new identities while confirming the altered geo-social legacy in postcolonial times remains of utmost importance.[7] Having lost their culture, identity, and languages, these Lokageet, in turn became emblematic of the cultural redemption of the *Rajbonshis* in their phase of crisis and in increasing the cultural consciousness of the people in West Assam. Her lyrical compositions, thereby, did not merely aim at reviving a lost folk music but also intended to rectify the postcolonial misgivings that considered the cultural values of Goalpara as a part of Bengali culture. Later these became the cult songs of the oeuvre after some of them were featured in Dr. Bhupen Hazarika's forthcoming movies. In fact, it was due to Dr. Hazarika and Pandey's constant endeavours that these regional folk songs, earlier referred to by the people of Western Assam as "Desi" songs in undivided Goalpara district, came to be known as "Goalporia Lokageet" in 1958. Further efforts were made by Dr. Hazarika to air Pratima Pandey's song on All India Radio in 1961. However, these songs were not enthusiastically received by Assamese society since these lyrical compositions were mostly sung by mahouts, farmers, and *maishals*, which defied the frenetic Assamese nationalism people nurtured wherein Rajbonshis were looked down upon as *Goalporia Bengalis*. Strong objections were also raised against Pratima Pandey's alleged "non-Assamese" status. However, as Hiren Bhattacharya, one of the eminent Assamese poets, later commented, it was Pratima Pandey who brought Goalpara culture closer to the Assamese.[8]

---

[7] Dr. Bhupen Hazarika made significant contributions to bringing Pratima Pandey to the fore as an artist of repute. During one of his visits to Gauripur in 1955, he was moved by Pandey's folk songs. Her mellifluous voice and her unique lyrical compositions led him to include her music in his forthcoming Assamese film *Era Bator Sur*, in which the two songs by Pandey—first, "Dung nori dung," a song sung by *phandis* while catching elephants, and, second, "O birikhasimilarè," a song about the unrequited desires of a lonely women—centred on a forgotten genre and language. For further details, see Jyotirmoy Prodhani, "Life as Lore: The Art and Time of Pratima Barua Pandey" (2008).

[8] Barman, Prafulla. *AsomNandiniPratima Pandey Barua*. Guwahati: Bishal Publishers, 2004, 17.

Pratima Pandey's Lokageet can be broadly divided into seven spectrums.[9] The first aspect, *Dehatatta*, or what could be called "materialistic spiritualism," is based on the ancient ideals of devotion to the immortal soul or the *Pramtatta*. The second aspect, *Biraha* or "tragedy," is the painful expressions of the wives to their husbands when the latter move out of the home for business purposes, something that was beautifully expressed in the form of the sentiments of these women. Furthermore, love affairs or "*prem*" became integral to the themes of Pratima Pandey's Lokageet, which remains the third significant aspect here. It centred on the motifs of union and separation, extramarital affairs, and so on. The life of the elephant-keeper or *mahout* could be treated as the fourth significant facet of these folksongs, considering his demanding profession that required him to stay away from his home for a long time withstanding the sun and the torrential rain, and leaving behind his dear ones to make a living. Fifth, the buffalo-keeper, or *maishal*, had to undergo similar agony and pain like the elephant-keeper. His flute and his *datura* have been romanticised as his only companion in braving such loneliness. The buffalo-keeper has been, in the process, elevated to high esteem through the artist/composer's imagination. Sixth, songs related to the Muslim community have found eminent presence here in an effort to uphold the varied social aspects of their community, like the mention of *sarees*, the red and white bangles made of conch, which were a type of artifice used by these Muslims parallel to their Hindu counterparts in certain areas like Dhubri and Agomoni that are depicted in the *Goalporia* folksongs. Seventh, mysticism remained an integral part of these folksongs wherein the divine love of Lord Krishna and his depiction as a lover becomes the focus of the artist. Pandey's Goalporia Lokageet, in this vein, could be stated to be expressing the secular ideas of this north-eastern Indian society. The noted folksong collector and composer Cecil Sharp has demonstrated how folksongs have been imbricated into the complex web of the anxieties and fear of nationalism, primitivism, and modernities. Sharp thereby comments on how folksongs are the "spontaneous music of the unspoiled, unlettered classes and created out of their pure natural instinct" (quoted in Hans 19). Folksongs, as these Goalporia Lokageet implicate, thereby become sociological documentations of people's perception about events, situations, and relations. Even though they are not scientific monographs, their capacity to hint at and suggest sociological details of the folk tradition makes them significant intangible archives of historical importance.

---

[9] Choudhury, Sanghamitra, and PratimaNeog "Folk Music as a Voice of Marginalized Society: A Comparative Study of Goalporia Folk Music of Assam and PlengPhueChiwit of Thailand," 2013, 283–84.

Folk music can be situated within the framework of folk media—the media directly related to the culture of the human locality in which communication is done—an idea that suits the immediate cultural context of the sender and receiver and thereby makes the process of communication more efficient. "No media have the power to replace folk media because folk media originated in the environment of our culture, belief and values and these are incredible!" states sociologist Indra Deva. Deva, in *Folk Culture and Peasant Society in India* (1989), further delves into the oral traditions of the peasants in the Indian subcontinent. Delving into its rich variety and content, he describes how "it consists of lyrical folk songs of numerous types, Ballads; heroic poems and epic lays; folk opera prose narratives such as marchen, legends and myths; proverbs and mnemonic formulae; riddles; and a variety of magical formulae and incantations" (1). Deva also notes how the elements of the orality of folk literature, in turn, become closely associated with the structures and specific aspects of one's social life (1–2). Situating the tradition of Goalporia Lokageet within this framework unveils how these folksongs constantly engage with the rural community while highlighting the rural media that was generated in the age-old folk tradition and rural backdrop of the Koch Rajbonshi evolutionary process. Its regional variety, its fundamental basis of articulation centred on regional customs, beliefs and faiths, attitude and habits, make this genre of folk music a continual process of interactive communication. Here, there are several issues to be discussed—What is the significance of folk music as an intangible cultural resource, and what is the importance of this approach and what problems of interpretation and evidence need to be overcome? Do goods possess intrinsic meaning or is culture responsible for creating it? Do people impose meaning on things, or do they discover it in them? These questions arise in all cultures and periods, but here they will be considered primarily in relation to the post-independent Rajbonshi community and Pratima Pandey's Goalporia Lokageet.

Given the territorial and geopolitical background of the Rajbonshis of Assam, one could well imagine the historical development of this community vis-à-vis their shared cultural and emotional legacies—the backdrop against which Pratima Pandey's lyrical nodes find existence. Pratima Pandey gathered the music of these rural and local marginalised folks, and contrived them in the domain of popular culture and mainstream cultural and social spaces. In this effort at creating a workable historical legacy, she remains the first female artist to have envisaged folk musical art as a repertoire of epistemic cultural resources reflecting the vibrant assets of the Rajbongshi heritage. Thus, Pratima Pandey's folk music could be considered as an evolutionary catalyst in advancing the folk and collective consciousness of the people, interrogating the reiterative processes of composition in the context of the postcolonial uncanny represented in the ideas represented during the 1950s.

Pratima Pandey's folksongs are suggestive of how the sociological aspects of the Rajbonshi community are used as tools of culture in structural patterns, and organised into meaningful relationships, while making visible the ongoing changes in the social and material condition of Goalpara lives. These Goalporia Lokageet are thereby not mere folk music but in turn also reveal personal information that lies beyond concrete data and allow us to grasp the nebulous concept of the culture. The kind of (in)animate communication rendered by Goalpara folk music mediate progress through the social world, while their diffusion bridges cultural boundaries and connects centres with peripheries. Additionally, the folksongs, as artefacts produced in reaction to specific moments and events, convey hidden cultural constraints, moral standards, social fears, and emotionally charged issues. Thus, if these folksongs are considered as a material resource and artefacts, it becomes necessary for material culturalists to take account of individual motivation and psychological taste, along with the consideration of how the meaning of any object is not separable from the opportunity and desire to acquire it. And when this framework is considered in terms of Goalporia Lokageet, it could be inferred that folk music now assumes more significance than material goods because it becomes a symbolic property triggering the personal and communal search for identity. While possession of physical property such as clothing and jewellery enable the anchoring of remembrance against a fleeting memory and a precarious identity in a mutable world,[10] folk music becomes all the more complex considering it constitutes a continual effort at keeping the idea of *memory* itself alive—an artifice prompted by the intensity of the desire to associate with their past histories while retaining their ostensible cultural properties. While possessions perpetuate significant memories for those who wear them (like jewellery and clothing), it could be inferred from Pratima Pandey's Lokageet that this kind of intangible communal possession perpetuate shared memories, where both personal and public memories are interwoven.

While delving into Pratima Pandey's folksongs as cultural recourses, Roland Barthes's observation in *The Pleasure of the Text* (1975) becomes significant:

> Every fiction is supported by a social jargon, a sociolect, with which it identities: fiction is that degree of consistency a language attains when it has

---

[10] For further information on material culture, refer to Richard Grassby's "Material Culture and Cultural History" (2005), 595–97.

jelled exceptionally and finds a sacerdotal class (priests, intellectuals, artists) to speak it generally and to articulate it. . . . Each jargon (each fiction) fights for hegemony; if power is on its side, it spreads everywhere in the general and daily occurrences of social life, it becomes *doxa*, nature. (27–28)

Pandey's effort at recounting the marginalised and lost existence of the Rajbonshi community could be placed within the framework of Barthes's ideas wherein he emphasises how each invented tale battles for hegemony, which later becomes an indispensable part of communal life. Considering how folklore has been, and continues to be, organised around communal affiliations, cultural productions, local community, ethnic identity, and nationalism, it has an intrinsic relation to power differentials that is fundamental to both the history and the future of the discipline.

Pratima Pandey's folk revivals are attempts at establishing a cultural articulation of the postcolonial identity crisis of the Rajbonshis. Her arrival in the scene is, in a way, her initiation of a formal claim for an extinct culture. However Pratima Pandey's Goalporia songs were neither popular nor did they reach all sections of the people until 1937. Though born into an affluent and aristocratic family, Pratima Pandey through her constant efforts enhanced the position of the Goalporia Lokageet, serving to retain and revive the originality of the Goalporia folk tradition until the very end of her life.

The uncanny spectre of the postcolonial past of independent India that presided over the region and dictated the songs' geopolitical and, thus, their cultural fate, remains significant. Thus, the cultural practice of folk music or vernacular music cultures could be identified within the discursive ideologies of revivalism of historical experience. However, within this tradition, the idea of "representation" itself becomes very significant, since the "re" of *representation* now entails contingent interventions and asymmetries of power that claims the representations of alterity through folk music, while calling out for deconstructive historicisation. Edward Said proposes how the idea of "representation"—the songs' construction and production, their movement and circulation from the annals of their history and their interpretations—becomes the very components creating "culture" (66). Philip V. Bohlman further argues how acts of musical representations engage in articulation of the unequal distribution of power between the "self" and the "other" (224). When Goalporia Lokageet are analysed within the framework of the politics of representation, it can be observed how this folk music was an articulation of the communities living a peripheral existence in Assam and beyond. Thus, Pratima Pandey's Goalporia folksongs and folk revivals could be read as a gesture loaded with political significance that has, in Said's words, "the power to narrate, or to narrate, or to block other narratives from forming and emerging" (xii), constituting the relationship between culture and imperialism.

Goalporia folk songs are reflective of the struggles and tribulations of common people—their hard labouring in the field, their agitations, struggles, pains, and exploitation are some of the common motifs woven through the fabric of the Goalporia Lokageet. Words like *Mahout, Baishal, Moishal*, and *Gariaal* feature in almost all these songs—a reflection of the engagement with lower-class workers, pointing to their socio-economic backwardness. A. L. Lloyd in *Folk Song in England* (1967) comments on how the articulation of political tension remains a chief motive behind the aspirations to recover a folk community, above and beyond its function to revive an association with a mythical rural past. Goalporia Lokageet have, indeed, remained synonymous with the history of the Koch Rajbonshis, while also being a crucial cultural reference to the folk geo-cultural mores of the peasantry of the region. Thus, this research analyses Pratima Pandey's Goalporia folksongs as a part of the material culture of the region, locating them within the discourses of the culture, ethnicity, folk consciousness, and history of the colonial past of Western Assam. Furthermore, Goalporia Lokageet, being collective registers of the Koch Rajbonsis, are transmuted into a significant cathartic space reflecting on the perception, social cognition, emotions, and culture and identity of the community, a glaring witness to the colonial history of Western Assam, and into a politics of dispossession—of land, identity, and culture.

References

Barman, Prafulla. *AsomNandiniPratima Pandey Barua*. Guwahati: Bishal Publishers, 2004. Print.

Barthes, Roland. *The Pleasure of the Text*. Trans. Richard Miller. New York: Hill and Wang, 1975. Print.

Ben-Amos, Dan. "Toward a Definition of Folklore in Context." *Journal of American Folklore* 84.331 (1971): 3–15. Web. 10 June 2017.

Bohlman, Philip V. "Music as Representation." *Journal of Musicological Research* 24.3–4 (2005). Web. 14 August 2017.

Choudhury, Sanghamitra, and Pratima Neog. "Folk Music as a Voice of Marginalised Society: A Comparative Study of Goalparia Folkmusic of Assam and Phleng Phue Chiwit of Thailand." *Eastern Anthropologist* 66.2–3 (2013): 279–91.

Cole, Ross Graham. *Ballads, Blues and Alterity*. University of Cambridge, 2015. Web. 15 August 2017.

Deva, Indra. *Folk Culture and Peasant Society in India.* Jaipur: Rawat Publications, 1989. Print.

Dunes, Alan. *Interpreting Folklores.* Bloomington: Indiana University Press, 1980. Print.

Grassby, Richard. "Material Culture and Cultural History." *Journal of Interdisciplinary History* 35.4 (Spring 2005): 591–603. Print.

Hans, Wisner. *A Rebel in Music.* Berlin: Allen Williams Book, 1978. Print

Lloyd, A. L. *Folk Song in England.* London: Lawrence and Wishart, 1976. Print.

Prodhani. Jyotirmoy. "Life as Lore: The Art and Time of Pratima Pandey Barua." *Indian Folklife* 31 (2008): 14–15. Print.

Said, Edward W. *Culture and Imperialism.* London: Vintage Books. 1994. Print.

Said, Edward. *Culture and Imperialism.* London: Vintage, 1994. Print.

Taylor, Archer. "Folklore and the Student of Literature." *Pacific Spectator* 2 (1948): 216–23. Print.

Tylor, Edward Burnett. *Primitive Culture: Researches into the Development of Mythology, Philosophy, Religion, Art and Custom.* London: J. Murray, 1971. Print.

BIOGRAPHIES OF *YAKSHA*:
OBJECT, STYLE, AND AGENCIES

SHAMBWADITYA GHOSH

Yaksha[1] *Manibhadra*, famously known as "Parkham *Yaksha*," was discovered in the village of Parkham situated in the south of today's modern city of Mathura in Uttar Pradesh, India. This colossal sculpture was presented to the Asiatic Society in 1820 and later transferred to the Government Museum of Mathura established in 1874 by Sir F. S. Growse, the then district collector of Mathura. The archaeological significance of Mathura was first identified by Sir Alexander Cunningham who conducted several archaeological excavations from 1861 to 1862. Later, a few more excavations in 1871 and 1873 provided a clear picture of the cultural significance of Mathura, especially during the pre-Christian era. While other amateur archaeologists like Sir. F. S. Growse mostly focused on Buddhist remains, Gregory Vogel highlighted the key aspects of the religious scenario of the area. In his reports from 1908 to 1912, Vogel wrote extensively on other cultic practices like the *Naga* and *Yaksha* cults.

The discovery of the *Yaksha* sculptures from the Mathura region gave impetus to these archaeological interpretations. It also helped create a historical chronology based on archaeological objects. Though scientific discussion based on archaeological objects began in the later decades of the nineteenth century, archaeology as a single independent discipline and method emerged in the last decades of the nineteenth century. The early nineteenth century witnessed the development of historical discourses on art that engaged with the style, features, and religious connotations of the Parkham *Yaksha* sculpture. The inscription on the pedestal of the sculpture mentions that it was commissioned by members of the *Manibhadra Puga* (a congregation) and made by *Gomitaka*, a pupil of *Kunika*. Several other giant

---

[1] A living supernatural being, spiritual apparition, or ghost spirit; also, a class of semi-divine beings. Described as sons of *Pulastya*; though generally considered as benevolent, occasionally imbued with *pishacha* and other malignant spirits. MWSE, 838.

Yaksha sculptures including those of the female counterpart of the *Yakshas*—the *Yakshis*—were discovered in these areas.

The socio-cultural context of this cult practice goes back to an older pre-urban environment in which standardised prescriptions of iconographical treatments were absent. We have very few remains of objects worshipped before the Mauryan period except the material examples of these giant sculptures of the *Yaksha* cult. Several other sculptures of similar cult practices along with their female counterparts have been discovered in Pawaya and Besnagar;[2] which shows the presence of this cult practice in wider geographical areas beyond the middle-Gangetic plains.[3] Several texts and inscriptional evidence substantiate the claim that this cult was quite prominent in urban centres, specifically among the mercantile communities and travellers, who had adopted *Manibhadra* as their tutelary deity. Two colossal images of *Yaksha*, similar to the Parkham sculpture, discovered in two neighbouring cities—Baroda[4] and Mathura, serve to substantiate this argument.

Before coming to the discussion of the Parkham *Yaksha*, we need to explore the socio-cultural and political context of Mathura as an urban centre. There is a considerable amount of research about the origin of the *Yaksha* cult, but focused studies on the sites are rare. G. Mitterwallner argues that the *Yaksha* cult has often been discussed with emphasis on its art history, at the cost of its social and cultural contexts. Studies of Buddhist *Nikaya* texts show that settlements began developing in Mathura around the sixth century BCE. Brahamanical *sutra* literature and *Jataka* stories provide prolific references to the extent of the development of crafts in northern India during the pre-Mauryan Haryanka, Saisunaga, and Nanda periods. But there was no specific mention of Mathura as a centre of craft-specialised, skill-based habitational sites.

These literary descriptions can be proved by archaeological evidence from excavations. Ample examples of painted greyware have been discovered in Mathura and in a nearby site, Sonkh. *Anguttara Nikaya*'s description

---

[2] The *Yaksha* image from Pawaya, the ancient *padmavati*, is now kept in Gwalior museum. The *Yaksha* figure from Besnagar, which has been identified as Kubera, is now kept in Vidisa State Museum. Chanda, Rama Prasad. "Four Ancient Yaksha Statues," *Journal of the Department of Letters*, vol. 4. Calcutta: CUP (1921): 3–6. Print.

[3] The *Yaksha* cult was distributed geographically. Buddhist literature, specifically the *Jataka* stories, describes this cult distribution. According to *Manimalaka jataka*, *Yaksha* Manibhadra had his "*Bhavana Chaitya*" in Magadha.

[4] Presently displayed in Mathura State Museum. Only the upper part of the sculpture is available. The estimated actual length of the sculpture is twelve feet.

provides information about the growing trend of urbanisation in the Gangetic valley, with emphasis on economic development and craft specialisations that enabled these settlements to develop into cities or *Janapadas*. But descriptions about Mathura reveal that it was not a fully developed city as is evident from the ambiguity surrounding the political nature of the city and its economic background. The momentum of political development was also affected by the use of iron tools in the Gangetic valley. George Erdosy explains the relationship between the promotion of agriculture and its catalytic role in the emergence of cities with a defined political framework. His argument was based on the theory of surplus production that led to the emergence of different, specialised, skill-oriented groups who played a pivotal role in the development of a stratified society. Ranabir Chakraborty argues that the spread of a village-based agricultural economy provided scope for political development, consolidating power into a new form of chiefdom or kingship.

As there was surplus production from agriculture, skill-oriented professions based on different craft specialisations flourished. This points out the essential shift in the cultural scenario, specifically, the emergence of "objects" that could be utilised in the economy, and simultaneously as objects of worship. The *Arthashastra* mentions these diverse professions, which were the precursors of the mercantile groups that emerged later. The *Baudhayana Dharmasutra*, *Ashtadhyayi*, and other *Pali* literature divide these groups into *Shreni*, *Gana*, *Puga*, and *Sangha*, depending on their functions and composition. Under the Mauryas, the economy was controlled by the state, as there were better roads and other facilities offered by the state, which resulted in the increased mobility of men and merchandise. Kautilya expresses concerns about the emergence of this new class, which could function as agencies of power.

The position of Mathura in this political and economic situation is not quite clear, as contemporary Buddhist literature does not describe the material culture of Mathura. Archaeological excavations prove that the outer fortification must have been made during the fourth century, which shows the increasing importance of this settlement, especially considering the fact that security walls were added to the existing settlement. It also ensures the security of the city-dweller. *Arthashastra* mentions the textile production of Mathura, which was quite famous in terms of its texture and quality.[5] While none of the Asokan edicts mention Mathura, the city finds space in Megasthenes's works (Arrian, Indica, VII) as Methora. *Patanjali*

---

[5] Varanasi and Mathura were famous centres of textile production, Jataka no. 297 (*Kama Vilapa Jataka*).

in his *Mahabhashya*[6] engages with the rapid development of Mathura as an urban centre. The *Mahabhashya* asserts that the people of Mathura were better than those of *Shankishya* and *Pataliputra* (*Sankashyakebhyasca pataliputrakebhyasca mathura abhirupatara iti*). R. S. Sharma has studied the economic development of Mathura extensively and examined how it emerged as an urban centre. However, he expresses concerns regarding the support from its rural areas, which were directly involved in the process of production. Geographically, Mathura was not a very fertile land owing to low rainfall, which made it unsuitable for the production of surplus crops.

The rapid development of infrastructural facilities including roads and means of transport during the Mauryan period (c.320 to c.200 BCE) facilitated the mobility of men and commodities, and provided scope for the exchange of ideas and cultural interaction. The geographic location of Mathura augmented its development as an urban centre. It was situated on the Rajagriha–Pushkalavati route, which was famous as *Uttarapatha*, which connected urban centres such as Rajagriha, Varanasi, Mathura, and Pushkalavati. The *Anguttara Nikaya* provides an account of cities in northern India during the time of Buddha; however, there are gaps in the information available about the settlements in Mathura. Although there is a general description of material culture in the upper Gangetic valley, details of Mathura as an urban centre are not known. Nevertheless, archaeological evidence suggests that Mathura developed as a flourishing urban centre in the first century CE.

The Mauryas adhered to very stringent statecraft, controlling the economy for their imperial achievements while simultaneously contributing to the development of agriculture and industrial production. The Mauryan government appointed record-keepers to keep track of transactions in the arena of trades and crafts in cooperation with the guilds.[7] Members of previous republican states who had lost their political power due to the extensive imperial network of the Mauryans staunchly opposed this monopolised system. Probably this was led by mercantile groups, as they had administered their own rules, including a different monetary system. But from the second century BCE, when state control became more flexible, these groups were able to widen their trade network. We observe repeated references to Mathura during this period.

Buddhist *Jataka* stories composed during the post-Mauryan period describe *Yakshas* as guardian deities. The habitats of these guardian deities

---

[6] The *Mahabhasya*, a commentary on *Panini*'s *Ashtadhyayi*, was compiled in the first half of the second century BCE.

[7] The Buddhist and Brahmanical resources reveal that the guilds were autonomous bodies with their own laws.

were defined very specifically, denoting their supernatural charisma. They were represented as dwelling in specific trees outside the city gates or toll gates, or in specific shrines made in palace gardens.[8] A. K. Coomaraswamy has worked extensively on the origin of the *Yaksha* cult and he writes that *Yakshas* were intimately connected with water, trees, and cities. In Buddhist literature, *Yakshas* are referred to as "*Rukkha Devata*," which signifies their malevolent character.[9] They were worshipped by a large number of groups including the aristocracy, merchants, and the common people.[10] Women, especially those who desired children, were the most devoted worshippers. Coomaraswamy has related the origin of the *Yaksha* cult with water cosmology and presented *Yakshas* as being synonymous with "*Deva*" or beings of purely divine origin. R. N. Misra has argued on the basis of the material remains that the cult of *Yaksha* was probably of non-Aryan origin. Popular forms of *Yaksha* worship were inherently related to nature worship, animism, and ancestral worship. Coomaraswamy relates the cult concept with the philosophical discourse of the *Upanishads*, which, over time, transformed into the plastic arts, providing a visual representation of cultic practices.

However, the earliest visual imagery of the *Yaksha* cult does not possess any sectarian affiliation. But scholars argue that the formation of the visual imagery of this particular cult was influenced by the Greco-Roman style, particularly in the case of Mathura. This argument was based on the economic situation in the second century BCE, which witnessed ideological and material exchange with the Greco-Roman world. But archaeological and textual information does not support the argument locating Mathura as a fully-grown urban centre during this time. Coomaraswamy, along with Vincent Smith and Growse, argues for the theory of the indigenous origin of the Mathura school of art, highlighting the characteristic features of *Yaksha* sculptures—robust, pot-bellied figures with grotesque facial features and crude representations without any classical refinement. Early Indian art has been viewed and comprehended predominantly through the lens of Indo-Sumerian and Indo-Iranian writings on the topic produced in

---

[8] *Yakshas* were identified and named according to their tutelary trees; it was quite common to name *Yakshis* after the trees they lived in, a famous example being the name *Salabhanjika*.

[9] As per the Buddhist sources, *Yakshas* were mellowed down by Buddha and transformed into benevolent deities. The Buddhist deity *Hariti* was very cruel and malefic; but she transformed into a benevolent goddess protecting children. Early Buddhist visual imagery depicts *Yaksha/Yakshi* sculptures.

[10] *Mahaniddessa* mentions the followers of *Manibhadra* and *Punnabhadra*, both of whom were quite popular among the mercantile groups.

the early nineteenth century. However, the presence of a pre-Mauryan style characterised by huge proportions and large dimensions could also be perceived and cannot be ignored. The incessant debate about the stylistic treatment of these images has led to some scholars arguing that they must be considered "primitive" due to the use of certain materials that were locally available. But this was a repository containing very specific patterns, designs, and motifs signifying the nature of art exclusive to that period.

There is no clarity regarding the particular religious or sectarian affiliations of the *Yaksha* cult, as the visual imagery does not fit with any particular sectarian belief system.[11] The epigraphic evidence collected from the Mathura region establishes the point quite clearly. Unlike the images that belong to the Buddhist and Jain sects, most of the *Yaksha* cult figures are not inscribed. Very few of them contain inscriptions dating back to the second century BCE, mentioning the name of the donor and the purpose of the donation. Two contemporary inscriptions mention the names of the donors and the sculptors. The inscriptions from Nagala Jhinga, and Parkham display the name of the same sculptor, Kunika, who was the pupil of Gomitaka. However, the name of the deity is not mentioned. Although similar cult images were discovered from other sites in neighbouring areas, epigraphic evidence is not sufficient to extract information about the sculptor, the patron, or the reason for patronage.[12] The fragmentary evidence of these epigraphic records is insufficient to obtain information regarding the actual ritual practices of this cult or to identify its followers.

Discussing the cultural contexts of these damaged inscriptions will help us comprehend how this cult came to be perceived later. Antiquarian pursuits entailed the collection, sourcing, and scholarship of objects, including manuscripts, for configuring and memorialising the past. In this particular case, we possess epigraphic evidence that can be used to "memorialise" the entire process of cult practice and its myriad experimentation in art forms. Therefore, we can hypothesise that the use of historical objects and topographies in pre-colonial India to create histories and to recall and use a specific aspect of the past can also be understood as examples of antiquarian pursuits.

---

[11] *Yakshas* are mentioned in Buddhist, Jain, and even Brahmanical canons; but there is no clear mention about their divine positions. They were given an important role in later Buddhist iconography; similarly in the Brahmanical religion, they have been associated with the God of wealth, *Kubera.*

[12] The sculpture of *Kubera* from Parkham, the pot-bellied male sculpture from Gayatri Tila, the plaque from Ral Bhadar showing a seated male and female, and the female figure from Mora, probably that of a *Yakshi*, indicate the presence of this cult practice.

Material culture and the creation of a defined cultural periphery through objects has been viewed over a period of time as an effective cultural exchange in the Indo-Sumerian and Indo-Persian contexts, specifically with regard to the artistic productions of the Maurya-Sunga period. Coomaraswamy provides a detailed list of such elements and procedural analogies, asserting that "so far as its constituent elements are concerned, and apart from any question of style, there is comparatively little in Indian decorative art that is peculiar to India and much that India shares with Western Asia" (11–14).

Although the influence of the Hellenist ethos shaped the vocabulary of the early Mauryan style, there already prevailed a tradition of depiction that did not have any classical refinement. Due to the identical style of depiction and dimensional execution, these examples were labelled "tribal" and "primitive." Such instances of "intermediaries" describing early Indian art has been a long-standing tradition, with travellers and writers from the Hellenist and Achaemenid world being predominant chroniclers. Transmission of Hellenist idioms into non-Hellenist art forms is not necessary to judge the meaning of Greek art. John Boardman's pioneering work "The Diffusion of Classical Art in Antiquity" elaborates upon the transmission of artistic features of the classical world from the eighth century BCE to the early centuries of the Common Era over large geographical areas, from Britain to China. He writes in detail of the material interests of the classical world—since the Greeks were not always the "intermediaries," the result of the transfusion of cultural forms, specifically in art forms, always depended on the needs of the recipients to make their own version of it. But for years, the European gaze denied the existence of "fine arts" in the ancient Indian context, since Indian arts did not confirm to the norms of European classical art. This long-standing view of the scholarship of the early nineteenth century contended the existence of an indigenous style and form that developed through experimentation.

These artistic executions with their own peculiar patterns and designs had specific features. Nihar Ranjan Ray argues that the "so-called Mauryan polish could be a deciding factor, but [the] non-availability of such polish throws light on the Mauryan court art, which was already on the wane" (67). The principal features of archaic solidity, robust presentation, and weighty volume found in the *Yaksha* figues stand in stark contrast to the features of the rounded and modelled figures in other examples of Mauryan art. The *Yaksha* figure from Parkham shows tight and stiff modelling with fully rounded arms and thighs representing an earthy heaviness that can be coded as smooth and lifeless inertia, with a flat treatment at the back.

Iconographical treatments vary across texts. *Yakshas* have been described with specific characteristics that define their visual presence. Buddhist and

Brahmanical texts discuss the two forms in which *Yakshas* are presented—as small, deformed, asymmetrical figures, often inducing laughter,[13] and as grandiose, benevolent, powerful figures offering protection to human beings. The former representation was more common. *Yakshas* presented in the latter mode were believed to be endowed with supernatural qualities that could save worshippers from danger. Manibhadra belongs to the latter group, which was also associated with other benevolent cult figures such as Kubera, Purnabhadra, and Panchika.

Textual references regarding *Yaksha* worship abound. In ancient India, special sanctuaries were built in order to install *Yaksha* statues in strategic locations on the outskirts of the city or at junctions and crossroads. These sanctuaries were called *yaksha-chaitya* or *yakshayatana*, indicating the cult status of *Yaksha* worship. The clearest references to Manibhadra's and Purnabhadra's devotees are available in the *Mahaniddesa*. There is an interesting assemblage of both *Yaksha* and Krishna cults in the Mathura region.[14] It is evident that votaries of the *Yaksha* cult belonged to various socio-economic groups, and their grip over the public psyche has been strong enough to continue into the present. Though the cult and the object have been separated from their original contexts, they have transformed into deities protecting villages. Even in the present era, an annual celebration is held in Parkham in Mathura district in honour of the *Yakshas*, reminding one of the ancient practices of the *Yaksha* cult.

References

Basham, A. L. *The Wonder That Was India*. Delhi: Rupa & Co, 2001. Print.

Boardman, John. *The Diffusion of Classical Art in Antiquity*. Princeton: Princeton University Press, 1994. Print.

Coomaraswamy, A. K. History *of Indian and Indonesian Art*. New York: Dover, 1965. Print.

—. *Yakshas: Essays in the Water Cosmology*. Ed. Poul Shroeder. Delhi: Oxford University Press, 1993. Print.

Chakrabarti, Dilip. *Colonial Indology*. New Delhi: Munshiram Manoharlal, 1997. Print

---

[13] The *Vamana Purana* narrates a similar story—that of *Yaksha Panchalika* who entertained Mahadeva by accepting yawning (*vijrambhana)* and lunacy (*unmad*). This became a source of laughter for others (*lokasya hasyakari*).

[14] In the *Dhammapada Attakatha*, while explaining the term *Vattasuddhika*, the writer mentions Punnabhaddavattika, Vasudevavattika, Baladevavattika, and Manibhaddavatika, indicating the presence of Vasudeva and Baladeva figures along with two prominent *Yaksha* figures.

Chakraborty, Ranabir. "*Prachin Bharater Arthanaitin Itihasher Sandhane*," *Itihash Granthamala*. Calcutta: Ananda Publishers, 2002. Print.

Cunningham, Alexander. *Report of the Year 1871–72, Archaeological Survey of India, Vol. III.* Varanasi: Indological Book House, 1966. Print.

Erdosy, George. *Urbanisation in Early Historic India*. BAR International Series, 430, Oxford: BAR, 1988. Print.

Guha, Sudeshna. *Artefact of History; Archaeology, Historiography and Indian Pasts*. New Delhi: Sage, 2015. Print.

Guha-Thakurata, Tapati. *Monuments, Objects, Histories: Institutions of Art in Colonial and Postcolonial India.* New York: Columbia University Press, 2004. Print

Hodder, Ian. *Entangled: Archaeology of the Relationships between Humans and Things*. Chichester: Wiley-Blackwell, 2012. Print

Johansen, P. G. "Recasting the Foundations: New Approaches to Regional Understanding of South Asian Archaeology and the Problem of Culture History." *Asian Perspectives*, 42 .2 (Autumn, 2003). Print.

Kenoyer, J. M. "New Perspectives on the Mauryan and Kushana Periods." *Between the Empires: Society in India 300 BCE to 400 CE*. Ed. P. Olivelle. New York: Oxford University Press, 2006.

Lahiri, Nayanjot. *The Archaeology of Indian Trade Routes Up to c. 200 B.C.* New Delhi: Oxford University Press, 1992. Print.

Luders, H. *Mathura Inscriptions: Unpublished Papers*. Ed. K. L. Janert. Gottingen: Vandenhoeck and Ruprecht, 1961. Print.

Mishra. R. N. *Yaksha Cult and Iconography*. New Delhi: Munshiram Manoharlal, 1981. Print.

Mitter, Partha. *Much Maligned Monsters: History of European Reactions to Indian Art*. Oxford: Oxford University Press, 1997. Print.

Mitterwallner, G. "Yaksas of Ancient Mathura." *Mathura: The Cultural Heritage*. Ed. D. M. Srinivasan. New Delhi. Manohar Publication, 1993. Print.

Ray, Nihar Ranjan. *Maurya and Sunga Art*. Calcutta: Quality Printers & Binders, 1965. Print.

Schnapp, A. "Towards a Universal History of Antiquarians." *Complumtum* 24.2 (2013): 13–20.

Shrimali, K. M. "Pali Literature and Urbanism." *The Complex Heritage of Ancient India: Essays in Memory of R. S. Sharma.* Ed. D. N. Jha. New Delhi: Manohar Publication, 2014. Print.

Singh, Upinder. *The Discovery of Ancient India: Early Archaeologists and the Beginning of Archaeology.* New Delhi: Permanent Black, 2004. Print.

Sircar, D. C. *Indian Epigraphy*. New Delhi: Motilal Banarasidas, 1965. Print.

Srinivasan, D. M. *Mathura: The Cultural Heritage*. New Delhi: Manohar Publication, 1989. Print.

Reports

1. Uttar Pradesh District Gazetteers, Mathura, 1968.
2. Indian Archaeology: A Review 1974–75, Archaeological Survey of India, Delhi.
3. Indian Archaeology: A Review 1976–77, Archaeological Survey of India, Delhi.

FOOD AND FOOD HABITS OF THE TRIBALS OF CHOTANAGPUR IN COLONIAL INDIA: WRITINGS, PERCEPTIONS, AND DISCOURSE

VINITA RAV

Food history is an arena that has come under academic scrutiny across the world. Many scholars have examined food products and food history as objects of academic inquiry. Most of the works were compiled with focus on one or more food items by observing and studying how the adoption of that particular food affected the history of the masses at a specific time. This essay explores colonial and ethnographic writings that discuss tribal food, with emphasis on the major causes that might have led to transformations in the food habits of the tribal people of Chotanagpur. Missionary and ethnographic writings, which include the writer's observations and collected folklore, are the major sources of information about food habits during the colonial period. These works showcase the writers' sentiments and perceptions of tribal food and food habits. The British colonial view of tribal food cultures also becomes evident through these writings, which influenced the policies of the Empire in tribal societies. As is well documented, ethnographers and missionaries were the first to translate tribal life, culture, and traditions into a language that could be understood by non-tribal people; it is also important to note that they were responsible for constructing stereotyped images of tribal subjects, which still persist in the non-tribal psyche.

Before discussing the tribal people and their food habits, let us investigate the Chotanagpur region and the story of the colonisation of clans in the area. Currently, Chotanagpur is an area surrounded by Madhya Pradesh in the west, West Bengal in the east, Orissa in the south, and Bihar in the north, and it is known as Jharkhand[1] (a land of forests). The transition

---

[1] As J. Reid mentions in the *Final Report on the Survey and Settlement Operations in the District of Ranchi*, "In the earliest references to the province of Chotanagpur it is called Jharkhand or the forests tract," (1). On 15 November 2000 India received its twenty-eighth state in the form of Jharkhand, which was separated from Bihar.

from Nagpur to Chotanagpur too can be seen as a conquest of essential resources for the benefit of the British Empire, which snatched the food, shelter, property, and forests of the clans, thereby triggering a prolonged battle between the local inhabitants, the British state, and the *Dikus*.[2]

During the colonial period, Chotanagpur consisted of the districts of Hazaribagh, Manbhum, Singhbhum, Ranchi, and Palamau. The main inhabitants of these districts were the Mundas, the Santals, the Oraons, the Paharias, the Turis, the Asurs, the Korwas, the Birhors, and the Kharias. According to the British official J. Reid, the Mundas were the first among the aboriginal tribes to arrive in Chotanagpur. At that time, Chiefs were assigned for the protection of the tribes from enemies. Outside interventions began when the family of chiefs intermixed with the Rajput families of Pacheto and Singhbhum, which helped the Rajputs, Brahmins, Baraiks, and other groups to settle down in Chotanagpur in large numbers. With the help of the chiefs, they soon established themselves as Jagirdars and Zamindars in this region. In 1616, Ibrahim Khan, who was sent by Emperor Jahangir to get diamonds, defeated the Raja of Chotanagpur, Durjan Sal. In 1765, Chotanagpur was gifted (along with three other provinces, namely, Bengal, Bihar, and Orissa) to the East India Company by Shah Alam II.[3]

The British policy towards Chotanagpur and its tribes gave more power to *Dikus* to exploit the tribal community. The commercialisation of forest resources strengthened the power of the Thikadars, the Zamindars, and the Mahajuns. "All the trees, with the exception of a few in the neighbourhood

---

[2] The term *Diku/Diku/Dikku* has been used by tribals to refer to non-tribal communities. Scholars working on the history of tribal communities in colonial India and in contemporary times tell us about the various images of non-tribals among tribes and the image of the tribal among non-tribals. In an essay in *Man in India*, S. C. Sinha, Jyoti Sen, and Sudhir Panchbhai describe the various meanings of the word *Diku* which is popular among the tribes. According to them, tribals used *Diku* as a word for "trouble-makers" (*Dik Dik karna*) and "exploiters." Interestingly, *Diku* is used for high caste Hindus. Lower caste Hindus were identified by their caste names, such as Chamar, Kumhar, Teli, etc. They conclude that the word *Diku* is used not only to refer to upper caste Hindus, but also to Muslims and Sikhs. They used the word *Diku* for those people whose languages were different from tribal dialects, for Zamindars and moneylenders. The word was largely used to denote exploiters. ("The Concept of *Diku* among the Tribes of Chotanagpur," *Man in India*, vol. 49, April–June 1969: 121–138). Nirmal Sengupta, in the book *Fourth World Dynamics Jharkhand* (New Delhi: Authors Guid Publications, 1982), writes: "The nineteenth century popular revolts in this area were specifically directed against the *Dikus*, which functionally meant 'a group of outsider-exploiter'" (32).

[3] Captain Camac was the first British Military Officer of Ramgarh, who came to Chotanagpur while campaigning against the Cheros of Palamau in 1769.

of roads, are the property of the Zamindars, and are rented out by them at price varying chiefly with the bazaar mirik or price of rice" (Ball 73). With the coming of the railways, the demand to cut down trees intensified, as timber was required for the construction of coaches and tracks. Sangeeta Das writes:

> The Indian Forests Act of 1878 provided for the constitution of "reserved forests" all over India, effectively excluding indigenous users from them [. . .] customary forest activities, not being conducted for earning profit, were termed wasteful, while the destruction of large areas of forests for the sake of the timber trade was a gainful utilisation of forests resources. (Ball 80)

Forests were an integral part of the lives of the tribal subjects. Their rituals and beliefs, as well as their livelihood, were linked to forests. They were essential for crop cultivation, the collection of wood, food, and medicinal herbs, for hunting and grazing cattle, and for protection from enemies. As such, forests were worshipped. Valentine Ball, writing on the flora of Manbhum, discusses the importance of forests as a source of drugs, fibres, dyes, lac, oil, and timber. But after the 1860s, under the guise of forest preservation, the British Empire snatched away most of the rights of the tribal people over the jungles. Only a chosen few could enter the forests and then only with licenses issued by the government. This led to huge transformations in the lives of tribal subjects, who were now forced to work in coal mines, in commercial projects involving the cutting of timber, in the construction of railways, or as bonded labourers for Zamindars and Thikadars. Valentine Ball, in the appendix to his book *Jungle Life in India* (1880), says:

> The reservation of forests tracts, which prohibits the inhabitants from taking a blade of grass from within the boundaries, has resulted, as I have pointed out, in the people being cut off from these food sources throughout wide areas, and many have been forced to migrate in consequence to other regions, not yet included in reserves, where they can continue to supplement their scanty cultivation with the production afforded to them by nature. (Ball 695)

In order to extend the railways and to increase cultivation, the colonial government supported deforestation in the early part of the nineteenth century. It was only in the late nineteenth and early twentieth centuries that the British government showed interest in forest conversation; by then, it was too late to save the ecology. Massive deforestation and new forest abandonment rules in the later period disturbed the dietary system of the tribal people, resulting in three famines in the late nineteenth and early twentieth centuries. Communities that had previously survived massive famines by taking recourse to forest produce, now perished due to hunger. It resulted in great distress, and led to dacoity, crop-stealing, and other crimes. The prohibition of access to forests, land alienation, shifts in work, migration, the banning of distilled liquor, and the introduction of alcohol and increased interaction with non-tribal society brought significant changes in the food habits of the tribes.

The distress soon led to uprisings. The Kol rebellion of 1831 is an instance. It made the British government realise that if the people of this area remained "illiterate," they might become a threat to the empire. To minimise the threat, it was necessary to introduce English education, which would mould the tribal subjects according to the will of the empire. It was with this objective that missionary schools imparting English education were established in this region. In Chotanagpur, three missionary groups were active: the Lutherian Mission (Gossner Mission), the S. P. G. Mission, and the Jesuit Mission. The first Christian mission established in Chotanagpur was named the Gossner Mission after the name of its founder, Father Johannes Evangelista Gossner. Apart from the establishment of schools in the region, the missionaries tried to learn local languages and documented the everyday life of the tribal people, their customs, beliefs, and traditions and their socio-economic status. Writings by the missionaries showed an empirical understanding of the clans. Other anthropological and official literature also played a crucial role in providing information about these tribes, their food habits, the geography and flora and fauna of the region, and the economy and social life of the people.

Paul Olaf Bodding (P. O. Bodding) worked extensively on tribal food habits in Chotanagpur. He was a missionary, a linguist, and a folklorist who worked mainly from Dumka in the Santal Pargana district. Bodding came to India in 1889 and until 1933 dedicated his time to learning the Santali language, collecting folklore, and publishing on them. Bodding's accounts of the food habits of the Santal tribes reveal that he regarded them as "nomadic" people attempting to move down the plateau. He mentions that they have been wandering across the region owing to their traditions, and that, because of the limited access to forests and the influence of non-tribal people, they had begun "adopting local habits, customs and practice, so that they may not be regarded as entirely alien" (428). He opines that they "still have to alter many of their ingrained habits" (445) and learn the value of money. Bodding also comments that "they (Santals) do not know how to get the maximum benefits from the soil and their methods are still primitive" (458). For him the Santals were still trapped in the past. He writes:

> The first thing that a Santal father makes for his boy to play with is a bow and arrow, a sure sign of the old mode of obtaining food supplies. They no

longer think of, or rely on, hunting as a means to this end; but the glorious
fascination of the chase and its possibilities hold a prominent place in their
minds. (429)

However, Bodding acknowledges that they knew of the edible products
found in the jungle only because they went on hunts, and that this
knowledge helped them survive during times of scarcity. They used seeds,
leaves, flowers, and other edible items found in the jungle when they were
unable to get enough grains to eat. The knowledge of alternative food items
saved them during famines. Bodding gives a long list of food articles that
the Santals cultivated or collected from jungles. He mentions some items
that were prohibited and also some types of vegetables and meat that were
eaten with great relish. He argues that the names of most of these food items
were recorded by Santal ancestors and that they had passed it on to the next
generation. While listing crops cultivated by the Santals, Bodding mentions
food items like potatoes and peas, which they generally bought from the
market.

Though Bodding's work elaborates upon the food habits of the tribes,
his emphasis was on the transitions that occurred due to the intervention of
non-tribal communities and Christian missionaries. He says that "under the
influence of their Hindu and (so far as pigs are concerned) their Mohammedan
neighbours, some Santals have ceased to eat the flesh of many animals"
(423). He asserts that this was the case only with wealthy Santals and that
poor people were not able to change their dietary habits, as they could not
afford alternative food items. Some of these writings, while depicting the
food habits of the tribes, also constructed images of human beings who were
"less civilised," "savage," "barbaric," and "racially inferior." For instance,
E. T. Dalton documents that the Birhor tribe was accused of engaging in
cannibalism. Although he argues that he does not believe it and that the
tribal subjects negated the "story," his work explicitly says that the Birhors
themselves accepted that their fathers were in the habit of disposing of the
dead by feasting on the bodies. Cannibalism has always been associated
with tribes and the non-tribal community upholds the stereotypical notion
that tribal people eat human flesh. Such misconceptions arise from ignorance
regarding the lives of the tribal subjects and also from the desire of the
mainstream to exoticise the tribals and present them as "mysterious" and
"bizarre." However, one could also argue that the tribal people themselves
propagated this (mis)conception in order to protect their communities from
the interference of non-tribals.

The tribes did not live in complete isolation from the non-tribal
community. They were always involved in trade and exchange of food items
and jungle products with the "settled" communities. For instance, salt and

oil were two major products for which the tribals were dependent on people living in the plains, and the latter obtained honey, other jungle products and animals from the tribals. As mentioned earlier, many Rajputs, Brahmins, and other castes had settled down in Chotanagpur with the help of the chiefs. Later, other Hindu communities like the Kumhars, the Dhobis, and the Gwalas also established their settlements in the area. Tribal folklore mentions these outsiders. Interestingly, the tribals considered people who belonged to higher classes to be *Dikus*. There was solidarity between the tribals and the subjects belonging to the lower classes/castes, as both were oppressed by the same group of people. Perhaps this explains why in the Santal *hul* of 1855, these people stood against the Mahajuns and Zamindars and helped the Santals.

The "outsiders" or non-tribal subjects influenced the culinary culture of the tribal society, as their folklore attests. Dalton mentions that the tribal people were prohibited from eating food with people of other communities. They were also not allowed to eat food prepared by "outsiders." Nevertheless, Dalton observes that the Oraons allow partaking of food cooked by others as long as it is without salt:

> The Oraons have a veneration for salt, and they are not absolutely prohibited from partaking of plain rice cooked by others, provided they are left to salt it themselves. The salt, it would appear, thus applied, removes the "taboo," and makes *fas* what is otherwise *nefas*. (Dalton 23)

While tribal belief systems are believed to be responsible for such restrictions, Dalton also mentions another specific reason in the case of the Santals—their hatred for "outsiders," especially Hindus.

> They (Santals) are not over-particular about food, but nothing will induce them to eat rice cooked by a Hindu, even by a Brahman. Unfortunately, during the famine of 1886 this was not known to us. The cooks who prepared the food distributed at the relief centres were all Brahmans, and it was supposed that this would suit all classes, but the Santals kept aloof, and died rather than eat from hands so hateful them (Dalton 213).

As discussed earlier, the Santals considered the Hindus to be *dikus* who were badly disposed towards them since the latter snatched their lands and imposed heavy taxes on them. Besides, the non-tribals believed themselves to be racially superior, thereby adding to the feeling of animosity. Sumit Guha argues that the idea of "racially inferior people" and "incompetent races" already existed in Indian society. Taking the example of the non-tribal groups' treatment of the hill tribes, he shows that the notion of 'racial difference' was engraved in the Indian psyche. While the Indian elites had their own motives in manipulating and representing the tribes in a particular way in these ethnographic studies, the colonial government had its own agenda and commercial objectives in allowing these studies to be conducted in the first place. Since the colonial empire wanted to exploit forest resources and acquire cheap labour, it became essential to learn and write about tribal societies. The British government encouraged ethnographers and survey officials to write about such societies with the intention of revealing the lives of these "mysterious" people. The ethnographers perpetuated their own prejudices and stereotypical notions about tribal communities, and this was nowhere more evident than in writings about tribal food cultures.

Food has always played a crucial role in determining the parameters of "modernity."[4] The status of the tribes and their food habits created and were located in a vicious cycle. Since the tribes were considered "uncivilised," their food habits were also perceived thus; and since their food habits were "unsophisticated," the tribes were deemed "barbaric." The texts studied illuminate the food habits of the tribal communities and their significance in the quotidian life of tribal subjects, thus serving as alternate histories of hitherto marginalised communities.

References

Ball, Valentine. "On the Jungle Products used as Articles of Food by the Inhabitants of the Districts of Manbhoom and Hazaribagh." *Journal of the Asiatic Society*, 36.2 (1867): 73–82. Print.

—. "Notes on the Flora of Manbhoom." *Journal of the Asiatic Society*, 38.2 (1868): 114–24. Print.

—. *Jungle Life in India*. London: De La Rue, 1880.

Bodding, P. O. *Studies in Santal Medicine and Connected Folklore*. Calcutta: A. Mittra, 1986. Print.

Dalton, E. T. *Kols of Chotanagpur*. Calcutta: Asiatic Society of Bengal, 1866. Print.

—. *The Descriptive Ethnology of Bengal*. Calcutta: Asiatic Society of Bengal, 1872. Print.

Damodaran, Vinita. "Gender Forests and Famine in Nineteenth-Century Chotanagpur." *Indian Journal of Gender Studies*, 22.3 (2002): 44–54. Print.

---

[4] Ishita Banerjee-Dube's lecture on the topic, "The Authentic, the Hybrid, and the Modern: Tales from 'Indian Cuisine,'" was given on 16 March 2016 at the University of Delhi.

Dube, Ishita Banerjee. "The Authentic, the Hybrid, and the Modern: Tales from Indian Cuisine." 16 March 2016, University of Delhi, Delhi. Lecture.

Guha, Sumit. "Lower Strata, Older Races, and Aboriginal Peoples: Racial Anthropology and Mythical History Past and Present." *Journal of Asian Studies* 57:2 (1998): 423–41. Print.

Gupta, Sanjukta Das. *Adivasis and the Raj: Socio-economic Transition of the Hos, 1820–1932*. New Delhi: Orient Blackswan, 2011. Print.

Mintz, Sidney. *Sweetness and Power: The Place of Sugar in Modern History*. Penguin: 1986. Print.

Polanyi, Karl. *The Great Transformation: The Political and Economic Origins of Our Time*. Boston: Farrar and Rinehart, 1957. Print.

Reid, J. *Final Report on the Survey and Settlement Operations in the District of Ranchi, 1902-1910*. Bihar and Orissa, Calcutta: Superintendent Government Printing, 1912.

Roy, N. B. "New Aspects of the Santal Insurrection." *The Santals: Readings in Tribal Life*. Ed., J. Troisi. New Delhi: Indian Social Institute, 1979. Print.

Roy, S. C. *Mundas and Their Country*. Ranchi: Crown Publication, 1912.

CONFLICT BETWEEN RIGHTS AND OBLIGATIONS IN FOOD COMMODIFICATION: A GANDHIAN APPROACH

ALOKE PRABHU AND LISA THOMAS

The evolution of societies based on the market system has led to a "rights"-based approach. The matrix of property rights and its market-centric development has created much conflict and discontent. The idea of food as a commodity has permeated the society by creating an exclusivity granted by property rights. It has led not only to an economic crisis but has had an effect on the political, social, and constitutional fabric of the country. Critics of neo-liberalism view conflicts concerning property rights from the vantage point of history, economics, environmentalism, culture, and law, in order to evaluate the impact of the commodification of food. Gandhian philosophy, known for its ethical and moral preferences, gives a perspective that holds significance for a market economy. The essay, therefore, attempts to delineate the intricacies involved in understanding the rights and obligations of the state through development of property rights, and its role in ensuring food security by the creation of respect, protection, and the fulfilment of its people's right to food.

The idea of property, both public and private, which has been in existence for centuries, undergoes a paradigm shift as scientific development and capitalism overtake the course of modern society. Property though, is defined as a "right" or "a relation," which, in simple terms, is relatable to a tangible good that exemplifies value. In a market system, this value is represented in the form of "commodity." When we commodify services or goods, it creates value in terms of its marketability and exchange. The notion of property, therefore, encompasses the idea of "commodity."

Emergence of property rights created the possibility of private property eclipsing common property. It helped in idealising the acquisition and creation of wealth as a natural human tendency. For example, the interpretation of John Locke's theory of property helped justify English colonial activities in North America by undermining the Native Americans' claim to their land.[1] It led to the creation of private property in a society that never had a sense of ownership and possession about land, material things, or even the fruits of one's own labour. The sense of community ownership and sharing through cooperation was destroyed by the notion of private ownership. Later, in the wake of the Industrial Revolution, Locke's theory of property was used to induce a dramatic shift in the property rights paradigm in England. The theory was used in support of the efforts of industrial property owners who quoted Locke to protect their property rights. The argument was made to resist state regulation and redistribution at the hands of the majority. Twentieth century interpreters identify Locke as a defender of capitalist accumulation and the rights of property,[2] and his idea is taken as a classic doctrine of the "spirit of capitalism" in which limitless and selfish accumulation is considered both just and desirable.[3] The establishment of the private property regime not only legitimised colonisation, but also legally justified and cemented the acquisition of material things, their ownership, and possession. The tri-continent became a site of the European endeavour to control and acquire material things in the form of land, its resources, and people. With the independence of Latin American, African, and Asian countries in the twentieth century, the acquisitive tendency of the colonisers found recourse in neoliberalism.

Gandhi, who critiqued colonialism, saw the legitimacy of private property underplaying community rights as a process that cannot be controlled easily, as it had permeated the very fabric of society. Gandhi believed that unbridled capitalism and the desire to "acquire" private property rights were inherently harmful to humanity since they promoted materialism. It was evidenced by the impact of capitalism on one of the basic needs for survival—the food rights of people in colonies.

In India, the acquisitive tendency was facilitated by the liberal property regime enforced by the state, which justified private property rights and believed that it can lead to greater growth and development or simply the creation of wealth. It was a right-based property regime rather than an obligation-oriented one. The emergence of cash crops in India during the colonial period, along with the development of trade relations with the Portuguese and the British, was an effect of capitalism and the resultant industrialisation and mechanisation. The cultivation of cash crops like

---

[1] See Barbara Arneil's *John Locke and America* (1996).
[2] See Leo Strauss's *Strauss: Natural Rights and History.*
[3] See C. B. Macpherson's *The Political Theory of Possessive Individualism: Hobbes to Locke*, 194–262.

indigo,[4] opium, coffee, tea, rubber, and other non-native crops[5] flourished during the period, resulting in an industrial scale of mechanised processes to create value. For a poor farmer, unless the British bought these crops, they were of no value.[6] This situation made farmers dependent on the British for their livelihood and it created great famines. This, along with the contribution of high taxes, control over trade in food grains, and the export of such grains[7] had immense tragic consequences.

The seeds of material culture, which made food a marketable commodity, were sown in the colonial era and came to characterise modern society. In India, the idea that the material well-being of a society depended on the production and manufacture of goods that could be traded with the British as per their needs and requirements led to the commodification of means of subsistence, especially food. A space within India for the farming of opium and cash crops led to a divide between farmers' needs and the needs of the trading-cum-political class of the British in British India (Kumarappa 130). It strengthened the argument that the introduction of new materials and the commodification of goods and materials led to new avenues for wealth creation, which in turn, could bring economic transformation and offer benefits to producers, traders, and the ultimate consumers of goods.

Commodifying goods in a market economy helps convert a commodity into money, making it an instrument of exchange and means of storage of purchasing power. This leads to better bargaining power (Kumarappa 137–38). In this process, the pattern of food production and consumption changed for good and its commodification also led to fissures in society. This became a matter of concern later. In the postcolonial period, the agricultural sector has been characterised by the dissociation of capital from primary production and a concentration of capital in processing and distribution. It led not only to the unequal distribution of wealth and income, but also to industrialisation and the homogenisation of goods, bringing in items that had not been commoditised until then. Reflecting upon such a sentiment, Gandhi, in *Harijan*, says that the modern technology could lead us to believe and indulge in materialism to such an extent that "the prospect of one being able to produce all that we want, including our food stuff, out

---

[4] See Prakash Kumar's *Indigo Plantations and Science in Colonial India* (2012).
[5] See *A Year in the Death of Africa: Politics, Bureaucracy and the Famine* (1986) by Peter Gill; *An African Winter* (1986) by Preston King; and *Imperialism, Colonialism and Hunger: East and Central Africa* (1983) by Robert I. Rotberg.
[6] See D. A. Washbrook's "Law, State and Agrarian Society in Colonial India," published in *Modern Asian Studies* 15.3 (1981): 649–721.
[7] See Irfan Habib's "Colonialization of the Indian Economy."

of a conjurer's hat" (quoted in Dasgupta 40), seems a possibility, albeit a frightful one.

The adoption of a material culture and the trade relationship that the colonised countries had with the West led to multiple crises. The impact of such trade relationships on food and farming in India is clearly visible in events like the famine in the Deccan during 1702–4, the Great Bengal famine of 1769–73, and the Indian famine of 1896–97. The Great Bengal famine almost exterminated the civilisation of Bengal with its appalling magnitude, killing around ten million people.[8] One of the major causes was the increased tax (which was raised to three to four times the existing land tax), trade tariffs, and the prohibition of hoarding of rice, as grain trading had become a monopoly of the British.[9] Likewise, in Africa, the colonial heritage created conditions for famine and food insecurity. Famines like the Great Ethiopian Famine of 1888–92, the Rumanumra Famine of 1918–19, the Rwanda Famine of 1944, the famine in Tigray, Ethiopia, of 1958, and the Sahel Famine of the early 1970s resulted from the economic intervention of colonial powers in commodifying land and labour and the production of cash crops instead of indigenous food crops.[10]

The shift from a market system run by the local community to a self-regulating one also led to the mass commodification of food. The modern free market economy, a product of industrialisation, with roots in the colonial era, is a space devoid of ethical and moral considerations. One of the economists who brought in the element of ethics to regulate the market system was Karl Polyani. He saw the self-regulating market as a disembedded structure, separated from its social base, creating cultural alienation. The market did not serve the society; rather, the society was required to serve the purpose of the market—i.e., the creation of wealth. Polanyi analyses the destructive impact of the new economic system by focusing on the transformation of labour and land into market commodities. This was a major point of criticism Gandhi raised against the use of mechanised production in farming. Labour (human beings) and land (natural resources) were commoditised, although they were never a direct product of human industry. Polanyi distinguishes between markets and the market system, which is the integration of all markets into a single national or international economy. He vigorously criticises the self-regulating economy, which is quite unlike the previous economic system. The latter

[8] See John Fiske's *The Unseen World, and Other Essays.*
[9] See Kumkum Chatterjee's *Merchants, Politics and Society in Early Modern India; Bihar: 1733–1820*
[10] See Peter Gill's *A Year in the Death of Africa: Politics, Bureaucracy and the Famine.*

was part of society and functioned in close collaboration with the local community. The self-regulating economy utilised a binary approach unrestricted by society, and it operated simply according to its own law of supply and demand with no link to the local community and, therefore, did not serve the community in any way. As Kaushik Basu says in *Beyond the Invisible Hand: Groundwork for a New Economics* (2010), a proper understanding of economics requires an understanding of economic relations that are, in effect, a part of the larger sphere of social and cultural interactions and institutions (104).

Gandhi favoured the earlier phases of human development when economic activity exercised a social function and remained linked to the local community, ensuring its sustenance. Labour was embedded in social relations, and mercantile society as such did not seek to create a separate economic system, as it evolved as an inherent part of society. The use of machinery in agriculture and food production should not be a medium of subjugation, but that of empowerment.

As Kumarappa observes in *Economy of Permanence* (1984), the dislocation and marginal existence of third world populations is better understood through the lens of Gandhi's argument that importing Western-style economic development effectively "dis-embeds" people's economic activity from their social relations, tears away the population from the social matrix that assured their cultural identity, and in the long run, may destroy their human self-respect. The commodification of food and the processes of production and manufacture exemplifies the deep roots of materialism created by a capitalist society that shatters the social and cultural systems of ethnic populations.

Liberal philosophers and economists assert that humans have, by nature, been barterers and hagglers and that the local market is, therefore, the earliest institution; capitalism is the result of its evolution. Polanyi, in countering this argument, brings in a new perspective—he suggests that historical research uncovers two kinds of markets, the external market, which traded in goods brought from distant lands, and internal markets, which traded in goods produced by local communities. These two markets have had different origins and their functions were separate. The external market was non-competitive, as the goods were unique and not locally produced; it encouraged the use of money or precious metals as a measure of exchange value and was a phenomenon seen in port cities or trading points. On the contrary, the internal markets were competitive, local, and based on bartering and haggling, as the goods that were transferred were mostly of daily use and available from different sources. Gandhi says that this situation is indicative of independence and a non-violent form of production, as everyone supports each other in a community and mutual trade sustains them. Being cooperative, it creates trust and gives value to what the people in the community care for—a product or a relationship. This is what he calls a "service economy" (Kumarappa 7). As Basu argues, trust, altruism, and identity equally promote a culture of economic transaction that seems to challenge the notion that selfishness is natural (104). Economic transactions based on such innate human reasoning too create value for goods. Such value can be based on time, fame, or acquisitiveness, and cannot be classified under a marketable value, especially in the case of food.

When considering the ethics of commodification of food from an economic perspective, like Polanyi and Gandhi, Wilhelm Roepke, an economist who has largely criticised the Keynesian approach to economics, attempted to understand the social and human implications of economics. Roepke, in "The Economic Necessity of Freedom" (1959), asserts that an economist has her/his own "occupational disease"—that is, "restricted vision" (227). He notes that economists generally find it hard to look beyond their own discipline or even to concede that the economy is part of a larger order on which other disciplines have an equal influence (234). This provincialism was magnified by the order of economism, the habit of viewing everything in relation to the economy and in terms of material productivity, making material and economic interests the centre of all activities. The drawback of economic research is magnified when societal complexity and the influence of other factors on people's choices and policies are ignored by economists. Roepke says that economism has invariably led them into the trap called "social rationalism"—the tendency to regard market mechanisms as value-neutral methods applicable to any economic or social order. Kumarappa considers this a shortcoming that leads to a blind alley of violence and destruction from which there is no escape. Hence, Kumarappa argues that one's actions should be based on spiritual appraisal, which values objects in their true setting and perspective. This, in turn, would create an economy of permanence, leading humanity to happiness and peace through the medium of non-violence (Kumarappa 38–39).

While analysing the commodification of food from a legal perspective, the state's role in fulfilling the citizen's right to food and its obligation to ensure food security has given rise to much discontent. In India, even after the enactment of the Constitution, the state continued supporting social forces that carried colonial legacies/interests. Even in a predominantly agricultural society like India, government policies led to the Green Revolution, which was an attempt to mechanise food production. The Constitution, on the contrary, gave the right to food a negligible place in the form of Article 47,[11] which indirectly talks of the right to food as a duty of the state intended to raise the level of nutrition and the standard of living, to improve public health. This article came under the section on the Directive Principles of State Policy, which mandates only an obligation on the part of the state to strive to achieve the stated objectives, negating the right of an individual to a basic necessity—food. Although the Directive Principles belong to the class of positive rights—an affirmative—they also impose the negative duty of non-interference in access to food rights.

India is also a party to the International Covenant on Economic, Social, and Cultural Rights, the main international instrument protecting the right to food. Again, the right is clearly articulated in Article 25 of the Universal Declaration of Human Rights, and it remains closely linked to the fundamental rights of the right to live with dignity and the right to life. The right to food includes solid and liquid food, which means safe water as well. It clearly shows that the government is liable to fulfil a set of duties that, many times, has vanished into the realm of obligations without any legal remedy available for its enforcement.

The government plays a major role in eradicating poverty and hunger, ensuring that the people have access to food of adequate quality and quantity and preventing actions that violate their right to food. After Independence, it took the state around sixty-five years to create a National Food Security Act, which was passed in 2013. Nevertheless, India has a score of 27.5 in the Global Hunger Index[12] of 2021 and is placed between Lesotho and Papua New Guinea. India stands 101st out of 116 countries. Even seven decades after Independence, poverty still remains a significant challenge. This indicates that the question of food rights looms large, even after the adoption of elements of the market economy by third-world countries. The effects of globalisation cannot be said to have positively affected the majority of people living in rural areas. Critics have identified the idea of "development" supported by technology, procured from the Western imagination as one that is destructive. Food security and food rights have been major concerns of philosophers and activists who criticised technocratic dominance propagated by development. As Kumarappa explains, the plentiful capital in Britain ignited the Industrial Revolution in the UK, while scarce labour and abundant natural resources led to mechanised production

---

[11] Article 47 mandates that the state shall regard the raising of the level of nutrition and the standard of living of its people and the improvement of public health as among its primary duties and, in particular, the state shall endeavour to bring about prohibition of the consumption, except for medicinal purposes, of intoxicating drinks and of drugs which are injurious to health.

[12] "Global Hunger Index Scores by 2021 GHI Rank—Global Hunger Index (GHI)."

(126–27) in the USA. But implementing the same model in India would have grave consequences, since capital and resources are scarce, while labour is available in abundance. Hence, the efficient utilisation of available resources necessitates the creative use of manpower as a form of production in India.

Gandhi's vision, which proposed the subsistence economy as an alternate economic model, shows a shift of focus from elite and middle-class society to the marginalised tribals and other underprivileged subjects who bear the brunt of the dominant models of development. The colonisers' idea of "development" that still continues to colonise the postcolonial tricontinent, deprives indigenous people of their share in the development and growth of their countries. Gandhi, who stressed the need to relate development to nature, visualised India as a cluster of villages in co-operation with nature and not in conflict with it. Similarly, Vandana Shiva, who was influenced by Gandhian philosophy, emphasises the need to reaffirm indigenous philosophies. She makes an analogy between the development of a seed and the development of a community that carries the essence of decolonisation.

It is self-generated and self-organised, and in societies, development should occur in the same way in which a community decides what our next stage should be, thereby symbolising a constant evolution from within in a self-organised way on the basis of Swadeshi (Jahanbegloo 74).

In the case of a subsistence economy, the ecological devastation caused by the commodification of food cannot be ignored. Movements like the Green Revolution, which was a result of industrial methods in agriculture promoted with the aim of mass production, led to large-scale crisis. In India, there is immense diversity in the arena of agricultural production. The diversity has been maintained because the country has not adopted industrial methods on a large scale. Environmentalists claim that India has the largest population of farmers and that ours is an agricultural society, not by accident, but by policy. Gandhi called India, "the land of village republics."[13]

Farmers are the most affected group when one considers the issue of securing food rights and food production. India, which had succeeded in overcoming severe malnutrition and becoming self-sufficient and self-reliant in food production, now promotes packaged food, including drinking water, as "good" food. The production of packaged food as a commodity is the direct outcome of globalisation. Vandana Shiva draws attention to the commodification of food by focusing on the root causes of the destruction

---

[13]   See the interview with Vandana Shiva in *Talking Environment: Vandana Shiva in Conversation with Ramin Jahanbegloo.*

of ecologically balanced methods of food production. She raises the notion of "seed globalization" (Interview) to demonstrate how the global seed economy works. Globalisation has commodified seeds, increasing their value and cost tremendously; this has led to the neglect of farmers, thus forcing them to commit suicide or incur huge debts. This new economy of globalisation, which pushes indigenous communities to the margins, boosts the market economy. The seeds artificially produced by private groups, popularly called hybrid seeds, may not be productive or useful for the farmers. However, this does not affect the economy functioning under the grip of the private sector, which is supported by globalisation. This situation, which is an effect of neocolonialism, takes one back to the British era, when the economy was largely controlled by the colonisers. The transfer of resources from rural areas to multinational companies, and the forceful separation of farmers from their own lands and resources cannot be ignored. Such acts reveal that the binary approach to development adopted by colonisers exists even today. Earlier, this was executed by creating colonies; now it happens through globalisation and economic policies.

As environmental critics point out, the internalised effects of colonialism make one believe that locally grown food is unhygienic and less nutritious, and therefore inferior to "nutrient-filled"' packaged food. The colonial strategy of inculcating shame and disregard in the colonised subjects for their own possessions, in order to make them appreciate the foreign, is thus evident in food cultures as well. Food becomes yet another means for the colonisers to exercise their power over the once-colonised countries, invading their culture and, thus, their economies.

The state collaborates with imperial powers, becoming perpetrators of violence over its own people to gain economic benefits. In Indian states like Orissa and Jharkhand, large-scale mining projects have had a negative impact on the food rights of marginalised tribal people. They have been evicted forcefully in order to promote the interests of private companies. The state-propagated denial of the right to food of the poor is visible in the amendment made to the Land Acquisition Act, in the formulation of "anti-terrorist" laws to curb protests and in the excessive importance accorded to "developmental" projects like the construction of dams, that separate indigenous people from their land, violate their right to life and dignity, and deny them rehabilitation, eventually nullifying their right to food. The clear difference in the perception of the West and the indigenous cultures regarding human rights helps one understand the difficulty in devising an appropriate blueprint for development. While the Western domain dictates that "human rights" must be the primary concern, indigenous cultures believe that it should be "life rights," which accommodates the rights of all living creatures and the earth. Walter Mignolo highlights the indigenous philosophy that upholds the idea that the aim of a human being should not be to live better than her/his neighbours, but to live in harmony with nature. The idea of "land ethics" (24) advocated by Aldo Leopold becomes significant in comprehending the need to adopt an eco-centric view of all rights, including fundamental rights. For enhancing one's quality of life and aesthetic indulgences, the health of the entire biosphere becomes an inevitable concern. The need for maintaining biodiversity cannot be overlooked.

The food culture of India has undergone radical transformation, with the focus shifting from indigenous systems to urbanised ones as a result of globalisation. Gandhi highlighted the pitfalls of urbanised food systems when he predicted severe consequences, not just on the right to food, but on ecology, on the parity of development, and on the harmonious existence of communities. Food has been transformed into a market-based commodity under a constitution located at the crossroads of rights and obligations. As Kaushik Basu argues, it also shatters the idea of development—it is difficult to say that we have developed from what we were a hundred years ago, especially when we take indicators like access to health, education, right to food, and livelihood into consideration. The free market society and the state make possible the creation of institutions of exploitation functioning within the purview of the laws and norms of the twenty-first century. The human, ecological, and social costs reveal that the market-based economic system has become a means to recolonise the world without physical conquest, in continuation of colonial hegemonic practices.

Conclusion

Gandhi, who fought against colonial hegemony in Africa and India, argued that self-rule can only be effectively achieved through *Swaraj*[14]—that is, by ensuring political sovereignty and spiritual freedom. Gandhi's idea of *Swaraj*, which was articulated more than a hundred years ago, becomes relevant in any analysis of the arena of material culture. The objectification of food as a market-based commodity emerged from the liberal interpretation of property rights. It also led to a culture of acquisition, which was promoted by free market principles, broadening the scope of property rights over not only the limited domain of private property, but over the land and its resources, both tangible and intangible. Human beings perceived nature as property to be acquired and subjugated, thereby developing a conflictual

---

[14] See M. K. Gandhi's *Indian Home Rule* (1909).

relationship with it. The basic rights of human beings—shelter, access to clean water, basic education, or nutritional food—which ideally should be protected under the constitutional framework, were read as market-oriented commodities. These became mere obligations for the state and were cast into a positive rights framework. It led to the creation of policies that were destructive in nature, like the acquisition of forest land and the over-exploitation of minerals and resources on land and in the sea. Huge infrastructure development projects in the form of dams, factories, and nuclear plants were undertaken and completed rapidly. The weakest people on the street were left to fend for themselves, deepening the chasm between the haves and the have-nots. Agrarian reforms were not people-oriented but machine-driven, based on mass production at the cost of diversified farming, leading to excessive use of pesticides and genetic modification of crops. Food began to be produced on an industrial scale, leading to homogenisation, wiping out diversified varieties. Even traditional knowledge systems and ideas about farming and cultivation were lost and small farmers were left without support. Poor cultivators were pushed to the verge of suicide, resulting in large-scale social and economic problems. To a large extent, this situation arose due to the exploitative presence of middlemen between the cultivators and the consumers. Gandhi exhorted everyone to undertake physical labour in some form or other, as it not only instilled a respect for the land in people, but also brought them the pleasure of earning their bread by the sweat of their brow. This ideal stands in stark contrast to the current scenario that deems physical labour degrading. Large-scale industrial production of food and the emergence of manufacturing technology led to the state compromising on food security, nutrition, and sustainability. The modernisation and mechanisation of food production could not wipe out hunger and poverty; rather, it brought malnutrition, inflation, and diseases. As Gandhi points out, we should be more mindful of the need of the poorest and the weakest person when policies are formulated; only those policies that help the poor can be deemed successful. Ironically, the majority of food-deprived people live in the countryside, where the bulk of the world's food is produced: 75% of the people who suffer from hunger live in rural areas in developing countries (IFAD 2011).

References

Arneil, Barbara. *John Locke and America: The Defence of English Colonialism*. Oxford: Clarendon Press, 1996. Print.

Chatterjee, Kumkum. *Merchants, Politics and Society in Early Modern India: Bihar: 1733–1820*. Leiden: Brill, 1996. Print.

Dasgupta, Ajith K. *Gandhi's Economic Thought*. New York: Routledge, 1996. Print.

Fiske, John. *The Unseen World, and Other Essays*. Boston: James R Osgood and Co., 1876. Print.

Gandhi, M. K. *Indian Home Rule*. Natal: International Printing Press, 1909. Print.

Gill, Peter. *A Year in the Death of Africa: Politics, Bureaucracy and the Famine*. London: Paladin, 1986. Print.

"Global Hunger Index Scores by 2021 GHI Rank—Global Hunger Index (GHI)-Peer-Reviewed Annual Publication Designed to Comprehensively Measure and Track Hunger at the Global, Regional, and Country Levels." *Global Hunger Index (GHI)—Peer-Reviewed Annual Publication Designed to Comprehensively Measure and Track Hunger at the Global, Regional, and Country Levels*, https://www.globalhungerindex.org/ranking.html. Accessed 14 Dec. 2021.

Gupta, Akhil. *Postcolonial Developments: Agriculture in the Making of Modern India*. Durham, NC: Duke University Press, 1998. Print.

Habib, Irfan. "Colonization of the Indian Economy, 1757–1900." *Social Scientist* 3.8 (1975): 23–53. Print.

Jahanbegloo, Ramin. *Talking Environment: Vandana Shiva in Conversation with Ramin Jahanbegloo*. New Delhi: Oxford University Press, 2013. Print.

King, Preston. *An African Winter*. Harmondsworth: Penguin, 1986. Print.

Kumar, Prakash. *Indigo Plantations and Science in Colonial India*. New Delhi: Oxford University Press, 2012. Print.

Kumarppa. *Economy of Permanence*. Varanasi: Sarva Seva Sangh, 1948. Print.

Leopold, Aldo. *A Sand County Almanac: And Sketches Here and There*. Oxford: Oxford University Press, 1977. Print.

Macpherson, C. B. *The Political Theory of Possessive Individualism: Hobbes to Locke*. Oxford: Clarendon Press, 1961. Print.

Mignolo, Walter. "From 'Human Rights' to 'Life Rights.'" *The Meanings of Rights: The Philosophy and Social Theory of Human Rights*. Ed.

Conor Gearty Costas Douzinas. Cambridge: Cambridge University Press, 2014. 161–80. Print.

Rotberg, Robert I., ed. *Imperialism, Colonialism and Hunger: East and Central Africa*. Toronto: Lexington Books, 1983. Print.

Roepke, Wilhelm. "The Economic Necessity of Freedom." *Modern Age* 3 (Summer 1959): 227–36. Print.

Strauss, Leo. *Natural Right and History*. Chicago: Chicago University Press, 1965. Print.

Timberlake, Lloyd. *Africa in Crisis: The Causes, the Cures of Environmental Bankruptcy*. London: Earthscan, 1985. Print.

Washbrook, D A. "Law, State and Agrarian Society in Colonial India." *Modern Asian Studies* 15.3 (n.d.). Print.

"THEY TOO HAVE A STORY": TRACING THE BIOGRAPHIES OF THE LOOMS AT SURAIYA HASSAN BOSE'S WORKSHOP

SOMEDUTTA MALLIK

Introduction: Putting the Fragments Together

Suraiya Hassan Bose's (fondly called Suraiya apa) weaving centre is called the House of Kalamkari Durries. The formal post reaches it at 1-86 Hussain Shah Wali Darga, Hyderabad-500008. The house is well known in the circle of textile connoisseurs, collectors, and researchers for reviving traditional Persian textiles such as *paithani*,[1] *himroo*, *mashru*,[2] and *jamawar*.[3]

With a Persian grandmother and an Indian grandfather (Etawah, Uttar Pradesh), Suraiya Hassan Bose grew up in a highly nationalist environment with the family participating actively in the Indian nationalist movement. After Independence, the family joined the cottage industry scheme launched

---

[1] *Paithani* is a traditional textile made of silk and zari. It got its name from the small town of Paithan in Maharashtra. It was first patronised by the legendary Satavahana ruler Shalivahana (c.200 BCE). The Mughal emperor Aurangzeb had a love for *paithani* sarees. Later in the nineteenth and twentieth centuries, the Nizams of Hyderabad patronised *paithani*. See http://grandeurmaharashtra.com/paithani-saree/, accessed on 27 May 2017.

[2] Both *himroo* and *mashru* are traditional Persian textiles woven with silk and cotton thread. It is said that they travelled from Persia to Aurangabad when Muhammed BinTuglaq shifted his capital from Delhi to Aurangabad in the fourteenth century. *Himroo* is locally called "Kam Khwab," which means "little dream," and *mashru* means "legal." See http://www.discoveredindia.com/maharashtra/arts-and-crafts/mashroo-and-himroo.htm, accessed on 27 May, 2017.

[3] *Jamawar* is an old Persian textile that travelled to Kashmir around five centuries ago. *Jama* means "robe" or "shawl" and *war* means "yard." It means this fabric was used to weave yard-long shawls. But now it is used for making *sherwanis*, *kurtas*, *salwar kameez*, and other garments. It was patronised by the Mughal emperor Akbar and techniques were further developed by the weavers of Varanasi.
See http://blog.utsavfashion.com/fabrics/jamavar-fabric, accessed on 27 May 2017.

during the Nehruvian era, and her father, Syed Badrul Hassan, became one of the founder members of the Cottage Industries Emporium[4] in Hyderabad. His untimely death, when Suraiya apa was four or five years old, forced her mother to bring her up single-handedly. Being an only child, she had to forego her dream of pursuing a career in medicine and join the cottage industry that was taken over by the government of Andhra Pradesh after her father's death.

While working there, Suraiya apa met an English lady who visited her shop. She advised her to meet Pupul Jayakar,[5] who was working to revive textiles and re-energise weavers in post-Independence India. Exposure to the larger textile world and association with Pupul Jayakar provided her with the opportunity to be acquainted with weavers from all over the country, which later helped her launch her own workshop. After a year or two, there was an international show in the 1950s in which Suraiya apa participated. Designers like Pierre Cardin, Hanae Mori, and Roberto Capucci were among the notable names in the show. Suraiya apa designed a dress with short sleeves and a beautiful motif of Lord Krishna on the front; the piece was highly appreciated by others. This brought her orders from foreign connoisseurs and business people who were enchanted with the exquisite textiles of India. She still remembers that the first export was to New York in the 1980s. Though she was able to establish herself as a prominent artist in Delhi, her uncle wrote to her to come back home to Hyderabad. Safrani, who worked in the Ministry of Foreign Affairs, had resigned by then and bought a vast area of land in Hyderabad. He asked Suraiya apa to launch any business enterprise she wanted. So, she had to return to Hyderabad to start in agriculture afresh. But her love for textiles

---

[4] Cottage industries are small-scale business enterprises functioning from a home or nearby workplaces, with equipment owned by workers. The National Planning Committee has provided a definition of a cottage industry: "industries in which a worker works with his own tools in his own home and with the aid of his family or hired labour not exceeding five persons" (Chitra 37). See http://www.mgutheses.in/page/titles_view.php?q=T%202203&word=#95 accessed on 27 September 2017. http://www.cottageemporium.in/history.php, accessed on 27 September 2017.

[5] Pupul Jayakar (11 September 1915–29 March 1997) was a writer and a prominent figure in Indian cultural activities. She is well recognised for her role in the revival of traditional and village arts, handlooms, and handicrafts in post-Independence India. She was an advisor to the prime minister on art and cultural relations. She was chairperson of the Handicrafts and Handlooms Export Corporation of the Government of India and president for many years of the Krishnamurti Foundation. See https://www.geni.com/people/Pupul-Jayakar/6000000001920398277, accessed on 27 May 2017.

compelled her to begin a business to export clothes. At this time, she came in contact with John Bissel, the founder of Fabindia and she began exporting items to his company. But she had to do something more to give shape to her passion for textiles. So, she launched her dream project by establishing looms that could produce old Persian fabrics like *paithani*, *himroo*, *mashru*, and *jamawar*. But it was difficult to find skilled weavers in these traditions since most of them had migrated to Pakistan after Partition. Finally, she contacted Syed Omar, a traditional weaver whom she knew, and he began to train others. The weaving unit began functioning with the help of Syed Omar, fondly called Omar Sahab, Abdul Khadar, a weaver from Varanasi, and Azmal and Gafoor from Hyderabad. Soon, Suraiya apa decided to engage women from the local area in order to provide them with financial security. But none of them were from the weaving community, which made things more difficult. Syed Omar undertook the task of teaching the women how to weave intricate designs and use various techniques for producing remarkable pieces of work. The first group of ladies who worked here were Parveen, Kausar, Balamani, and Manju.

As part of the research for this essay, I utilised extensive fieldwork. I conducted interviews with people who were and are directly and indirectly associated with the weaving house. These were not formal conversations, but informal chats. I obtained an overview of the everyday activities in the weaving house through the weavers' narratives and also through close observation. Through the narratives, stories, memories, remarks, and complaints, I attempted to unearth the history of the objects in the house.

In order to develop the methodology of my research, I analysed two sets of literature. The first was *The Social Life of Things: Commodities in Cultural Perspective* (1988), edited by Arjun Appadurai, which I chose in order to understand the historiography of object studies. It helped me trace the entangled socio-cultural relationships built around an object and the politics that emerge from the relationship. Another piece of literature I analysed is a short story titled "Shilpi" (2016), written by Manik Bandyopadhyay in Bengali, which engages with how the body of the weaver, the fabric, and the loom bind each other.

The Loom: House of Weaving

In this section, I will scrutinise different types of crafts such as making looms, weaving fabrics, and making threads in spinning wheels in the weaving house of Suraiya apa. My endeavour is to study the objects in this house, which are socially, culturally, politically, and emotionally attached to the people residing there. I will trace the different trajectories of the objects through the memoirs of Suraiya apa, Omar sahab, and the weavers of the house—Nasreen, Hasmat, Shobha, Shesamma, Yasmin, Zarina, and Bipasha. I will look and think through craft.

"Here is the Dargah, madam!"

The words of the cab driver shook me out of my reverie and I found myself standing under a gateway on Shaikpet Road. It was a hot day in August 2016. I was going to meet Suraiya apa. The pink boundary wall with two entrances had the name of the house written on it: "House of Kalamkari Durries."

The weaving house is called "Loom." It has a single spacious rectangular hall, the size of which is approximately 1480 cm × 850 cm. It has four windows on the right wall and four windows on the left wall and one on the front wall. The inbuilt shelves appear on both sides. The roof of the house is built of asbestos. There are translucent parts in between the asbestos sheets so that light can come inside. When I entered the Loom, I found Omar Sahab engrossed in making the *jala*.[6] He knows whenever someone enters the house. He greeted me with a smile and a humble "*adab*."[7] He usually sits on the floor on a *durrie* next to a *mashru* loom, and makes *jala* in a wooden frame that is approximately 70 cm × 46 cm × 27 cm in size. A number of white threads are set up as warp on the frame, and they are tied horizontally to another set of threads to prepare the *jala*. The place where he sits provides him with a view of the entire house.

Omar Sahab's place opens into a narrow passage with a row of pillars in the middle. The looms are set up on both sides of this narrow way, making it congested; the arrangement hardly leaves any space for more than one or two people to move together. Thus, the looms, the pillars, the seats, and the other objects create a zigzag path where we move between looms, pillars, shelves, and seats; this prevents crowding. Ten looms are installed in the room and one at the front end of the hall. The looms make two rows with the pillars in the middle and they face each other. They also make aisles on the sides of the windows and shelves. The weavers also sit facing each other like the looms. The pile of threads, an aluminium kettle for making tea, a lunch box, and an earthen pitcher always stand within reach of the weavers. The row just next to the entrance has five looms. In another row there are five looms. And one stands near the front wall.

There are four types of seating arrangements in the Loom: (i) Omar Sahab sits on the floor, (ii) the person who handles the *jala* sits at the table,

---

[6] *Jala* is the graph of the designs in *himroo* weaving.
[7] *Adab* is an Urdu word referring to a hand gesture used mainly by South Asian Muslims when they greet someone.

(iii) the weaver sits on a plank of wood placed at the mouth of the pit, and (iv) Suaiya apa and the visitors have chairs and stools.

The walls are covered with objects—calendars, group photographs, certificates, paper-cuttings, and stickers. On the front wall, just next to the window, a recent Telugu calendar has been hung. The rest of the objects are placed on the five pillars in the middle. A laminated newspaper cutout has been hung on the first pillar. It faces the *mashru* looms on the left row. It contains an article about Suriya apa and the weavers in the Loom. The news article, titled "Weave Me a Warm Magic," has a picture of Suriya apa and Rokeya, one of the weavers who later left the workshop. The report was published on 3 October 2005 in the magazine *Outlook*. It speaks about Suraiya apa's journey as a revivalist of traditional textiles and her dream to have a loom in every house. There are four pictures that are displayed on the next pillar. A framed certificate and photograph are placed on the side of the pillar that faces the entrance and two group photographs face the left side and the rear wall. The framed certificate is that of the fourteenth Godfrey Philips Bravery Award[8] presented to Smt. Suraiya Hassan Bose. An image of Suraiya apa is displayed under the certificate. The group photo on the left wall of the pillar facing the retired *mashru* looms shows Suraiya apa and Omar sahab with sixteen weavers. The weavers are, from right to left, Naziya, Narsamma, Sobha, Ruksana, Sajida, Hasmat, Zulekha, Shabana, Parveen, Zakira, Nasreen, Rokeya, Farzana, Parveen, Malan, and Fouziya. Among them, only three are still working—Sobha, Nasreen, and Hasmat. The rest of them have left the workshop for various reasons. The photograph was taken on 8 December 2005 by Kundalu, the cashier in the office. Another photograph hanging on the back of the pillar shows only the sixteen weavers. This photograph was also taken on the same day. Both the photographs are covered with plastic sheets, using the price tags as sticking tape. The next pillar shows a photocopy of the same news article, "Weave Me a Warm Magic." The paper is pasted with Sellotape. Another pillar has a recent Arabic calendar on the front. An Islamic religious picture hangs on the front of the last pillar. It is rendered in three colours: blue, white, and black. The picture depicts a set of two minarets flanking an Islamic dome and the image of the Great Mosque of Mecca. Over these lies a halo—a white half-circle. A book, probably the Quran, is kept in the front. The book is flanked by two stands of *agarbatti* on either side.

---

[8] The Godfrey Phillips National Bravery Awards was instituted in 1990. The award is given to common citizens for their selfless acts of physical bravery and social acts of courage that can inspire others. This award is presented annually. See http://www.godfreyphillips.com/bravery-awards, accessed on 25 April 2017.

The Looms

Two Retied *Mashru* looms

The two retired looms sit next to Omar sahab. On entering the room, the first loom we encounter is a *mashru* loom. The *mashru* loom is a frame loom. It has a wooden frame that has to have a minimum size of eighteen to twenty inches. *Mashru* is a mixed fabric made of silk and cotton. Silk threads are used in the warp, while cotton threads are used for the weft. Thus, the cloth produced has a silk design on the outer surface and cotton inside. Cotton can easily absorb sweat. The *mashru* loom is complex in design since it has eight *rach* and eight *dam*. Omar sahab sits just next to the *mashru* loom. It stands first in the left row; however, it is not in use now. It was installed some ten to twelve years back after Suraiya apa and Omar sahab travelled to Ahmedabad in Gujarat and decided to set up the *mashru* looms. But since *mashru* weaving is a very complex process, only Omar sahab and Shesamma, one of the weavers, could do it. Because of this difficulty and Omar sahab's bad health, *mashru* weaving was abandoned around five years back. Typical small *butiya* (dots) that appear on *mashru* were woven in this loom. The thread they used was *gas-silk*, dyed by Md. Sukur of Goshamahal, Hyderabad. Md. Sukur was a *rangrez* (dyer) from Jaipur, Rajasthan. This particular loom is 230 cm × 233 cm × 197 cm. It has eight *dam*[9] and eight *rach*[10] and a *hatta*.[11] A wooden plank, which is 67 cm above the floor and 285 cm × 31 cm × 4 cm in size, is placed as the seat of the weaver. The red warps are still in the loom. A piece of kalamkari covers the warp.

Another *mashru* room is placed next to it. It is smaller than the first one. It is also a frame loom with a size of 238 cm × 201 cm × 178 cm. It was made along with the first loom. A carpenter called Ramu had built both of them and Shesamma used to work on this loom. Both the *mashru* looms were closed at the same time and for the same reason. The loom consists of eight *rach* and eight *dam* and a *hatta*. The weaver's seat is 201 cm × 33 cm × 3 cm in size. There are two stickers pasted on the frame. One of them bears the words "No god but God" with an image of Mecca.

---

[9] *Dam*, "peddle."
[10] *Rach*, "harness."
[11] *Hatta*, "reed."

Two Retired *Himroo* Looms

The *himroo* loom is essentially a pit loom which consists of four *rach*, one *fruit-ka-rach*, four *dam, naka, paga*, and a *hatta*. A *himroo* loom stands next to the two *mashru* looms. Though *himroo* is still being woven in the weaving house, this loom sits idly, because most of the weavers have left. A similar fate has befallen the next one. The first *himroo* loom was made some fifteen years back. It was last used around five or six years ago. The loom is 264 cm × 275 cm × 201 cm in dimension. The pit of the loom is 115 cm × 87 cm × 56 cm in size. All the pits in this room are about the same size. The weavers who used to weave in this loom have left their marks on three. They are pasted on the *hatta*. One of them stands in the middle with an image of a mosque. The other two flanking it have Arabic calligraphy, including the inscription "Allah" in Arabic. Perhaps the weaver who worked on this loom wrote it with a pencil. Another one, located next to it, is approximately 264 cm × 272 cm × 201 cm in size. Five *charkha* (spinning wheels) are placed in   between the frame of the loom. The weavers sit there and use the spinning wheels to sort out the thread (*taga kholna*).

Durrie-ka-loom

Next to the two *himroo* looms, the last one in the row is the *durrie* loom, which is 104 cm × 278 cm × 122 cm in size. *Durrie* loom is usually a pit loom. The loom has two *rach* and two *dam* like a *paithani* loom. No jala is needed to weave the *durries*. It was installed some six years back to produce *durries*. *Durrie* is a heavy cotton carpet weaved in the Indian subcontinent. This loom was bought from Warangal and installed here. It was set up to see whether the weavers could master the skill of weaving durries. But only Shesamma, one of the experienced weavers, used to work on this loom. She is the only one among the group who knows how to weave a *durrie*. She produced a few *durries* that are still in use in the house. After working for a year, she had to leave this loom because there was a huge demand for *himroo* and fewer *himroo* weavers were in the house. Thus, the loom remains idle now.

Nasreen-ka-loom

The five looms make another row that forms the right side of the entrance. The first loom that is opposite to Umar Shab's seat and the *mashru* loom is the *himroo* loom. It is called *Nasreen-ka-loom*. Nasreen Begum had been working on it for twenty-two to twenty-five years, though others have also used it. That is why it is fondly called "Nasreen-ka-loom." It is the largest loom with a size of 269 cm × 289 cm × 212 cm. It is a pit loom and was initially a *paithani* loom. It is one of the oldest looms in the house, and was built around 1985–86. In 2001, it was mended into a *himroo* loom by adding two more *rach*s and *dam*s.

It was 27 December 2016 when I went to the Loom house in the afternoon, after the lunch hour. I saw that Nasreen and Shobha were working on the Nasreen-ka-loom. While Shobha was sitting on the table and lifting the *jala* for Nasreen, the latter was sitting on the loom seat and weaving a piece of *himroo*. A box next to her contained small rolls of threads. The Nasreen-ka-loom was designed by Omar sahab, who learned to design and make looms while working in the Furnishing Society in Darulshifa, Kalikhabar, in Hyderabad. The Nasreen-ka-loom was made for him by Carpenter Ramu.

Darga Ramesh, commonly known as Ramu, continues the legacy of his grandfather's (and later, his father's) carpentry business. He had begun working when he was fifteen. His father, Darga Satyanarayan, was in the business of making doors, windows, and furniture. Satyanarayan's association with Suraiya apa began thirty years back when she was involved in agriculture. He had made ploughs for her farm. When she launched the weaving unit, Satyanarayan was given charge of making looms. He had not studied a loom in detail before; nor did he have any drawings of it. Hence, he had to meticulously follow the instructions of Abdul Khader, the master weaver from Benares. It was a *mushroo* loom that he built. After that, when Ramu joined his father, he got an order for four *himroo* looms from Suraita apa. The wood and other materials were provided by the weaving centre. Omar sahab gave instructions regarding the design and measurements. He also decided which wood would be used for various parts of the loom. *Tik*, *babul*, and *neem* wood were used. Teak wood was used for making the frame, *bhim*,[12] and *amboda*.[13] *Neem* and *babul* wood were used for making the more fragile parts like the *hatta*, *rach*, and *dam*, since they were less expensive and hence the production cost could be reduced. Ramu charged between Rs 2000 and 3000 as the labour cost for each loom. This was around 1995. Three men worked for seven to ten days to finish the job. He made ten looms for Suraiya apa. The last loom he made for the weaving unit was in 2008. Ramu runs his workshop, Shri D. Ramesh Wood Works, from the ground floor of his house, with four men working there. Though the looms have never broken down, small scale repairs are often made since the

---

[12] *Bhim* is the horizontal post that lies between two sides of the frame on which the woven cloth is rolled up.

[13] *Amboda* is the instrument used to lift the *jala*.

threads and the strings that are attached to *naka, paga*,[14] and *dam* can be torn if the loom is used roughly or hastily.

Nasreen joined the workshop twenty-two years back. She learnt weaving from Umar Shab. After Nasreen's husband passed away, she was compelled to join a job to run the family. She began her career by lifting the *jala*, which is done when the *katla*[15] is in between the threads of the warp. As she learned weaving, she moved to the seat of the weaver on the loom. Nasreen informs us that the process of throwing the *katla* appears very easy. She realised how difficult it is when she was learning the role. Initially, when she could not move the *katla* evenly, the thread of the warp would be torn and the fabric would be damaged. Omar sahab would scold her for this and he would rectify the error with his mastery of the art. Thus, the woven fabric would appear flawless and she would learn how to correct the mistake. Now she knows how to make a *jala* and how to set up the warp in the loom. When she first began weaving, the continuous beating of the reed used to cause pain in her shoulder and pressing the *dam* used to cause leg cramps. Slowly all such pain vanished and Nasreen's body gradually picked up the rhythm of the movement of the *katla*, the reeds, and the thread of the weft.

Nasreen's first woven fabric was *paithani*. Along with her, Parveen, Zakira, Malan, and Parvati worked on this loom. All of them were trained by Nasreen, but none of them work in the unit anymore. This loom was in the old workshop. Nasreen also worked there. In 2001, the loom was shifted to the Loom House. Nasreen and Parveen used to weave *paithani sarees* in it when it was a *paithani* loom. The borders of the sarees were three metres long and the *pallu* was woven afterwards. Two weavers used to work on two sides of the saree to render the border designs. But when Suraiya apa decided to turn the *paithani* loom into a *himroo* loom, many changes were brought in. For instance, earlier it had two *dam,* two *rach*, and eighty counts of *phanni*. But now, two more *dam* and *rach* and sixty counts of *phanni* have been added.

As Nasreen has worked with this loom for several years she has a personal attachment to it. She has pasted a newspaper cut-out of a zebra on it. I also found newspaper cut-outs of film stars. Yasmin has pasted photographs of people who used to work on this loom two or three months previously. Nasreen is a fan of old Bollywood songs. She plays Hindi songs on her phone while weaving. Other weavers enjoy that too.

---

[14] *Naka* and *paga* are two sets of horizontal (*paga*) and vertical (*naka*) strings. These strings are lifted in order to lift the warp to pass the shuttle in between the threads.
[15] *Katla*, "shuttle."

Retired *Himroo* Looms

There is another *himroo* loom with a size of 269 cm × 267 cm × 200 cm sitting idle next to Nasreen's loom. It had been a *jamawar* loom. A typical *jamawar* loom has eight *rach* and eight *dam* like a *mashru* loom, while a *himroo* loom has four *rach*s and four *dam*s. It was built in the 1990s and was turned into a *himroo* loom fifteen years previously. Only Omar sahab and Nasreen Begum can weave *jamawar* in the weaving house. Nasreen worked on this loom for one or two years. But there was hardly any order for *jamawar*. Thus, Suraiya apa decided to close the loom. It is a pit loom with a wooden plank with a size of 180 cm × 21 cm × 3 cm functioning as the weaver's seat. *Jamawar*, too, needs *jala* for the design. Another *himroo* loom, which is 269 cm × 275 cm × 200 cm in size, also stands idle in the workshop. It was set up around fifteen years ago.

Hasmat-ka-loom

The next loom in this row is a *himroo* loom. It was built around thirty years ago when Satyanarayan, Ramu's father used to work here. This pit loom was also designed by Omar sahab. The most striking thing is that Satyanarayan made the loom based only on the instructions given by Omar sahab. He had never seen a loom before. Teak, *neem*, and *babul* woods were used to build it. The frame is made of teak and other parts such as the *hatta* and *rach* are made of cheaper woods like *neem* and *babul*.

Thirty years ago, when the loom was installed at the earlier weaving unit, it was intended for weaving *paithani* fabrics. Abdul Khadar was a weaver from Varanasi. He used to sell *saree*s in Hyderabad when Omar sahab worked at the Furnishing Society in Kali Khabar. Omar sahab and Khadar sahab met at the Furnishing Society. Thus, when Omar sahab joined Suraiya apa in 1985 in her old workshop, he invited Khadar sahab. Khadar sahab was the first person to work on this loom. He used to weave *paithani sarees*. After he passed away, this loom became the favourite of Hasmat Begum. Now it is called "*Hasmat-ka-loom*" (Hasmat's loom). Hasmat has been working on this loom for the last twenty-five years. Hasmat initially had no experience weaving and it took Omar sahab six to eight years to teach her the interrelations between warp, weft, and the count of threads.

Hasmat joined the weaving centre to support the family after her husband became unable to work. At first, she learned to handle the *jala* with *amboda*. While sitting at the table and handling the *jala*, she used to observe the hand movements of the weaver when she moved the *katla* and interlocked the threads in the fabric. The first time she was at the loom in the workshop, she got nervous seeing the number of strings of *naka* and *paga*. It was very complex for her. Initially, Hasmat used to pull the thread too tightly while throwing the *katla* before beating the reed. Gradually, she realised that it makes the thread in the cloth dense and the cloth consumes more threads. Omar sahab or Suraiya apa would point out such errors. Now she can identify mistakes and correct them. While speaking to someone, she sometimes keeps her elbows on the woven cloth and inattentively puts pressure on it, which tears the threads of the unfinished woven fabric. If the cloth is torn at the beginning, then she has to start again. But if it is torn in between, the full fabric is sold. Even a small piece of *himroo* textile is sold at the workshop.

Hasmat told me that she prefers to work in the workshop because it is near her house and most of the workers are women. It gives her a sense of security and comfort. Once she enters the Loom House, she removes her *burqa*. She dons it again before going home. The workshop is almost a domestic space for her, with Omar sahab being a father figure. Though she is not happy with the wages, she is unwilling to leave this job since Omar sahab says that weaving earns them respect. When someone asks what job she does at Suraiya apa's place she replies with pride that she is a weaver. But she hardly has any knowledge of the history of the textiles woven in the workshop. She is more concerned about the quantity produced.

Sometimes Shesamma also works in this loom. Shesamma has pasted a sticker of Lord Shiva, Goddess Parvati, and Lord Ganesha together on the left side, and stickers of the Goddesses Laxmi and Balaji on the right side of the *hatta*. She offers her prayer to the deities whenever she sits at the loom. Hasmat makes scratches on it to remove the image. She says: "hamare isme aysa nehi hota. Photo nehi lagate" ("In our religion, photos are not used"). When I asked about the scratches on the picture, she was apologetic in her tone as if she were compelled to do it.

The Functional *Himroo* Loom

The last loom in this row is also a himroo loom with a size of 269 cm × 276 cm × 200 cm. Earlier, Bipasha used to work on this pit loom. After she left the job, Shesamma took up the job. She sits on a wooden plank that is 180 cm × 22 cm × 3 cm in size. She has pasted a sticker of Lord Ganesha on the *hatta*.

The Isolated *Paithani* Loom

At the front, next to Omar sahab's place, there is a small *paithani* loom. It is a frame loom with two *rach* and two *dam*. It is 138 cm × 104 cm in size and is meant for weaving *paithani* borders. Sometimes Shobha works on this loom. The weaver's seat is 104 cm × 24 cm × 2cm in size.

Walking around the looms in the Loom House, I saw the stories behind their origin and use, as well as their current state, unfolding before my eyes. I got to know who made each loom, who worked them, why some looms are now resting while some are still hard at work. The spatial relationships between the looms as objects and as houses was revealed in all their nuances through the stories they narrated.

Concluding Thoughts

My interest in objects and their biographies emerged from readings of texts by Arjun Appadurai, Igor Kopytoff, and Manik Bandyopadhyay, among others. Consequently, it helped me develop a methodology for my research. For the last eleven to twelve months, I have been visiting Suraiya apa's weaving unit regularly and talking to Suraiya apa, Dominic Hassan, Zeenath, Omar sahab, and the weavers. Those informal chats and interviews offered me narratives centred on each loom, its journey from the carpenter's house to the Loom House, and its relationship with the carpenter, the weavers, Omar sahab, and Suraya apa, who regularly interact with it. I got to know about the looms from the anecdotes, complaints, and memories of the people I met there and those who had already left their jobs in the workshop.

Each worker shares a distinct relationship with each of the looms. For Suraiya apa, the workshop is not only her workplace, but a place of devotion. Though she never weaves, she can easily locate flaws in the weaving. This expertise is the result of long years of experience. At the age of 87, she still visits the workshop every half an hour and gives instructions to the weavers. It shows her passion both for the looms and for the fabrics. Omar sahab, like Suraiya apa, is so passionate about textiles that even after undergoing major heart surgery, he travels everyday for one and half hour to reach the weaving house. He finds it difficult to spend time at home on Sundays, and spends the entire day making the *jala*. Occasionally, he chats with Suraiya apa or the visitors. His conversations with Suraiya apa centre mostly on their old experiences and memories. He becomes nostalgic whenever he talks about his journey and experience. Omar sahab keeps on narrating the stories of his life like an old storyteller. But the sad part is that the people around him are hardly interested in listening to him. The weavers are concerned only with the act of weaving and the quantity of fabric they are able to produce each day, rather than the historical and aesthetic aspects of traditional techniques of weaving. Weaving flawlessly and uninterruptedly gives them greater satisfaction. Though there are grievances regarding the wages, there is certainly a sense of pride and adoration for this profession that stops them from leaving the weaving house. Dominic Hassan stands apart from others in that he is genuinely concerned about the Loom House, the production and the business as a whole. Weaving as a craft attracts him as a means of production and a source of money; however, the aesthetic aspects and techniques are also of immense interest to him.

After conducting fieldwork for almost a year, I have been able to collect a handful of disjointed stories. The lack of fluidity in the narrative disturbs me; yet it is this very factor that encourages me to return to the Loom House. As I have already mentioned, the year-long fieldwork was an attempt to hear the voices of the looms and other objects in the Loom House. It was a struggle to hear the tales of the objects as well as the people there. However, there are many more stories that remain unheard. I have to return to hear those tales, as objects constantly whisper to me: "We too have stories."

References

Appadurai, Arjun, ed. *The Social Life of Things: Commodities in the Cultural Perspective.* New York: Cambridge University Press, 1988. Print.

Bandyopadhyay, Manik. *Manik Bandyopadhyay Rachanasamagra 5.* Kolkata: Paschimbanga Bangla Akademi, 2016. Print.

THE MAKING OF A "TRANSGRESSIVE" SUBSTANCE: THE CASE OF CANNABIS IN HIMACHAL PRADESH

PRASANJEET TRIBHUVAN

This essay examines how material objects gain influence in society so as to metamorphose into what Taussig calls "transgressive" substances (xiii). I study the influence of cannabis in the Kullu district of Himachal Pradesh and its ability to affect individual lives and engender rapid social change in the region. My focus here is two-fold: one, to examine how cannabis in the form of locally produced hashish (popularly known as *charas*) attains influence in the region to become transgressive; and, two, to study how local society engages with cannabis and to attempt to interpret the effects of this engagement.

Cannabis is indigenous to large parts of the lower to mid-altitude (up to 3500 m) Indian Himalayas. It has been traditionally cultivated for various purposes. In the Kullu district of Himachal Pradesh, cannabis and its products have been used in food, clothing, and medicines, and for pleasure (owing to its intoxicating properties). The branches of the plant have been used for a long time to produce hemp, which is used as a fabric in coats to keep warm during harsh winters. This hemp is also used to make slippers due its durability and ability to weather harsh physical and climactic conditions. Parts of the plant have been used regularly in local food preparations. Cannabis seeds are used to make spicy chutney to be eaten with local bread made of fermented rice called *sidhu*, especially in winter, to keep warm. Sharma has documented several medicinal uses of the plant in the villages of Himachal Pradesh. Oil from cannabis flowers has been used to ease muscle pain, especially in the case of menstrual cramps. Buds from the plant are boiled in milk and used as cure for impotence. Cannabis leaves are used as a de-wormer and diuretic to cure stomach problems and diarrhoea. There are recorded instances where cannabis was used to wean people from alcohol since the latter was considered to be more harmful than cannabis. In addition to this, *charas* produced from cannabis flowers has always been valued in Himachal Pradesh for its psychotropic properties. It is traditionally consumed in social gatherings, smoked in hookahs or *chillums*, along with cups of tea and snacks. Charas also assumes a sacred character as the favourite intoxicant of Shiva, a significant Hindu deity. Historically, the use of cannabis and its products was normalised in the villages of Himachal Pradesh to such an extent that its presence and influence in the domestic and social spheres almost went unnoticed. In Miller's terms, cannabis has been a "humble" (18) object in the hill societies of Himachal Pradesh, of great utility, but subsumed under a web of social relations in such a manner that its influence was only limited to its utility and ubiquity.

In the last couple of decades, especially in the post mid-nineties, cannabis lost its "humility" in most parts of Himachal Pradesh, including in the Kullu district. While its utility has increased for individuals and families, so has its ability to cause great distress, disturbance, and agitation in society. Cannabis is no longer subsumed within local social structures and relationships. It has become a social "actant" (Latour 21), possessed of an almost human-like ability to influence society and steer individual life trajectories. While doing so, cannabis joins the ranks of the other "powerful" or "transgressive" objects described ahead.

How do Material Objects become Transgressive?

Transgressive substances are powerful materials and objects that display an almost human ability in influencing society and shaping individual life trajectories. These objects cause disturbance and turbulence in the social orders they affect. The term "transgressive" possibly comes from Foucault's notion of "transgression." For Foucault, the act of transgression not only breaches boundaries but continuously creates new ones, since the existence of transgression is impossible without the existence of limits. Transgressions and boundaries constitute an inseparable binary. Hence, when transgression occurs, new territory is added in terms of practices, ideas, values, and geography, thereby reconstituting the social. This process engenders transformation in all aspects of social life. This is exactly what transgressive substances do—possessed of a transformative power, they affect every aspect of social life. How do some material objects gain such a degree of influence in society?

Objects that constitute material culture possess the potential to affect societies in myriad ways and their power to influence human life increases under some conditions. For Taussig, fetishisation is the most significant process contributing to the ability of material objects to influence society (14). Fetishes are those properties of material objects that are of social rather than natural origin. However, in some cases, these social "properties" become attached so deeply to an object that they become an integral part of it, and it becomes extremely difficult to differentiate them from the natural properties of the object. Over years, the social properties of objects become their second nature, and socialised human beings fail to see the difference between the object's natural properties and those attached to it socially. In a way then, fetish is "the most aggressive expression of the social life of things" (Pels 91). Fetish bestows on material objects an inimitable ability to act like human beings by presenting inanimate objects with an aura of agency. In its commercial, religious, and academic usage, "fetish" signifies something that is manufactured, as opposed to something that is naturally found.

Hornborg argues that although the phenomenon of the fixation of the label "fetish" to objects has been present since ancient times, conditions of modernity provided a fertile ground for its widespread prevalence. Institutions and processes like colonisation and globalisation, spawned by modernity, successfully freed objects from their social contexts and physical and moral worlds, so that they were available for maximum utilisation and exploitation. Objects that were bereft of their social contexts were ready to be used and exploited by modern society. Social relations that performed the function integrating objects into social worlds were gradually replaced by fetish relations that strove to exploit objects to their maximum potential. The result of this process of objectification of social relations was that objects appeared powerful enough to control human life; and in the most practical terms, they did. Commodity fetishism, where material objects control human life owing to their economic significance, describes arguably the most crucial aspect of social life after modernity.

Another significant relationship is the relationship between fetish and desire that forms an intrinsic part of human–object relationships today. The desire that attracts human beings to objects is also constitutive of a fetish relationship. Such an economy of desire, Dant points out, is important in finding the reason behind social values of certain objects and why humans have an intrinsic desire to relate to such objects (by consuming them). He shows how social value can be mediated through material culture. In such cases, fetishism causes certain objects to be over-determined at the level of their social value (16–18). The processes of fetishisation, both as functions of reified social relations that impart human qualities to objects and those of over-determination that make them desirable within the social milieu, impart power to material objects to influence social relations.

The process of fetishisation with regard to objects has been closely linked to the *circulation* of those objects within and outside different political and cultural regimes. Pels writes that the processes of fetishisation and circulation implicate each other since they are mutually dependent. The circulation of objects in different cultural and political regimes confers them with meanings and they transition in and out of those meanings. Circulation affects the cultural, brand or commodity status of the object as its meanings change because of differences in the spatial and temporal contexts of such circulation. Objects can be commodities, brands, or gifts at different points in their biography and can simultaneously be a few other things. Circulation of objects and their continuous transition from one phase to another has significant influence on individuals and on the societies in which they circulate. Hence, the circulation of objects, acting complementary to processes of fetishisation, contributes significantly to the power of material objects.

Processes of fetishisation and circulation constitute fragments of human history that animate material objects and empowers them to influence society. In most cases, these processes are tied together and work in different combinations that overlap each other as they continuously redefine different aspects of material objects, and in the process, empower them. However, in some instances, the material aspects of objects—their physical properties and their chemical make-up—are often downplayed in favour of their socio-cultural contents. Study of the materiality of objects, which, in the most part, addresses their physical existence and their bio-chemical make-up, has gathered great emphasis in the arena of material studies in recent times. This emphasis mostly stems from the belief that material studies have traditionally explored objects as containers of metaphors, signifiers, and similar languages. Materials however are different from language because they exist irrespective of their interpretation by society. Material objects have the ability to affect us because of what they are, and not just because of what we make of them. Materiality, on its own, or in most cases, in conjunction with the socio-cultural processes described above, plays an important role in making specific material objects influential in a society.

Finally, historical socio-economic, cultural, and political conditions predispose certain regions or countries to stronger influence by material objects than other locales. It is not mere coincidence that most studies of powerful material objects affecting particular regions are based in formerly colonised countries. Taussig's work on cocaine in Colombia, Mintz's work on sugar in Jamaica, and West's work on coffee in Papua New Guinea illustrate how global power relations shaped by colonisation played a major role in empowering these objects in the respective regions. Regional ecology also plays an important part since materiality is closely connected with ecology, especially in the case of naturally occurring materials or those objects that are synthesised from such materials. For example, sugarcane thrives mainly in tropical climates and, hence, it has been particularly influential in tropical areas such as Jamaica and other Caribbean island nations.

Thus, materiality, regional peculiarities and historical and continuing fetishisation and circulation work concurrently, and in different capacities, to make specific objects powerful in a region, country, or society. Let us now examine the particular case of cannabis in the Himalayan state of Himachal Pradesh in India.

From Humility to Illegality

Global circulation of cannabis ensured a number of socio-cultural meanings and values being attached to it. Cannabis use was documented in Europe and other Western countries much later than in India or other countries in South Asia. Official accounts of the appearance of cannabis in Europe dates back to the thirteenth century, when slaves from East African countries were transferred to work in emerging European colonies, or to Europe for manual work (Booth 19). Although the plant was not native to Europe and was brought to the continent by slaves from Africa, it had become quite popular and was mainly used for its hemp. Cannabis was widely cultivated in Spain, England, France, and other European countries, although not for its psychoactive properties. In Europe, the cannabis plant was simply known as "hemp." It was rarely used as an intoxicant and Europeans were largely unfamiliar with the intoxicating properties of the leaves and flowers of the plant. It was cultivated mainly for its fibre, which was used for manufacturing ropes, paper, and cloth. From around the thirteenth century through the seventeenth century, the hemp of the cannabis plant was used on a large scale to make fibres for various purposes throughout Europe. When the new continent of America was discovered, the European countries, which almost instantly rushed there to establish their colonies, saw huge amounts of land and, hence, huge potential to grow hemp.

Not long after the doors of the global East were opened to Europe because of advances in shipping technologies, eager White travellers began journeying to the "magical" world of what was then called the East Indies and brought back stories from these new coasts. They wrote treatises on their life in these "exotic" lands, describing ways in which Indians and Chinese used cannabis and its various products in their medicines, as a source of intoxication and enjoyment, and during religious ceremonies and rituals. For these young men, this new use for the already familiar hemp was a novelty and a source of great curiosity (Courtwright 23). It was, however the doctors who first wrote about the use of cannabis on a large scale in India to cure a large number of ailments. For example, books like Da Orta's *Colloquies on the Simples and the Drugs of India*, first published in the year 1563, not only enlisted the medicinal uses of cannabis, but also—in great detail and sometimes with greater embellishments—discussed the psychoactive properties and use of cannabis in India. Both real and exaggerated accounts of cannabis consumption and its perceived effects were regularly recorded in such accounts. However, many of these authors and travellers confused the effects of cannabis with those of opium. This was because opium and cannabis looked similar to their unfamiliar eyes. The folly of confusing opium with cannabis continued for a very long time in Western literature, and has been of some disservice to the understanding of cannabis and its effects.

Another breakthrough was *Confessions of an English Opium-Eater* by Thomas De Quincy, first published in 1821. It gave rise to a new form of literature consisting of unabashed writings centred on intoxication and intoxicants. Walter Benjamin's *On Hashish*, first published in 1927, talks of his experience of hashish. The books of these authors, along with the works of what is known as the "decadent" generation, comprising artists like Arthur Rimbaud and Keats, further popularised cannabis and its ability to induce intoxication. Later, authors such as William S. Burroughs and Jack Kerouac, whose writings were part of the beat movement of the 1950s and 60s, were also greatly influenced by the so-called decadent generation of artists (Roszak 54). European and North American artists of the nineteenth and twentieth centuries played a significant role in associating certain ideas and values with cannabis and the act of its consumption. These values informed meanings and practices that would later play a significant role in socio-cultural movements such as the Rastafarian movement of the 1930s and the hippy movement of the 1960s and 70s. Both these movements were responsible for positioning intoxication as a means to liberation; cannabis, as a potent intoxicant, became a significant representative object for these movements. Literature produced on cannabis in the early nineteenth century, and subsequent socio-cultural movements that used it as an icon, were successful in fetishising it to a great extent. The utility value of cannabis was far exceeded by its socio-cultural value, thus creating fertile ground for its fetishisation.

In the US, literature produced on cannabis was a great source of anxiety for certain groups that formed a major chunk of the middle- and upper-middle-class population (Booth). National newspapers highlighted the claim that hashish caused people to act violently and hurt each other. The fact that the word *assassin* is linguistically derived from the word *hashish* was used frequently to claim that consumption of cannabis caused its consumers to commit violent crimes.[1] Stories like these were cleverly embedded with news of "violent," "high" Mexicans killing middle-class American citizens, in a deliberate attempt to malign both the immigrant population and the immigrant object. Fiction seemed to go hand in hand with reality to give hashish the notoriety of being an inducer of violence in humans. Some individuals who were in a position to influence laws and policies were particularly wary of the new "drug" from the Orient. Special sections were dedicated in newspapers and journals to make the youth aware of the "dangers" of cannabis abuse. Literature on cannabis written during this time in the US was driven by a political context influenced by a general mistrust of both humans and things from foreign lands. The credit of bringing cannabis under the ambit of strict prohibition laws goes, among others, to Harry Aslinger, the then director of the Narcotics Bureau in America (Courtwright 121). Aslinger made a strong case against cannabis in the hearings of the Marihuana Tax Act of 1937 and quoted a number of cases in which perpetrators of violence had consumed cannabis (it was later found that most of these cases falsely implicated cannabis as a reason for violence). As a result of the efforts of Aslinger and his colleagues, cannabis came to be outlawed in the United States for years to come. Cannabis became an outlawed "drug," a prohibited object or "dope," as it continued its westward journey from the Asian subcontinent to Europe and to America.

Discourse generated around cannabis and its consumption in the West attributed meanings of illegality and moral depravity to cannabis and the act of its consumption. The fetish around it had now become powerful enough to influence the material lives of those involved with it. The position of power that the US and Europe enjoyed on a global scale ensured that countries across the globe were gradually forced or volunteered to criminalise cannabis. The Single Convention on Narcotic Drugs, adopted in 1961, included cannabis as a controlled substance in addition to opium, heroin, cocaine, and morphine, mostly due to the efforts of the US.

---

[1] Historical records show the existence of a radical religious group that had gained notoriety for their violence against their victims. According to a myth, individuals in the group were made to consume large amounts of hashish before they went on their periodic rampages. Hashish was seen to provide them with the strength and moral crudity to commit such heinous acts. Hence they were called *hashishins* which might have later evolved into *assassins*.

Accordingly, it was classified as a substance that required the highest level of regulation by the state in terms of its production and consumption.

In India, initial efforts at bringing cannabis and its consumption under the ambit of law were undertaken by the colonial British government. In the late nineteenth century, officials of the British Empire expressed concern regarding the effect of cannabis on the people of India, which was the colony consuming the largest amount of cannabis. It was used by a large number of people in India in different forms. Consequently, the Indian Hemp Drugs Commission Report of 1894 was prepared, based on large-scale research on the consumption habits of cannabis (Kaplan 12). Data was collected on a quantitative basis with samples of mediocre sizes taken from a number of districts in the country with the help of district administrators, doctors, and local policemen. The scope of this report makes it one of the most inclusive sources of quantitative data available on cannabis consumption and its effects in India. The results of the report did not warrant a strict law to be enforced on the consumption of the drug; it did not confirm any reports of direct deaths due to cannabis. Moreover, most respondents denied having any knowledge of the moderate consumption of cannabis causing grievous harm; however, most of them reported that heavy use of cannabis caused severe damage to the body. The report highlighted the large-scale use of cannabis for religious and medicinal purposes in the country, which made criminalisation of the drug harmful to the interests of successive governments, as they would have lost their popularity if they had banned a "sacred" and "useful" object in India. After the publication of this report, little was done by the government to prohibit or curtail the use of cannabis in the country.

The issue of the criminalisation of cannabis in India was subsequently not addressed before the Single Convention on Narcotic Drugs of 1961 discussed above. Being one of the signatories to the convention, India was to enforce an act that would effectively lay down rules for the control, prohibition, and regulation of narcotic drugs and other psychotropic substances within its boundaries. Cannabis and its products were also to be included in the list, and since the use and circulation of cannabis was prevalent across the country, a period of a maximum of twenty-five years was given to formulate and effectively implement this act. Accordingly, the Narcotic Drugs and Psychotropic Substances Act, commonly known as the NDPS Act, came into force on 14 November 1985. The NDPS Act applied to the whole of the country; it criminalised cannabis and its products by declaring a gamut of activities surrounding cannabis, including its production, circulation, and consumption, illegal.

Cannabis and Transgression in the Parvati Valley, Himachal Pradesh

Climatic and geological conditions in many parts of Himachal Pradesh are conducive to the growth of cannabis and it grows wild in these regions. Cannabis also grows naturally in various parts of the Indian subcontinent. Plants that are found in other regions are used to produce *ganja* (weed made from cannabis leaves and buds), *bhang* (a paste made by grinding cannabis leaves together), and *charas* (a black, amorphous substance obtained from the bud of the cannabis plant). *Ganja* and *bhang* are used as intoxicants. Of the three, *charas* is the most potent. Good quality *charas* is produced in the Himalayas, since the combination of sunlight and the temperate weather of the region is conducive to its production.

Kullu district in Himachal Pradesh sees the largest magnitude of *charas* trade by volume in all Himachal Pradesh and all India. Most of this *charas* comes from the areas of the Parvati Valley and Manali. The Parvati Valley is steep sided with a length of 130 km up to the town of Bhuntar. With more than one hundred villages, it is an important administrative region in the Kullu district in terms of population and area. The economy was traditionally dependent on agriculture and forest resources. Horticultural products including apples, walnuts, plums, and forest products like honey, medicinal herbs, and wood have historically been important commodities in the valley. In the late nineties, *charas* emerged as the most lucrative commodity in the region and remains so up to now. The production of *charas* does not require privately owned land, since cannabis used for the purpose is mostly cultivated on forest land. Since production of *charas* is illegal, people involved in any stage of its production are at risk of prosecution. This risk has only helped increase its profitability. Today, money earned from *charas* trade exceeds or equals that earned from traditional sources of income for most households. This money is used to support other economic endeavours including horticulture and tourism, and also for meeting household needs, the education of children, marriages etc. It has been instrumental in considerably raising the purchasing capacity of households in the region. Tourism, one of the most important economic activities in the region, is co-dependent on the *charas* trade. "Drug tourists" form a significant chunk of total tourist influx in the valley and such visitors were among the first to come to the area. *Charas* and the subcultures it creates in the valley attract young tourists who form the backbone of the tourism industry. The historical global circulation of cannabis and its fetishisation add value to *charas*. Tourists travel to the Parvati Valley in large numbers not only to taste the *charas*, but also to experience expressions of cannabis cultures from different parts of the world.

The illegality of cannabis and its products contributes significantly to making it powerful. The profitability of *charas* production and trade, and the promise of a better life attract many individuals and families towards it. For example, members of all households in the five villages where I conducted ethnographic studies were involved in the trade. The illegality of activities related to cannabis is negotiated by stakeholders including villagers, tourists, and policemen by actively managing the trade as a public secret. Public secrets are information and facts that are shared within the members of a society, generally known to all, but hardly spoken on occasions and spaces considered to be public (Taussig 19). The management of a public secret is a social practice that involves performances from participants who inhabit the space where the public secret exists. The management of *charas* production and trade in Parvati Valley as a public secret involves strategies that make use of knowledge coded in local socio-cultural institutions and practices. It is also a matter of performance as it requires regular reinforcement of certain meanings and properties of cannabis that challenge its illegality. For example, local villagers often invoke the traditional use of cannabis in the region and its sacredness owing to its relation to the Hindu God, Shiva, to justify their participation in what is otherwise an illegal activity. Similarly, the recent decriminalisation and legalisation of cannabis in parts of the USA and other western countries, and prevalent pro-legalisation discourse, are cited by both cannabis traders and policemen (who are often involved in the trade and allow local producers and traders to escape arrest with the aim of obtaining monetary or other kinds of benefit from the trade).

Public secrecy enables participants in the trade to earn money; but it does not guarantee immunity from state action, as is evident from the arrests that take place intermittently in the valley. The office of the superintendent of police at Kullu reported around 510 cases registered under the NDPS Act in Kullu district in 2012 alone; about 279 kg of *charas* was seized from "smugglers." Youngsters who enter the trade at the age of twenty or even younger, spend most of their youth in prison. Time spent in prison continues to affect individuals and their families even after they are released. The process of managing the public secret and living under its influence affects local society deeply. The fear, paranoia, and guilt of engaging in an illegal trade manifests itself through strained social relationships and broken families. Since the cultivation of cannabis is illegal and punishable by law (often leading to long-term imprisonment and hefty fines), large-scale cultivation has shifted to forested areas in the upper reaches of mountains in the Parvati Valley. Tracts of forest land have been cleared by burning to make way for cannabis plantations. During February and March, one can see flames in the upper forests of the region, with smoke billowing up into the air. Such modes of clearing forests leads to long-term damage to the ecology, which may have serious consequences in the years to come. However, in the absence of a locally comprehensive study, the extent of ecological imbalance caused by cannabis cultivation in the environmentally sensitive region cannot be gauged with certainty.

Cannabis-centred tourism has had far-reaching effects (other than its obvious impact on the local economy) on society in the Parvati Valley. It influences youth cultures, and shapes the lifestyle and worldview of its young men and women. The diffusion of cultures encouraged by large-scale tourism in the region has contributed to the emergence of a dynamic youth culture, which is a mosaic of cultural influences that enter the valley through different sources. The cultural plurality ushered in by tourism can be observed during important social events like marriages, village *melas* (festivals), naming ceremonies, etc. Values, ideas, and practices brought to the valley by tourists influence important life decisions taken by the youth. In many cases, residents of the valley actively participate in cannabis sub-cultures in order to mingle with tourists, cultivate close relationships with them, and exploit these links for economic and personal gains.

The introduction of global cannabis sub-cultures to the valley has influenced the consumption practices of many with respect to cannabis and other intoxicants. As discussed earlier, cannabis in its various forms has been traditionally consumed in the region. However, recent trends do not reflect the traditional ethos centred on cannabis consumption. Global cannabis cultures tend to link the consumption of the drug with other, potentially more addictive and harmful substances. Cannabis-induced drug tourism has introduced substances like cocaine, opium, heroin, ketamine, MDMA, and acid in the region. Drugs are brought into the valley by a network of tourists and local dealers or those from outside, and are sold locally at a profit. Easy access to drugs for economic gains and the influence of underground drug subcultures has led to a huge increase in drug consumption amongst the residents, especially the youth. Psychological problems among the local youth and intermittent cases of death due to drug overdose in the last decade stand testimony to the impact cannabis consumption has on the young population in the region.

Negotiating the influence of cannabis in the Parvati Valley is a process that constitutes a continuous struggle between the human will to utilise an object and the obduracy and power of the object that resists such utilisation. This makes the continuing interaction between cannabis and the social order a necessarily fecund avenue affecting the resident society in multiple ways. Further, interactions with the local society only seems to extend the reach of cannabis to every aspect of human life in the Parvati Valley, progressively transgressing boundaries and reinforcing its power over institutions and practices. The power of the material object and its ability to influence society is thus also embedded in the efforts of the society to utilise the object and resist its ability to affect human life adversely. Thus, while histories of circulation and fetishisation, and the ambiguous, yet desirable, materiality of cannabis and its products make it powerful enough to engender social change in the Parvati Valley, the engagement of the local society with cannabis at various levels fuels its transgression into every aspect of social life in the region. Transgressive objects—because of their utility, desirability, and unpredictability, and the inherent threat they pose—elicit almost total engagement from the society they affect, and it is this property that facilitates transgression. Cannabis is made transgressive not only by its illegality, but also by its economic utility that draws the residents of the valley to negotiate its illegality. The ambiguous yet desirable materiality of cannabis, as well as the attempts of the social order to exploit this materiality, makes cannabis transgressive.

Conclusion

The facets of a material object that make it influential are accrued through various processes and experiences it encounters on account of its historical and continuing association with human beings. Such an association entails an indistinguishability between features of objects that are considered "natural" and those that are "cultural," i.e., those that are inscribed in the objects due to their historical circulation in society. In such a situation, the material properties of objects, which are otherwise considered "given" or "naturally" associated with it, need to be re-examined to assess how social processes have rearranged the "material" in the material object. Laws and moral frameworks that govern the circulation of objects also shape the knowledge that is produced about them to a large extent. In many cases, as in the case of cannabis and its products, laws and moral judgements are inclined to conflate socially inscribed properties of cannabis with its natural, material properties. Such conceptions of cannabis prove to be faulty from their inception because they do not take into consideration the fact that a clear delineation of the natural properties of an object vis-à-vis its social properties is extremely difficult, if not impossible. Studies on objects like cannabis tend to locate their starting point at legal or moral definitions of objects, and miss crucial aspects of human–object relationships. This essay has used the framework of material sociology to study a morally ambiguous substance, known for its narcotic properties and referred to as a "drug" in studies that have attempted to examine its impact on society. The moral universe(s) associated with cannabis is not a pre-given for the essay, but is a consequence of its properties and various processes that work in conjunction with each other to incessantly build them. One has to bear in mind, then, that the object is in the continuous process of being constructed at the material and discursive levels through its interaction with society. This essay re-emphasises the need to study the historical and present engagement of an object with the social order, to better understand its materiality and significance. While arguing in favour of repositioning the starting point of studying substances like cannabis, this essay hopes to prepare common ground for studies on drugs and narcotic substances to engage with the fertile discipline of material sociology.

References

Benjamin, Walter. *On Hashish.* Trans. H. Eiland and M. W. Jennings. New York: Harvard University Press, 2006. Print.

Bernard, Lewis. *Assassins: A Radical Sect in Islam.* Texas: Pheonix Publications, 2003. Print.

Booth, Martin. *Cannabis: A History.* New York: Picador, 2005. Print.

Courtwright, David. *Forces of Habit: Drugs and the Making of the Modern World.* London: Harvard University Press, 2001. Print.

Da Orta, Garcia. *Colloquies on the Simples and Drugs of India.* London: Henry Sotheran, 1913. Print.

Dant, Tim. *Material Culture in a Social World.* London: Open University Press, 1996. Print.

Foucault, Michel. "A Preface to Transgression." *Language, Counter Memory, Practice: Selected Essays and Interviews,* ed. and trans. D. Bouchard. New York: Cornell University Press, 1977, 29–53. Print.

Kaplan, J. *Marijuana: Report of the Indian Hemp Drugs Commission, 1893–1894.* Silver Spring: Jefferson Publishing, 1969. Print.

Latour, Bruno. *Reassembling the Social: An Introduction to Actor–Network Theory.* London: Oxford University Press, 2005. Print.

Miller, Daniel. *Stuff.* Sydney: Wiley Publications, 2009. Print.

Mintz, Sidney. *Sweetness and Power: The Place of Sugar in Modern History.* New York: Penguin USA, 1986. Print.

Pels, P. "The Spirit of Matter: On Fetish, Rarity, Fact and Fancy." *Border Fetishisms: Material Objects in Unstable Spaces,* ed. by Patricia Spyer. London: Routledge, 1998, 91–121. Print.

Roszak, Theodore. *The Making of a Counter Culture.* San Francisco: University of California Press, 1969. Print.

Sharma, G. "Ethnobotany and Its Significance for Cannabis Studies in the Himalayas." *Journal of Psychedelic Drugs*, 9 (1977): 337–39. Print.

Taussig, Michael. *My Cocaine Museum.* London: University of Chicago Press, 2004. Print.

—. *The Devil and Commodity Fetishism in South America.* North Carolina: UNC Press, 1987. Print.

West, Paige. *From Modern Production to Imagined Primitive: The Social World of Coffee from Papua New Guinea.* New York: Duke University Press, 2012. Print.

PERAMBULATING REEDS:
AN ANALYSIS OF TAPAN SINHA'S *HARMONIUM*

SUVADIP SINHA

In the first volume of *The Church Missionary Intelligencer and Record: A Monthly Journal of Missionary Information* in 1876, a report published under the title of "Visit of Sir W. Muir" contains the following in a paragraph:

> After tiffin the bells chimed for Divine Service in the church of the Epiphany. The service was in Santali. The Rev. A. Stark read the evening prayers. Bhim, catechist, read the lessons. The singing and chanting were rendered in a very hearty manner, accompanied by the harmonium. The church was filled in every part. (166)

The report ends with a rather long list of achievements of that particular chapter of the missionary in converting the local indigenous people into Christianity. Compare this with the way Tapan Sinha's film *Harmonium* (1963) begins with an evocative effort at firmly placing the musical instrument within the socio-cultural milieu of the Bengali community. Before the film begins, there appear epigrammatic lines on inter-title cards:

> It's said that paddy, rice, coal and cow-dung cake are
> Truer than laughter, flute and song,
> Yet one can see in the secluded corner of a Bengali home,
> One harmonium!

Although this essay is not an attempt at excavating the historical journey of the harmonium, separated by almost one hundred years, these two appearances of the same musical instrument reveal an interesting material transition and possibility for us. From being an accompanying instrument within the broader machinery of colonial oppression, it managed to certify itself as an inherent part of the Bengali bourgeois cultural milieu. Almost immediately, the harmonium is located in a process of material circulation that instils the pulse of what Arjun Appadurai calls "social life" (5) in an inert object. In his analysis of the social life of things, Appadurai contends:

> Even if our own approach to things is conditioned necessarily by the view that things have no meanings apart from those that human transactions, attributions and motivations endow them with, the anthropological problem is that this formal truth does not illuminate the concrete, historical circulation of things. For that we have to follow things themselves. . . . Even though from a *theoretical* point of view human actors encode things with significance, from a *methodological* point of view it is the things-in-motion that illuminate their human and social context. (5; emphases in the original)

Although Appadurai's formulation, in its effort at giving independence to the "things-in-motion" (5), runs the legitimate risk of dehistoricising the circulation itself (see Pels "The Spirit of Matter"), following a thing through its journey and circulation can certainly reveal hidden nodal points of human history. Following the circuitous journey of a musical instrument in the film *Harmonium*, I argue that the thing-in-motion—in this case, the harmonium travelling from its feudal abode to an urban middle-class location to a brothel—is invested with both narrative and signifying impetus to reveal the particular "human and social context" (5) it dwells in. This essay aims to chart the curious journey of the instrument in Sinha's film to argue that the cinematic life of the harmonium provokes us to imagine an object-oriented worlding that de- essentialises the subject–object binary.

Comprising three separate narrative segments, this film becomes a whole by only being materially sutured by the travelling harmonium. The harmonium, the main object of attention, interestingly, goes through various circuits of valuation—use-, exchange-, and sign-value—to shift from one destination to another. The narrative centrality of the harmonium is not essentially dependent on that circuit. Rather, the journey, the network of destinations—both spatial and cultural—is what emerges as the stage of performance for the inanimate possession. The film complicates the material journey of the harmonium from a family heirloom in the feudal world, to a bourgeois possession in a middle-class household, to a pure source of pleasure in a brothel, by juxtaposing the journey of a thing with the complex dynamics of class and gender.

Before engaging in an analysis of the film, I think it would be worthwhile to recapitulate the journey of the harmonium as a musical instrument in India. Invented in Paris in 1842 by Alexandre Debain, the first version of the modern harmonium reached India in the nineteenth century through Christian missionaries. In fact, this could purportedly be considered a return of the instrument to the land of its origin.[1] In tandem with the existence of devotional music as an inherent part of everyday life in India, the harmonium soon caught the fancy of the native population. But the over-sized and typically large European pedal-harmoniums were not suitable for the Indian lifestyle for a variety of reasons.[2] The invention of the current form of the hand-held harmonium is credited to a Bengali gentleman, Dwarkanath Ghose, who was an employee of the British musical instrument merchant Harold and Co. in Calcutta. Realising the limitations of the pedal-harmonium in the Indian context, the ingenious Dwarka, as he was better known, improvised on the existing model to come up with a hand-held version. Eventually, encouraged by his British employers, Dwarkanath opened his own shop in Bowbazar area in Calcutta and founded his company, Dwarkin and Sons, in 1875 (this is the make of the harmonium shown in Sinha's film). Dwarkin remains to date the most well-known and sought-after brand of harmonium in India. This story certainly bears traces of the material impact of colonialism: the harmonium as an object emerges as an ambivalent space, a space where colonialist hegemony is accepted, appropriated, and, implicitly contested. Historicising the material emergence of the harmonium might help us fathom and, possibly, underscore the ambiguity that I attempted to point out at the beginning of this essay.

When it comes to such representation of an affective attachment with an inanimate object in Indian and Bangla cinema, Sinha's film is surely not unique. We can recollect an emotionally charged moment in Satyajit Ray's *Jalsaghar* (1958) when the almost bankrupt feudal lord Biswambhar stands in his dilapidated music room and looks at the dust-covered chandelier and other possessions that remind him of his glorious past. *Ajantrik*, a 1958 film directed by Ritwik Ghatak, is a profoundly philosophical narrative of a small-town taxi driver's enchanted and affective relationship with his malfunctioning car, Jagaddal. A similar theme reappears in Ray's *Abhijan* (1962), where we see a taxi driver and his assistant's emotional attachment with their car.[3] In 2015, a Tamil film about a seventy-year-old man's obsessive attachment with an old valve radio, *Radiopetti*, won the KNN Audience Award at the Busan International Film Festival. Beyond these

---

[1] Charting the history of the evolution of the harmonium as a musical instrument, Kraig Brockschmidt (2003) points out that the instrument is believed to have originated in the East, most probably China. The modern harmonium evolved from the primitive harmonica of ancient China (9–11).

[2] See, Brockschmidt 18–19.

[3] In recent years, a similar interest in inanimate objects has returned to Bangla cinema. *Laptop* (2012, dir. Kaushik Ganguly) and *Obhishopto Nighty* (The Cursed Nighty, 2014, dir. Birsa Dasgupta) are two examples.

more prominent examples, we have seen less explicit articulations of similar materiality in numerous Indian films. Notwithstanding the presence of such a large number of these film-texts, the discipline of Indian cinema studies has remained overtly humanistic and has not paid sufficient scholarly attention to these materialities. The assumption that the human figures on screen can be read and interpreted without paying attention to their object world is a limited one. We need to follow and engage with these things on screen in order to fully fathom the ontologies of their human counterparts.

In an interview sequence in the British film *Ghost Dance* (1983) by Ken McMullen, Jacques Derrida poignantly comments: "[Cinema] is the art of allowing the ghosts to come back." Are these ghosts necessarily remnants of living beings? Or, can they be of spirits of inanimate objects too? The haunting presence of things, objects, and commodities has long been adding to the ephemera of cinema screen (think "Rosebud" in *Citizen Kane*). As in literary narratives, cinematic narratives, too, are often entwined with the presence of inanimate objects—"things charged with effects" (Stern 320). Bresson once demanded, "Make the objects look as if they want to be there" (101). And, Siegfried Kracauer proposes, "[F]ilms in which the inanimate merely serves as a background to self-contained dialogue and the closed circuit of human relationships are essentially uncinematic" (46). Discussing cinema's ability to instil life into inanimate things, film-maker Jean Epstein says:

> I would even go so far as to say that the cinema is polytheuristic and theogonic. Those lives it creates, by summoning objects out of the shadows of indifference into the light of dramatic concern, have little in common with human life. These lives are like the life in charms and amulets, the ominous, tabooed objects of certain primitive religions. If we wish to understand how an animal, a plant or a stone can inspire respect, fear and horror, those three most sacred sentiments, I think we must watch them on screen, living their mysterious silent lives, alien to the human sensibility. (295)

How does the camera infuse the objects—"constellations of meaning" (Moore 73)—with their own will? What does this organised sovereignty do to their historical possibility? Furthermore, how does their audacious presence on screen affect our understanding of their human counterparts? These questions will keep haunting us throughout this thesis. Now Bresson's direction relates directly to the organisation of *mise en scène* and cinematography. The narrative possibility invested in the objects can certainly go beyond this. Think of how Vertov deployed the object on screen in his commercial for Soviet toys (1924) to conceptualise a Marxist critique of capitalist consumption, or in *Kinoglaz* (1924) to show the backward revealing of the production history of a commodity like meat. The intellectual engagement with things on screen, despite its limited volume, has remained diverse in its approach. These works have drawn upon psychoanalysis, Marxism, feminism, and, in some cases, theories of everyday life, to explain the ontological, historical, and referential significance of objects on screen.

As I have argued elsewhere, such affective attachments with inanimate objects cannot always be read through the Marxist idea of commodity fetishism.[4] Since Marx's idea is deeply premised upon an assumption of a post-Enlightenment, protestant ontology, it essentialises and universalises an unbreachable gap between the subject and the object. It also fails to consider the porous and permeable boundary between an object's commodity form and its status as a singular thing. Igor Kopytoff in his canonical essay urges us to explore the biographical possibilities of an object in order to identify the permeability between the singular and the commodity. Arguing for recurring transitions between commoditisation and singularisation, he points out that the cultural biography of the commodity, which is fluidly contextualised and recontextualised as it enters and exits the economy of exchange, needs to be studied in order to invalidate the historically deterministic distinction between "things" and humans. To undertake such a project, he calls for a biographical inquiry into the life of things and a rigorous attention to their moves through personalised rituals of exchange. Resonating Marcel Mauss's argument about pre-capitalist exchange as a process of treating objects as "personified things that talk and take part in the contract" (55), Kopytoff calls for the epistemic necessity for doing the biography of a thing. He argues that to do so,

> [. . .] one would ask questions similar to those one asks about people: What, sociologically, are the biographical possibilities inherent in its "status" and in the period and culture, and how are these possibilities realized? Where does the thing come from and who made it? What has been its career so far, and what do people consider to be an ideal career for such things? What are the recognised "ages" or periods in the thing's "life," and what are the cultural markers for them? How does the thing's use change with its age, and what happens to it when it reaches the end of its usefulness? (66–67)

Sinha's *Harmonium* provides us with meticulous opportunities for answering all these questions by showing the musical instrument's continuous journey through commoditisation and singularisation.

---

[4] Sinha, 2017.

The opening scene itself shows the first transition. It is an unusual setting of exchange. The location is a visibly plush parlour in a feudal household; the setting is an auction. As an auctioneer shouts, "Item No. 5: one mahogany bed. Double bed. One hundred years old. Think, for hundred years there has been so much love, affection, arguments on this bed." And then the prospective buyers start bidding. Then comes, "Item No. 6: a harmonium. It's there in that corner. Dwarkin make. It's a thing of taste. You won't get this thing anywhere else. It starts with two-hundred rupees." As the lonely lady of the house watches, "love," "affection," and "taste" are abruptly translated into economic figures according to the erratic mood of the auction. The musical instrument is just another item on a list of things to be auctioned. The human emotions and memories invested in these objects are blatantly used to embellish the price of these objects; the personal belongings are transformed into collectibles in the marketplace of the bourgeoisie. It is the scene of the fall—the fall of a family, of a value-system, and a social topography. The auction scene is followed by a flashback revealing how the musical instrument was brought to instil a taste for music in a little girl—the older lady of the opening scene—of a zamindar family. The opening auction scene serves as a pretext for the feudal house being sold off and the landlady, the young girl of the flashback sequence, leaving the ancestral home. The manager (Gangapada Basu) of the estate has gradually usurped the entire property through deceits and scams. The flashback further shows the little girl with her in various sequences in which they are enjoying the harmonium's music.

Gradually the narrative reveals the harmonium, albeit obliquely, as a traveller through various material impersonations to render a historical, cultural, and contextual continuity to the social transformation. After the auction, the harmonium reaches an urban, middle-class household from its feudal abode. From the feudal household, the narrative cuts to a city scene where the harmonium travels through the signboard-laden streets of the city to reach the cramped quarters of a middle-class family. From its reified status in the zamindar household, the harmonium in its urban dwelling becomes some sort of a symbolic and utilitarian acquisition. While the materiality of the harmonium as a musical instrument and as a source of aesthetic pleasure is conspicuously fulfilled in the zamindar household, in the household of the middle-class family in the city, the harmonium becomes a device for preparing the girl of the family as a prospective match in the marriage market. Her parents hope to make their daughter more valuable as a possible match by giving her some music lessons. Thus, the harmonium arrives. The unwitting instrument rather inadvertently performs its ultimate duty. The family appoints a young man from the neighbourhood, with whom the girl is already in love, as the girl's music teacher. This only works as a facilitator for their romance of which the families are unaware. After the girl elopes with her music teacher, the families break into an ugly squabble. Intriguingly, the girl's parents unequivocally hold the harmonium responsible for the disaster. As soon as the eloping couple is apprehended and brought back by the police, the girl's father decides to sell the harmonium. And, the harmonium goes back to the system of exchange. Along with the discernible presence of class dialectic, this segment is further complicated by the introduction of gender relations. The use of the harmonium to make the unmarried girl more marriageable is indicative of the gendered appropriation of value: the bourgeois family crassly strips the harmonium of its materiality as a source of aesthetic pleasure to deploy it to fulfil the motives of a patriarchal society.

Now moving towards an even inferior class position, the harmonium is purchased and taken to a city brothel. As the harmonium winds down to find its final abode among the impromptu musical soirees of the women of the brothel, the biography of an object is persistently intertwined with the movement of human beings across various class and cultural layers. The plot showing the prostitutes' quarters is certainly the most dramatic one. Depicting the story of one particular girl (Shyama) who has landed in the brothel through sheer misfortune, this part of the story presents the harmonium in its most inconsequential incarnation. The events of this part are not in any way facilitated or threatened by the harmonium, for it simply remains a source of aesthetic pleasure here. A fugitive criminal who is Shyama's husband, an elderly woman who is also the guardian of the house, an impassioned singer (Ratan) who is especially close to and sympathetic with Shyama, and several other women form the human world. The harmonium comes to the brothel as an impulse buy. As soon as it arrives, the whole group breaks into a spontaneous singing session. It remains a participant in the regular musical soirees. Apart from this, the harmonium has no more narrative role to play here. As Shyama's husband kills Ratan, this segment comes to an end.

The final part of the film returns to the woman who had been the original owner of the harmonium. This particular part of the film forms a kind of parallel text in the film. It runs simultaneously with the journey of the harmonium. The feudal landlord's daughter, ousted from her estate, has ended up in the city. Living in absolute penury, she takes up a job as a housekeeper-cum-governess for a family. She keeps her family identity a secret. Eventually her employer, a widower, finds out about her musical acumen and requests her to train his daughter. The narrative reaches its denouement with the harmonium ultimately brought to the same household.

The erstwhile owner unexpectedly finds the prized possession of her childhood returning to her; and the film ends with her singing a song she had learnt from her father, with scenes showing glimpses from her childhood.

The categories of "productive labour," which produces value, and "unproductive labour," which consumes value, appeared first in Adam Smith, who writes in *The Wealth of Nations* (2007 [1776])[5] that "the labor of most respectable orders in the society is . . . unproductive of any value. . . . In the same class must be ranked . . . churchmen, lawyers, physicians, men of letters of all kinds; players, buffoons, musicians, opera-singers, opera-dancers, etc." (271). It is interesting to note how Marx, extrapolating from Smith, considered musical instruments (exemplified by the piano) to be part of what he thought of as "unproductive labour":

> What is *productive labour* and what is *not*, a point very much disputed back and forth since Adam Smith made this distinction, has to emerge from the direction of the various aspects of capital itself. *Productive labour* is only that which produces *capital*. Is it not crazy, asks e.g. . . . Mr. Senior, that the piano maker is a *productive worker*, but not the piano player, although obviously the piano would be absurd without the piano player? But this is exactly the case. The piano maker reproduces *capital*; the pianist only exchanges his labour for revenue. But doesn't the pianist produce music and satisfy our musical ear, does he not even to a certain extent produce the latter? He does indeed: his labour produces something; but that does not make it *productive labour* in the *economic sense*; no more than the labour of the mad man who produces delusions is productive. (*Grundrisse* 305; emphases in the original)

Marx's interpretation of the music producer could easily be extended to encompass the corpus of music appreciation, patronage, and so forth. From within the logic of production, the harmonium in this film has no

---

[5] In the canonical section entitled "Of the Accumulation of Capital, or of Productive and Unproductive Labour," Smith writes: "There is one sort of labour which adds to the value of the subject upon which it is bestowed: there is another which has no such effect. The former, as it produces a value, may be called productive; the latter, unproductive labour. Thus, the labour of a manufacturer adds, generally, to the value of the materials which he works upon, that of his own maintenance, and of his master's profit" (270). Marx retheorised the difference between productive and unproductive labour by arguing that the former produces surplus value for capital, while the latter does not. Unproductive labour, for both Smith and Marx, represents everything parasitical, wasteful, and adventitious to capitalism—a perversion of labour. See, in this context, Hannah Arendt's analysis of these two forms of labour in *Human Condition* (1998).

"productive purpose" after it is first bought. The importance of the exchange value of the harmonium, properly monetised, is evocatively overlooked in the thingly message conveyed through the film. Sinha tries to capture its symbolic value with reference to the cultural life of the Bengali community. The representation of human historical change in this film is subtle. Apart from the initial uprooting of the lonely feudal woman from her ancestral home and the auctioning of her belongings, there is a narrative smoothness in the film that is designed to make the audience oblivious to the tumultuous changes the film subtly captures. It is through meticulously following the unproductive biography of the harmonium that we can remain attentive to these changes. Instead of seeing the harmonium as an already-coded human possession or as a merely fetishised commodity, we need to move away from, as Bill Brown suggests, a simplistic and humanist thing–object dialectic in order to understand how this seemingly inanimate thing asks us to disavow the subject–object binary.

The biographical sojourn of the harmonium represents the end of the feudal era and the beginning of an urbanised, bourgeois existence in Bengal, even though this apparently linear movement is not without slippages. One of the slippages would be the segment dealing with the brothel. This brothel sequence adds a unique dimension to the narrative. Insofar as the social subjectivity and class hierarchy are intricately linked, the harmonium's position as a source of pure pleasure in the feudal household and the brothel unravels an extremely intriguing disposition. The harmonium unwittingly blurs the class distinction between the two extremes of social hierarchy: Shyama is the daughter of a travelling performer whom we come across at the beginning of the film. By the end, the performer's daughter has become a prostitute in the city. The journey of the performing woman, synchronised with the journey of the harmonium, shows how the rise of the bourgeois middle-class turned both the musical instrument and the performer into commodities in modern, monetised society. There is a perceptive connection between the arrival of the harmonium amongst the middle-class family as the agent for making the girl more marriageable and the decline of Shyama into prostitution in the city. The juxtaposition of the body of the actress-prostitute and the commoditised status of the harmonium is reflective of the melancholy of monetised modernity:[6] an approximate replication of the philosophical connection Simmel makes between money and prostitution.[7]

---

[6] In this context, see Dorothy Rowe's "Money, Modernity and Melancholia in the Writings of Georg Simmel" (2005).

[7] Georg Simmel makes an interesting comparison between the monetised society and the trade of prostitution: "Money serves most matter-of-factly and completely for venal pleasure, which rejects any continuation of the relationship beyond sensual

But amid the bourgeois world of the city, it is the spontaneous gatherings of commoditised women over songs and dance around the harmonium that rejuvenate its sensuous materiality.

It is undeniable that there are human possessors of the musical instrument; yet, Sinha continuously inserts slippages that subverts the tyranny of the human possessor/inanimate possession binary. Rather than the human characters always deciding the fate of the inanimate thing, it is the inanimate thing, sometimes inadvertently, that determines the destiny of its human cohabitants. Through its spatial journey, the peripatetic harmonium generates a new temporality. This new temporality connects, fascinates, appropriates, and transforms the human characters. Only through a humanist way of watching can the harmonium be mistakenly understood as transparently legible and intelligible through the desires, pleasures, and actions of its human possessors; an object-oriented reading, however, enables a counter-intuitive reading of the narrative. Almost none of the human characters have full control over the life of the harmonium. The musical instrument escapes the subjects' control and insinuates itself to bring unexpected narrative consequences. This convinces me to argue that it is not audacious enough just to say that by following the biography of an object, we can uncover the biography of human subjects. In fact, things exhibit the potential of altering those human biographies. While doing so, this speechless (not mute) inanimate thing delights us "in evoking a world that is not just distant and long gone but also better—a world in which, to be sure, human beings are no better provided with what they need than in the real world, but in which things are freed from the drudgery of being useful" (Benjamin 19). By transitioning from being useful to useless, from cherished to saleable, from general to singular, the harmonium becomes "different things in different scenes" (Brown, "Thing Theory" 9). Simultaneously a "quasi subject" and "quasi object" (Latour 51), this seemingly uncomplicated inanimate thing emerges as the protagonist, a profoundly cinematic being, to lend its fungible infungibility to render its human co-actors tangible.

---

satisfaction: money is completely detached from the person and puts an end to any further ramifications. When one pays moneys one is completely quits, just as one through with the prostitute after satisfaction is attained" (Simmel, *Individuality and Social Forms* 121).

References

Appadurai, Arjun. "Introduction: Commodities and the Politics of Value." *The Social Life of Things: Commodities in Cultural Perspective*. Ed. Arjun Appadurai. Cambridge: Cambridge University Press, 1986. 3–63.

Benjamin, Walter. *The Arcades Project*. Tr. Howard Eiland and Kevin McLaughlin. Cambridge, MA: Harvard University Press, 2002.

Bresson, Robert. *Notes on Cinematographer*. Tr. Jonathan Griffin. London: Quarter Books, 1986.

Brockschmidt, Satyaki Kraig. *The Harmonium Handbook: Owning, Playing and Maintaining the Devotional Instrument of India*. Nevada, CA: Crystal Clarity Publishers, 2003.

Brown, Bill. *A Sense of Things*. Chicago: University of Chicago Press, 2003.

—. "Thing Theory." *Critical Inquiry*. 28.2 (2001): 1–22.

Kopytoff, Igor. "The Cultural Biography of Things: Commoditization as Process." In *The Social Life of Things: Commodities in Cultural Perspective*. Ed. Arjun Appadurai. Cambridge: Cambridge University Press, 1986. 64–94.

Kracauer, Siegfried. *Theory of Film: the Redemption of Physical Reality*. Princeton, NJ: Princeton University Press, 1997.

Kellar, Sarah, and Jason N. Paul, eds. *Jean Epstein: Critical Essays and New Translations*. Amsterdam: Amsterdam University Press, 2012.

Latour, Bruno. *We Have Never Been Modern*. Tr. Catherine Porter. Hemel Hampstead, UK: Harvester Wheatsheaf, 1993.

Marx, Karl. *Grundrisse: Foundations of the Critique of Political Economy*. Tr. Martin Nicolaus. London: Penguin, 1973.

Rowe, Dorothy. "Money, Modernity and Melancholia in the writings of Georg Simmel." In *Metaphors of Economy*. Ed. Nicole Bracker and Stefan Herbrechter. Amsterdam: Rodopi, 2005. 27–80.

Simmel, Georg. *Georg Simmel on Individuality and Social Forms: Selected Writings*. Ed. Donald N. Levine. Chicago: University of Chicago Press, 1971.

Sinha, Suvadip. "Magical Modernity: The Fallacy of Affect in Ritwik Ghatak's *Ajantrik*." *Cultural Critique*, 95 (Winter 2017): 101–30.

Smith, Adam. *Wealth of Nations*. New York: Cosimo, 2007.

Stern, Lesley. "Paths that Wind through the Thicket of Things." *Critical Inquiry* 28.1 (2001): 317–54.

The Church Missionary Intelligencer and Record: A Monthly Journal of Missionary Information. "Visit of Sir W. Muir," 1 (1876).

ABOUT THE CONTRIBUTORS

Arundhathi currently teaches in the Department of English and Cultural Studies at Christ University, Bangalore, India. She completed her PhD at the Advanced Centre for Women's Studies, Tata Institute of Social Sciences (TISS), Mumbai, researching women's experiences of everyday mobility and the usage of local trains in Mumbai. Her areas of research interest include mobility, feminist media studies, and urban studies.

Jibu Mathew George is Professor in the Department of English Literature, the English and Foreign Languages University, Hyderabad, India. He holds MA degrees in English literature, philosophy and religion, and political science, an MSc degree in applied psychology, and a PhD in English literature. His areas of research are meta-questions in the humanities, philosophy, and history of religion, continental philosophy, philosophy of history, hermeneutics, philosophy of literature, European cultural history, literary modernism, twentieth-century literary theory, mythology and folklore, life-span psychology, and Holocaust studies. He is author of three books: *Ulysses Quotīdiānus: James Joyce's Inverse Histories of the Everyday* (2016); *The Ontology of Gods: An Account of Enchantment, Disenchantment, and Re-enchantment* (2017); and *Philosophical Meta-Reflections on Literary Studies: Why Do Things with Texts, and What to Do with Them?* (2019). A three-volume international anthology of essays entitled *De Natura Fidei: Rethinking Religion across Disciplinary Boundaries*, edited by George, is in press. He featured in the Oxford Academic Index of Critics (the Year's Work in English Studies) in 2018. He was Research Fellow at the Zürich James Joyce Foundation, Switzerland, in 2008. In the same year he also received a DAAD Scholarship for studies at Technische Universität Dresden. He is editor of the literary studies issues of the *English and Foreign Languages Journal*; and pre-publication reviewer for Springer, Dordrecht, Routledge, New Delhi, and Orient Blackswan, Hyderabad.

Roshin George is Associate Professor of English at St. Thomas College, Kozhencherry, and an approved research guide at Mahatma Gandhi University, Kottayam. Her doctoral thesis is on postmodernism and contemporary Indo-Anglian fiction, and she is interested in contemporary literary theory. She has published research articles in renowned literary journals including the *Atlantic Critical Review*, *Kakatiya Journal of English Studies*, and *Quest*, as well as in anthologies.

Shambwaditya Ghosh is a research scholar at the Department of History, University of Delhi. He has received awards and fellowships from the Indian Council of Historical Research, Charles Wallace India Trust, and Nehru Trust for the Indian Collection at Victoria and Albert Museum for studying archaeological archiving and museum display techniques. He was also selected for the British Museum International Training Programme and Senior Fellowship. He studied Ancient Indian History, Culture and Archaeology from Visva Bharati, Santiniketan, followed by a post-graduate diploma in archaeology from the Institute of Archaeology, Goverment of India, New Delhi, and an MPhil in history from Dr B. R. Ambedkar University Delhi. He worked previously for the Indian National Trust for Arts and Cultural Heritage (INTACH), New Delhi, and the Center for Art and Archaeology, American Institute of Indian Studies, Gurgaon, and City Palace Museum, Jaipur.

Nilakshi Goswami is a Fulbright Nehru-Postdoctoral Research Fellow 2020–2021 and a CURA Fellow (Institute of Culture, Religion, and World Affairs) 2021–2022 at the Department of Anthropology, Boston University. She holds a PhD in English literature from the English and Foreign Languages University and a BA and MA (English Literature) from Delhi University. Nilakshi is currently working on the role of new media and popular culture in the construction of gendered identities in Southeast Asia. Her research interest broadly centres on gender and sexuality studies, popular culture, and comics and graphic novels.

Minu Susan Koshy works as Assistant Professor in the Department of English, Marthoma College for Women, Kerala, India. She is an approved research guide at Mahatma Gandhi University, Kerala, with Mar Thoma College, Thiruvalla, as the research centre. She has published extensively in national and international journals and has served as the resource person at several conferences. She is a reviewer for the *Journal of Global South Studies* and a member of the editorial board of *Education, Society and Human Studies*. Her books include *Narrating Childhood Trauma: The Quest for Catharsis* (DC Books-Expressions, 2015), a translation of the Malayalam anthology *Tattoo* (Authorspress, 2015) by Jacob Abraham, an edited collection of poems by Elizabeth Kuriakose titled *Gossamer Reveries* (Authorspress, 2019), and *Mapping the Postcolonial Domestic in the Works* *of Vargas Llosa and Mukundan: Tales of the Threshold* (Cambridge Scholars Publishing, 2020).

Édison Lopera Pérez majors in basic education optional humanities and Spanish. He participates in several student research projects that focus on the teaching of Spanish as native language and the implementation of new pedagogic strategies. He is interested in linguistics and Colombian cultural studies.

Somedutta Mallik is an art historian and curator who presently works with Dhi Artspace, Hyderabad. Her research interest lies in material memory, anthropology of objects, and oral history. Her post-graduation thesis traced the biographies of the looms in Suraiya Hasan Bose's workshop. Mallik's curatorial projects include *Allegories of Threads* (2021), which featured artists Gözde Ilkin, Sharmistha Kar, Shruti Mahajan, and Sumana Som; *Metaphor: The Magic It Holds* (2020), featured artists Ajith AS, Arjun Das, and Subhankar Bag; and *A Voice to a Voice*, the seventh edition of the International Print Exchange Programme (IPEP), India (2019) among others. She holds a master's degree in art history and visual studies.

Russell McDougall is Professor Emeritus in the School of Arts, Humanities and Social Sciences at the University of New England in Australia. He has published widely on African, Australian, and Caribbean literatures. His most recent publications are *Postcolonial Literatures of Climate Change* (Brill, 2022—co-edited with John C. Ryan and Pauline Reynolds), *Letters from Khartoum: D. R. Ewen, Teaching English Literature, Sudan, 1951–1965* (Brill, 2021), and *Tracking the Literature of Tropical Weather: Typhoons, Hurricanes and Cyclones* (Palgrave Macmillan, 2017—co-edited with Sue Thomas and Anne Collett). He is also executive editor (with Mala Pandering and Michael Griffiths) of the new Postcolonial Lives series for Brill.

Indrani Mukherjee is Professor in the Center of Spanish, Portuguese, Italian and Latin American Studies, Jawaharlal Nehru Univerity, India. She teaches Latin American studies and her area of interest includes comparative literature, decolonial feminist studies, and new materialism. Her latest publication is a co-edited book entitled *Posthumanist Nomadisms across Non-Oedipal Spatiality*, published by Vernon Press, 2021.

Juan Ignacio Muñoz Zapata holds a PhD degree in comparative and general literature at the University of Montreal, has published articles on Latin American cyberpunk novels and film, Amazonian literatures, and ecocriticism. Currently, he conducts research projects on edusemiotics, symbolic systems, and comparative literature at Tecnológico de Antioquia, Medellín (Colombia).

Aloke Prabhu is Associate Professor of Law at Jindal Global Law School, O. P. Jindal Global University, Haryana.

Vinita Rav is a PhD student from the History Department at the University of Delhi. Her research interests focus on the tribal food and food habits of Chotanagpur region in the period 1850–1950. She completed her MA and MPhil degrees from the History Department, Delhi University. Her MPhil was on socioeconomic shifts of tribal women of Chotanagpur region. She is currently working on the research project "Role of Indian Army in First World War," which is conducted through the Ministry of Defence.

Álvaro Sánchez Giraldo majors in Spanish language and literature Teaching at Tecnológico de Antioquia. He studies graffiti communities in Medellín, Colombia.

Suvadip Sinha is an assistant professor of South Asian literature and culture in the Department of Asian and Middle Eastern Studies, University of Minnesota, Twin Cities. His primary research areas are Indian cinema, modern South Asian literatures, and philosophy of the nonhuman. Sinha's research articles have been published in journals like *South Asian Popular Culture*, *Interventions*, *Feminist Media Histories*, and *Cultural Critique*. He is a co-editor of *Postcolonial Animalities* (Routledge, 2019). His monograph, *Entangled Fictions: Nonhuman Animals in an Indian World* is forthcoming from Routledge.

Jennifer Yvette Terrell received her PhD in politics from the New School for Social Research (2014). From 2012 to 2016 she held a joint position in the Department of Law and the Institute for Gender and Women's Studies at the American University in Cairo. She is currently in South Africa conducting fieldwork for a project on rights and their spatial and temporal dimensions in the current post-apartheid politico-legal regime.

Lisa Thomas teaches English at Jindal Global Law School, O. P. Jindal Global University, Haryana.

Prasanjeet Tribhuvan is a Social Anthropologist. He completed his PhD from the Department of Sociology, Delhi School of Economics, Delhi University in 2017. He is currently an Assistant Professor of Sociology at IIT, Rajasthan (Jodhpur), and a former fellow at IIAS, Shimla. His research interests are mainly in the areas of STS, anthropology of material objects, and ethnographic studies of communities in ecologically sensitive regions. Apart from his main research interests, Prasenjeet is interested in listening to different genres of metal music and following metal biographies.

Sarah Zia is a journalist at a leading Indian daily and an independent researcher. Her areas of research interest include mobility studies, media, and identities.